Teacher's Handbook

ECCE ROMANI

A Latin Reading Program
Second Edition

5

From Republic to Empire

Longman

Ecce Romani Teacher's Handbook 5, Second Edition From Republic to Empire

ISBN 0 8013 0448 2
(78258)

Cover illustration by Nancy Carpenter

This edition of ECCE ROMANI is based on ECCE ROMANI: A LATIN READING COURSE, originally prepared by The Scottish Classics Group, copyright © The Scottish Classics Group 1971, 1982, and published in the United Kingdom by Oliver and Boyd, a division of Longman Group. This edition has been prepared by a team of American and Canadian educators:

Authors:
Carol Esler, Boston, Massachusetts
Ronald B. Palma, Holland Hall School, Tulsa, Oklahoma
David J. Perry, Rye High School, Rye, New York
Coordinator:
Professor Gilbert Lawall, University of Massachusetts, Amherst, Massachusetts
Consultants:
Dr. Rudolph Masciantonio, Philadelphia Public Schools, Pennsylvania
Dr. Edward Barnes, C. W. Jeffreys Secondary School, Downsview, Ontario
Shirley Lowe, Wayland Public Schools, Wayland, Massachusetts

Acknowledgements

Extract from Plutarch's Life of Sulla, translated by Rex Warner in *Fall of the Roman Republic (Six Romasn Lives)*, is reprinted by permission of Viking-Penguin Books Inc. Copyright © 1954 by Viking-Penguin Books Inc.

Extract from *Pliny: Letters and Panegyricus*, translated by Betty Radice, is reprinted by permission of the publisher, William Heinemann Ltd., and the Loeb Classical Library, Harvard University Press. Copyright © 1969 by William Heinemann Ltd.

Extract from *The Art of Rome*, by Bernard Andreae, is reprinted by permission of Editions de Art Lucien Mazenod. Copyright © 1973 by Editions de Art Lucien Mazenod, Paris.

Extract from *The Ancient Romans*, by Chester G. Starr, is reprinted by permission of Oxford University Press. Copyright © 1971 by Oxford University Press.

Extract from *Greece and Rome* (Cambridge Introduction to the History of Art), by Susan Woodford, is reprinted by permission of Cambridge University Press. Copyright © 1982 by Cambridge University Press.

Extracts from *Roman Civilization Sourcebook I: The Republic*, edited by Naphtali Lewis and Meyer Reinhold, is reprinted by permission of Harper & Row, Publishers. Copyright © 1951 by Columbia University Press.

Photo credits, page 108: Alinari/Art Resource, NY. All other illustrations originally appeared in *Orbis Pictus Latinus* by Hermann Koller, © 1976, 1983 by Artemis Verlag Zurich and München.

Longman
95 Church St.
White Plains, N.Y. 10601

Associated companies:
Longman Group Ltd., London
Longman Cheshire Pty., Melbourne
Longman Paul Pty., Auckland
Copp Clark Pitman, Toronto
Pitman Publishing Inc., New York

ABCDEFGHIJ-CT-959493929190

Contents

troduction to Book 5 / 4

aching Notes

  Part I
     Chapter 54 / 7
     Chapter 55 / 14
     Chapter 56 / 17

  Part II
     Chapter 57 / 20
     Chapter 58 / 24

  Part III
     Chapter 59 / 29
     Chapter 60 / 34
     Chapter 61 / 38

  Part IV
     Chapter 62 / 44
     Chapter 63 / 52
     Chapter 64 / 58

  Part V
     Chapter 65 / 66
     Chapter 66 / 72
     Chapter 67 / 77

ibliography / 82

atin Vocabularies / 87

ppendix: Supplementary Materials / 90

Introduction to Book 5: From Republic to Empire

I. Overview

In this volume of ECCE ROMANI, students will be reading for the first time exclusively in original Latin authors. Except for some abridgments, usually minor, these texts are entirely unadapted. In addition to introducing students to extended reading in authentic Latin, *From Republic to Empire* also aims to introduce them to the broader aspects of the Latin-speaking world, especially the characteristically Roman arts of politics, war, and administration. The readings that deal with these topics (Parts II, III, and IV) are framed by an overview of the period from 64 B.C. to A.D. 14 (Part I) and by a final section (Part V) which returns the student to the lives of individuals, where the ECCE ROMANI program began.

The readings in Part I (Chapters 54–56) are taken from Eutropius' *Breviarium ab urbe condita*, a handbook of Roman history written in the late fourth century A.D. These readings will give students an overview of the transition from Republic to Empire and will introduce some topics that will be treated more fully in the following Parts.

Part II (Chapters 57–58) provides a glimpse of the political violence that characterized the end of the Republic, typified by the murder of Clodius and the trial of Milo; the episode is represented here by excerpts from Asconius' commentary on Cicero's *Pro Milone* and passages from Cicero's oration itself.

Part III (Chapters 59–61) shows the results of this political disruption as it finally broke out into civil war in 49 B.C., as seen in selections from Cicero's letters and Caesar's *De bello civili*.

Part IV (Chapters 62–64) shows the ultimate result of the civil wars, the establishment of the Principate as a new form of government, and the concern for justice, public works and services, and an orderly civic life that the early Principate offered its subjects in exchange for some of their political freedoms. Readings come from Augustus' own *Res gestae*, Pliny's correspondence with Trajan, and Eutropius.

Part V (Chapters 65–67) combines some of the themes from earlier books of the ECCE ROMANI program with the themes of political history dealt with in Parts I–IV of *From Republic to Empire*. Selections from the *Satyricon* of Petronius (Trimalchio's tomb and autobiography) touch upon many aspects of everyday life in the first century A.D. and provide a humorous story very different from the material in the first four Parts. Two letters of Pliny draw interesting portraits of two people: his friend Fannia, whose life illustrates the darker side of the Principate, and his uncle, who was killed in the eruption of Mt. Vesuvius. On completing *From Republic to Empire*, students will have come full circle and will have returned to the typically Roman emphasis on the family that they first encountered in *Meeting the Family*.

II. Teaching the Texts

The passages from Eutropius are approximately at the same linguistic level as the stories at the end of the fourth student's book, and so provide a smooth transition into *From Republic to Empire*. Since the passages are authentic Latin, however, they offer new opportunities: mature subject matter and style, the satisfaction and pride of "communicating" directly with ancient authors, and expanded possibilities for discussion of important political, cultural, and literary issues.

Some preparatory work is usually desirable before having students translate the passages, e.g., introductory discussion of background and content, oral reading, introduction to new vocabulary, and gradual approaches to the general sense of the passage (through the comprehension questions provided). The teacher will find many suggestions for such preparatory activities in the teaching notes that follow. Only after students are thoroughly familiar with the form and content of the reading will they be expected to produce a formal translation, either written or oral, of the text.

Both before and after formal translation, there are numerous opportunities for lively discussion of the issues raised in the readings. These passages have been chosen, in part, for their relevance to important social and political questions that are still very much alive today. Students should enjoy working out for themselves, with guidance from the teacher, the parallels between their own experience (both as private individuals and as citizens) and that of the Romans. Many such parallels are suggested in the teaching notes, in addition to those mentioned in the discussion questions in the student's book.

Since many of the readings in this volume are drawn from the works of major Latin authors, it should also be possible to begin guiding students toward an appreciation of some of the literary qualities of Latin literature: the artful placement of words to achieve nuances of meaning and emphasis; the choice of one synonym rather than another; and balance and parallelism of words, phrases, and clauses to clarify and enhance meaning.

The texts also provide abundant practice in critical reading and in assessing the reliability of primary sources historical and cultural evidence. For example, students are asked to examine the contrasting claims of Cicero and Asconius on the murder of Clodius and the evidential value of epitaphs for Roman social history and of Pliny's letters for the early history of Christianity. It is clearly of the highest importance that citizens of a democracy be accustomed to think critically about the sources as well as the content of what they see, hear, and read. The questions, writing projects, and notes provided in both the student's book and the teacher's handbook are intended to guide the teacher to encourage students to acquire the habit of asking themselves not only "What does this say?" but also "Who is saying it?" and "What are his biases, his intentions, and his personal involvement in this issue?"

II. The Format of the Book

Because we are now dealing exclusively with original texts, the format of *From Republic to Empire* differs somewhat from that of the earlier ECCE ROMANI volumes. Each chapter presents a main reading, which is broken up into segments labeled A, B, C, etc.; comprehension questions follow each segment of text. Each segment is about 20 lines in length and is intended to be covered during one class period. (In a few cases two short readings, such as 59C and D, could be covered in one period.) Text is printed on right-hand pages only; extensive vocabulary lists and notes appear on the opposite (left-hand) pages. Grammatical items appear at the end of the chapter or occasionally between reading segments. References are given by chapter, segment, and line numbers; thus, 55A:2 means Chapter 55, section A, line 2.

V. Grammar and Vocabulary

Part I contains no new grammar, but is designed to provide a thorough review of the major topics presented in the third and fourth student's books. This will be particularly useful for those students who begin *From Republic to Empire* after a summer vacation. There are special review sections on participles, ablative absolutes, infinitives and indirect statement, and the subjunctive. In addition, the teaching notes for Part I suggest points of departure for reviewing other material, such as the comparison of adjectives, which is not given a special section.

The major new grammar in this book involves the gerund and gerundive, some additional subjunctive usages (fear clauses, relative clauses, independent subjunctive, and conditions), and special and impersonal verbs. In addition, there is a great deal of material designed for review and synthesis of grammar studied previously. It should be emphasized that students at this intermediate level of Latin, who have been taught all the basic structures, still need continuous review. In addition to the formal review sections, the teaching notes in each chapter point out examples of structures that can be used for review.

The teaching notes also point out structures that students will encounter in the readings and that will be formally taught in a later chapter (e.g., conditional sentences). In most cases it is better not to discuss these until the formal presentation is met. These structures are identified so that teachers can give extra help with the reading, if required, since they know that students are encountering something they have not yet studied; also, once the topic in question is formally introduced, the teacher may wish to find additional examples from previous readings.

The teaching notes also identify some structures, present in the reading, which are never formally presented in the ECCE ROMANI program (e.g., clauses of proviso, clauses of doubt, etc.). In most cases these will not cause problems in comprehending the text, and there is usually no need to discuss them formally, although some teachers may wish to do so. Some of these structures are included in the section titled Syntax found at the end of the student's book.

The treatment of vocabulary is somewhat different from that in previous books. In order to accommodate the very large number of new words that students will meet in these unadapted texts, and to speed up the reading process, each segment of text is accompanied by a facing vocabulary list. Students are *not* expected to memorize all words in these lists, since many of them will not occur again in this book. We have designated with an asterisk (*) all new words that occur in Colby's *Latin Word Lists* for the first three years. In addition, we have placed asterisks next to a very few words that are not in Colby but that occur several times in this text.

We have also printed a number of review words in the facing vocabularies, if we felt it unlikely that students would remember them. For example, the verb condō is first presented in Chapter 34. Since it does not occur again until Chapter 54, most students would have to look it up. Condō is therefore glossed and marked with a bullet (•). About three-quarters of the words with bullets are also listed in Colby; for typographical reasons, we only printed one symbol. Generally, words with asterisks or bullets are *not* repeated again in the facing vocabularies. The message to the student is "An asterisk means an important word; a bullet means a word you have met before but may not remember. Learn these!" We suggest that students be held responsible, even out of context, for words that are marked in these two ways. This system of facing vocabularies is an efficient way to help students get through the reading while building their vocabulary; it is also very similar to the system used in the Longman Latin Readers, which many students will use after completing *From Republic to Empire*.

The end vocabulary contains all words with asterisks or bullets as well as the words that are not printed in the facing vocabulary lists, either because they are presented in previous chapters of ECCE ROMANI or because students are expected to deduce them. As in the previous volumes of ECCE ROMANI, words to be deduced are listed in the notes for each chapter. In the end vocabulary, words for which students should be held responsible are identified by the chapter and reading in which they first appear (54d means Chapter 54, Reading D). In the facing vocabulary lists, the words are listed in the format used in Books 2–4 (principal parts and third-declension genitives spelled out in full). In the end vocabulary, we follow the format used in the *Oxford Latin Dictionary*; principal parts and genitives are abbreviated to save space.

V. Supplementary Materials

There is no Language Activity Book to accompany *From Republic to Empire*. Experience with the earlier edition has shown that the activities found in the LAB, so important for thorough mastery of the material in the earlier books, are less essential at this point in the student's study of Latin. We have, however, provided a few additional exercises on important grammatical points; these are printed in the Appendix to this teacher's handbook and may be reproduced by teachers who are using *From Republic to Empire*.

In addition to the grammar exercises, the Appendix contains Word Study sections, cultural background readings, and supplementary Latin passages, including several inscriptions. All this material is in reproducible form and may be copied as the teacher wishes. Space considerations prevented this material from being included in the student's book, and in any case not all teachers may wish to use it.

VI. Sequencing and Pace

From Republic to Empire has been designed to be completed within one semester. There are forty readings, most of which can be completed in one class period. Since the average public school semester contains about ninety days, this leaves about forty days for grammar, cultural activities, review, and testing. Those who have less time available (e.g., teachers in some independent schools, which have a shorter school year) may find it necessary to omit some material. We strongly suggest that *all students read Part I*. Teachers may then pick and choose material from Parts II–V to fit their needs. Of course, if time is available and teachers desire to spend more than a semester on this book, there is noth-

ing wrong with that; teachers should adapt the program to fit the needs of their schools and students. However, we felt it important to limit the book so that it could be covered in one semester (usually the first half of the third year), leaving the rest of the year for advanced readings.

Those who have used the earlier edition of Book 5 titled *Public Life and Private Lives*, will find this revised edition more tightly focused, since all the readings in Parts I–IV are related to the theme of transition from Republic to Empire. The current book is also more manageable, since there are fewer Latin texts to cover, and the format has been revised to provide additional help for students. The price for these changes has been the elimination of much of the material in the earlier edition that focused on the daily lives of individuals. Some items were included in the Appendix to this teacher's handbook precisely because they focus on individuals; we suggest that these are particularly worth using to balance the large amount of historical and political material in the student's book.

VII. Philosophy of This Handbook

In this handbook, we have tried to offer as many suggestions, ideas, and resources as we could. We recognize that teachers come to the teaching of Latin with varying backgrounds, that *From Republic to Empire* will be used by students of differing ages and levels of ability, and that each district or state imposes its own requirements on the teacher. Therefore, the teacher should not feel obliged to follow every suggestion or read every book mentioned in this guide; that would be almost impossible in any case. Teachers should pick and choose according to their interests and needs and those of their students. Three examples should make this clear. (1) Many suggestions are offered for student reports or projects; these will be limited by the time available, if by nothing else. (2) The teaching notes point out many constructions found in the reading that can be used for review; to review each one of these every time it is mentioned would probably be quite boring for a class, in addition to taking up much time. (3) The reading notes also point out literary and stylistic features that may be taught; older, more able students will clearly be able to do more in this area than younger or weaker ones. In all cases teachers, who best know the needs of their students, must pick and choose what to use.

Teaching Notes

PART I

The End of the Republic and the Establishment of the Principate

CHAPTER 54: THE LATE REPUBLIC

. The aims of this chapter are:

a. to introduce students to the organized study of Roman history and to provide necessary background for the readings from Eutropius
b. to review participles, the ablative absolute, infinitives, and indirect statement.

. Translations

A. During the consulship of Marcus Tullius Cicero the orator and Gaius Antonius, in the 689th year from the founding of the city, Lucius Sergius Catilina, a man of very noble ancestry, but of very wicked character, formed a conspiracy to destroy his country with certain men, distinguished indeed but daring. He was expelled from the city by Cicero. His associates were caught and strangled in the jail. Catiline himself was defeated in battle by Antonius, the other consul, and was killed.

In the 693rd year from the founding of the city, C. Julius Caesar, who later on ruled [as dictator], became consul with L. Bibulus. Gaul and Illyricum were assigned to him, with ten legions. He was the first to defeat the Helvetii, who now are called the Sequani, then by conquering in very serious wars, he proceeded as far as the English Channel. Moreover, within nine years he subdued almost all Gaul, which is between the Alps, the Rhone River, the Rhine, and the Ocean, and which stretches in circumference 3,200 miles. Soon he made war on the Britons, to whom before him [his time] not even the name of the Romans had been known, defeated them and, after receiving hostages, made them subject to tribute. Moreover, he levied on Gaul an annual tax of 40,000,000 sesterces, under the title of tribute. And he attacked the Germans across the Rhine and defeated them in very extensive battles.

B. Now next an accursed and lamentable civil war followed, through which, beyond the disasters that happen in battles, even the fortune of the Roman people was changed. For Caesar, returning victorious from Gaul, began to demand a second consulship and in such a way that without any doubt it would be offered to him. There was opposition from Marcellus the consul, from Bibulus, from Pompey, from Cato, and he [Caesar] was ordered to return to the city after disbanding his armies. Because of this injustice, he came against his country with an army from Ariminum, where he had soldiers assembled. The consuls with Pompey and all the Senate and the entire nobility fled from the city and crossed over into Greece. In Epirus, Macedonia, [and] Achaea the Senate prepared a campaign against Caesar under the leadership of Pompey.

Caesar entered the empty city and made himself dictator. Then he headed for Spain. There he defeated the very strong and brave armies of Pompey with their three leaders L. Afranius, M. Petreius, [and] M. Varro. Then he returned, crossed over into Greece, and fought against Pompey. In the first battle he was defeated and put to flight; however, he escaped because Pompey did not want to follow since night intervened, and Caesar said that Pompey did not know how to win and that only on that day could he [himself] have been conquered.

C. Then in Thessaly at Old Pharsalus they fought, with huge [numbers of] troops drawn up on both sides. Pompey's battle line had 40,000 foot soldiers, 600 cavalrymen on the left wing, 500 on the right, and in addition the auxiliary troops from all the East, the entire nobility, innumerable senators, ex-praetors, ex-consuls and those who had already been victorious in great wars. Caesar in his battle line had less than 30,000 foot soldiers, [and] a thousand cavalrymen.

Never up to this time had greater [numbers of] Roman troops come together in one place, nor with better leaders; they would have easily subdued the whole world, if they were led against barbarians. Then they fought with a huge struggle, and Pompey was defeated in the end and his camp ransacked. He himself was put to flight and headed for Alexandria, in order to get reinforcements from the king of Egypt, to whom he had been given as a protector by the Senate because of his [the king's] young age. He, following expediency rather than friendship, killed Pompey, [and] sent his head and ring to Caesar. Upon seeing this Caesar is said to have even shed tears, as he gazed at the head of such a great man, once his son-in-law.

D. Then Caesar, after settling civil wars throughout the whole world, returned to Rome. He began to behave rather arrogantly and against the custom of Roman liberty. Therefore, when he bestowed by his own will even honors which previously were awarded by the people, and did not stand up for the Senate when they approached him, and did other royal and almost tyrannical things, a conspiracy was made against him by sixty or more senators and Roman knights. Notable among the conspirators were the two Brutuses from that family of Brutus, who had been the first consul of Rome and who had driven out the kings, and C. Cassius and Servilius Casca. Therefore Caesar, when on the day of the Senate [meeting] he had come among others to the Senate House, was stabbed with twenty-three wounds.

Almost in the 709th year [from the founding] of the city, civil wars were renewed after the death of Caesar. For the Senate favored Caesar's assassins. Antony, the consul from Caesar's faction, tried to defeat them in civil wars. And so, with the state thrown into confusion, Antony was judged an enemy by the Senate because he was committing many crimes. Sent to pursue him were the two consuls, Pansa and Hirtius, and Octavian, a young man 18 years old, Caesar's nephew, whom he had left as heir in his will and had ordered to bear his name. This is [the man] who later on was called Augustus and got control of affairs. These three leaders set out against Antony and defeated him [battle of Mutina, 43 B.C.]. However, it turned out that both victorious consuls perished. Thus three armies obeyed the one Caesar Augustus.

3. Background

   a. Eutropius' *Breviarium* is, as its name suggests, a short summary of Roman history. Eutropius treats no topic at great length but rather moves quickly from one event to the next. Thus, even though we pick up Eutropius' account in the middle of Book VI, there is no great need for the teacher to explain at length what has gone before. It is important, however, for students to have a basic understanding of Roman government and of some of the events that led to the downfall of the Republic. Students therefore should not begin the Latin text until they have read and understood the introduction to Part I. The exercises printed in the Appendix (page 91) may be used to help ensure mastery of this material. Although Eutropius is not a traditional author in American schools, his Latin is, for the most part, quite straightforward and is an ideal vehicle for students to use in making the transition from the composed Latin of Books 1–4 to the reading of authentic Latin. Eutropius himself is a slightly mysterious figure; almost everything we know about him is printed in the last paragraph on page 11 of the student's book.

   b. The late Republic was a period of volatile, even chaotic politics. The reading notes below will provide the basic information necessary for the teacher to understand the various events involved, but it is strongly suggested that, for a more complete background, teachers should read

the sections covering 64 B.C–A.D.14 in any of the standard histories of Rome, such as those of Sinnigen and Boak (*A History of Rome to A.D. 565*) or Scullard (*From the Gracchi to Nero*). This background will be useful for Part I, and it will be even more essential for teaching Parts II and IV.

   c. It is also important for teachers and students to have an understanding of the Roman constitution. Pages 8–9 in the student's book present the basic facts, but the teacher should be aware of the following points which are not discussed in the student's book.

    1. The offices of tribune and aedile were not an obligatory part of the **cursus honōrum**; one could, legally, go from being quaestor to being praetor. However, since the aediles were in charge of public entertainment, most politicians chose to run for this office in order to curry favor with the voters by providing lavish spectacles. The tribunate was, of course, only open to plebeians. Tribunes could veto ("I forbid") any decree, motion, act, or law. The extent of this authority, originally designed to protect the **plēbs** against the power of the nobles and their monopoly over magistracies, had grave consequences for the Republic in its waning years, when the tribunate became the personal political tool of ambitious men.

    2. Two offices in the **cursus** that are not mentioned in the student's book are those of dictator and censor. The former was an exceptional magistracy. In time of crisis, the Senate could ask the consuls to appoint one man to rule the state for no more than six months; he was not subject to some of the limitations on the powers of ordinary magistrates. This office is important for our purposes because Julius Caesar held it, but he became **dictātor perpetuus**, not subject to the six-month limit. Censors had the job of keeping the roll of citizens up to date. Since this also entailed determining who could belong to the Senatorial order and who to the **equitēs**, it was a politically powerful position.

    3. The chart printed on page 13 of this handbook may be reproduced and used when discussing Roman government.

In addition, the teacher should help students to understand the rather closed nature of Roman politics. During the Republic, political power was concentrated in the hands of a few families who had one or more consuls among their ancestors. In modern terms, it was as though only members of families such as the Kennedys could be elected to high office; men without this background did enter politics, but it was extremely difficult for them to be elected to the praetorship and especially the consulship. This senatorial class (**nōbilēs, bonī,** or **optimātēs**) ruled by a combination of birth, wealth, and patronage. The absence of political parties in the modern sense (although conservative and liberal elements did exist) is noted by Syme (*The Roman Revolution,* p. 11): "The political life in the Republic was stamped and swayed, not by parties and programs of a modern and parliamentary character, not by ostensible opposition between Senate and People, **Optimātēs** and **Populārēs, nōbilēs** and **novī hominēs,** but by the strife for power, wealth, and glory." For an excellent discussion of **dignitās,** that value which in so many ways drove the political process, see "Dignity," *A History of Private Life, Vol. I,* pp. 101–102 (this entire chapter, entitled "Where Public Life Was Private," is well worth reading, since it discusses many issues that are important for dealing with the texts in *From Republic to Empire*). Students will have a chance to develop their understanding of politics during the Republic further in connection with Part II.

4. Teaching the Text

a. After completing the Introduction (pages 8–11), but before beginning work on the Latin text of Chapter 54, it might be advisable to give students an overview of *From Republic to Empire* and to situate Part I within it. It is important for students to understand that from now on they will be dealing exclusively with authentic Latin; this would be a good time to read *To the Student* (page 7) with the class, and then to explain that Part I will provide an overview of the transition from Republic to Empire and that some of the topics introduced in summary form in Part I will be examined in more detail in Parts II–IV.

b. Since *From Republic to Empire* uses a format that is somewhat different from that of the first four student's books, be sure that students understand the mechanics of the book: how to use facing vocabularies, line numbers, and the meaning of the asterisks and bullets. Reassure students that they will not be required to memorize all the words in the lists, and explain what you do require of them (we suggest assigning the words with asterisks and bullets). You may find it helpful to work through the vocabulary list before beginning the reading of the text. It should be noted that Part I contains a good deal of new vocabulary. Especially notable are the many political and military words, most of which will occur again in Part III and which are also important for students who will be taking standardized tests, such as the College Board Achievement Test, which tend to assume that the student has learned words of this type.

c. In general, the same approaches to the text that are familiar to students from the first four books should be used in dealing with the texts in this book. Start with an oral reading, either by teacher or students. Point out any potential stumbling blocks which are not covered in the notes; do not, however, discuss new points of grammar. Just as in Books 1–4, new features are often encountered in readings before they are to be discussed formally (e.g., the gerundive **dēlendam** on line A:4).

Some teachers find it helpful to prepare overhead transparencies for each text section. (This can be done by photocopying the page from the book—use the enlargement feature if your machine has one—then trimming off any unneeded material such as illustrations and running the photocopy through a transparency maker.) An overhead often focuses students' attention better than simply looking at the book, and one can use erasable markers to highlight important items, mark words that agree, etc. (Such transparencies are also good for reviewing a passage, perhaps with books closed.)

d. Students can then answer the comprehension questions, which are designed to give the general sense of the passage as a prelude to formal translation. The comprehension questions often make good homework assignments, which will prepare students for translation in a following class period. (However, we suggest that for the first couple of readings, at least, all work on the text be done in class to allow students to become comfortable with the new book and to get used to Eutropius' style). Formal translation and close grammatical explication, if required, will follow.

e. After reading about Caesar's arrogant behavior (D:1–6), which led to his murder, teachers may wish to use the supplementary reading *Political Jokes about Caesar* (page 92). See pages 13–14 for answer key and discussion.

5. Reading Notes

A.

a. **M. Tulliō Cicerōne ...** (1–2): The two methods of identifying a year (mentioning the consuls and giving a number A.U.C.) were first introduced in Chapter 34. This is an ideal opportunity to review them. Unfortunately, however, Eutropius is not always precisely correct about his dates. The normal method for converting A.U.C. dates to B.C. is to subtract the A.U.C. date from 754. But 689 subtracted from 754 gives 65, not 64 (formation of the conspiracy) or 63 (Cicero's consulship). The dates given in line A:9 for Caesar's consulship, and in D:13 for Caesar's murder, are likewise one year off.

b. **dēlendam** (4): It is doubtful that Catiline really wanted to "destroy" his country; he, like many other ambitious aristocrats, wanted to get power into his own hands. The exact nature of this conspiracy and of Catiline's motives have been the subject of endless debate; was he simply making use of the economically unfortunate to advance his own ends, or did he have a genuine desire to help the poor? In any case, it must be remembered that Cicero's speeches against Catiline, which so many of us have read, are masterful pieces of propaganda. For more information, see the standard histories of Rome; see also *Social Conflicts in the Roman Republic*, especially pp. 124–132, for discussion from a different point of view.

c. **Gallia et Illyricum** (11): Make sure that students know where the maps are (page 31, general map of the Empire, and page 18, map of civil war sites) and encourage them always to locate any place that is unfamiliar to them on the map.

d. **Helvētiōs** (12): The Helvetii and Sequani in Caesar's time were separate tribes. Either by Eutropius' time the earlier tribal allegiances had become obscured, or Eutropius was not being very careful here.

e. **quadringentiēs** (21): Suetonius, *Divus Julius* 25, confirms this figure of 40,000,000 sesterces. The value of ancient coins is notoriously difficult to translate into modern monetary terms, and students always want to know "How much is it worth in our money?" A Roman legionary earned 25 denarii (=100 sesterces) a year. For a quick summary of coinage, see the third teacher's handbook, page 11, note 7; for a very detailed history of Roman coinage, see "Coinage, Roman," *The Oxford Classical Dictionary*, pp. 261–263.

f. **trāns Rhēnum** (21): Eutropius is wrong, in that Caesar never fought large battles across the Rhine; he did cross the Rhine to "show the flag" and make the Germans less inclined to cross into Gaul and stir up trouble. Also, Britain did not become a Roman province until the time of Claudius; Caesar did not establish any lasting presence on the island.

B.

a. Word to be deduced: **congregātōs** (8).

b. **Catōne** (7): M. Porcius Cato (called "Cato of Utica" to distinguish him from his famous great-grandfather, "Cato the Censor") was one of the staunchest opponents of any attempt to subvert the Republican form of government. M. Calpurnius Bibulus was another Republican, Cato's son-in-law. He was elected consul in the same year as Caesar (mentioned in line A:10) and tried without much success to hinder Caesar's designs. In frustration he finally retired to his house and took minimal part in the government, and the year was humorously referred to as "the consulship of Julius and Caesar."

c. **Pompeiō** (6): Many texts print the name **Pompeius** with a long e. We print it short following the treatment of W. S. Allen (*Vox Latina*, pp 38–39), who points out that in words such as **eius**, **Pompeius**, and **Troia** the i-consonant is actually to be pronounced *double*; it is the double consonant that accounts for the long syllables found in these words in poetry, not the vowels themselves, which are short by nature.

d. **ab Arīminō** (8): Eutropius does not mention the Rubicon river, just to the south of Ariminum, which formed the southern boundary of Caesar's province. It was as he crossed the Rubicon that Caesar exclaimed **"Ālea iacta est"** ("The die is cast"), a **sententia** first introduced in Chapter 30.

e. **dictātōrem** (14): Caesar's innovation was to make himself **dictātor perpetuus**; the office of dictator was designed to be of no more than six months' duration. See the coin reproduced on page 30 of the student's book. In connection with this coin, it should be noted that Julius Caesar was the first living Roman to be portrayed on coins, a fact that must have seemed to his contemporaries yet another proof of his autocratic designs.

f. **Hispāniās** (15): Caesar went to Spain first because Spain was Pompey's base. Pompey was governor of the province and had large armies there, yet Caesar felt he could defeat them since Pompey himself was not there to command them. In one stroke he weakened Pompey's forces considerably and forestalled any threat to his control of Italy while he pursued Pompey to Greece.

g. **M. Varrōne** (16–17): Marcus Terentius Varro was later pardoned by Caesar and had an illustrious career as a scholar and antiquarian. His *Rerum rusticarum libri III* and part of his *De lingua Latina* have come down to us. It was Varro who calculated the date of the founding of Rome as 753 B.C., a calculation which became the standard for reckoning Roman history.

C.

a. Word to be deduced: **victōrēs** (6).

b. **Palaeopharsālum** (1): The battle of Pharsalus will be covered in detail in Chapters 60 and 61.

c. **rēge** (14): Ptolemy XIII was born in 63 B.C. and came to the throne of Egypt upon his father's death in 51. His father, Ptolemy XII Auletes, had cultivated friendly relations with Rome to such an extent that he was expelled from his throne by an angry populace in 55 and then restored by Roman troops. His young son was likewise under the protection of Rome. The decision to murder Pompey in 48 was made by Ptolemy XIII's ministers, since the king was only fifteen years old.

D.

a. Words to be deduced: **cīvīlibus** (1), **tyrannica** (6), **committēns** (17).

b. The plural **bellīs cīvīlibus** (1) probably refers to the several campaigns Caesar fought in his struggle against Pompey and his Republican supporters.

c. **Annō . . . nōnō** (13): on the problems with Eutropius' dates, see above, page 9, note Aa.

d. **Octāviānus** (19): The name of the young man was Gaius Octavius. After his adoption, he became Gaius Iulius Caesar Octavianus. Eutropius uses Octavianus not Octavius—he is thinking in "post-adoption" terms. Modern historians usually refer to him as Octavian when discussing the civil wars and as Augustus when discussing events after 27 B.C.

e. The title **Augustus** (22) was granted to Octavian by the Senate in 27 B.C. and means "sacred" or "revered." Students will study Augustus' career in more detail in Part IV.

6. Review: Participles

a. Participles require considerable attention. They are met frequently in reading; they can be translated in many different ways; they appear frequently in that common construction, the ablative absolute; and the rules of time relations that apply to them apply also to infinitives in indirect statement. If students are weak on the forms of adjectives and on the rules of agreement, these also should be reviewed at this time.

b. Exercise 54a: Make sure students understand that they are to look for participles used simply as adjectives, that is, not as part of compound verb tenses (e.g., **dēcrēta est** [A:11]) or as part of ablative absolutes. Answers:

  dēprehēnsī (A:6) modifies **sociī**
  victus (A:7) modifies **Catilīna**
  victōs (A:19) modifies **eōs**
  aggressus (A:22) modifies the subject of **vīcit**
  rediēns (B:4) modifies **Caesar**
  congregātōs (B:8) modifies **mīlitēs**.

c. Exercise 54b: Only one translation is given below. Encourage students to work out which of the possible alternatives best fits the context. Suggested translations:

1. Catiline, because he wished to destroy his country, formed a conspiracy with others.
2. The consul Cicero drove Catiline, who was about to harm the state, from the city.
3. Catiline, after he was driven from Rome, went to his army.
4. Many people heard Cicero speaking in the Forum against Catiline.
5. C. Iulius Caesar recruited soldiers when he was about to go to Gaul.

6. Caesar defeated the Gauls who were fighting for their freedom.
7. A large number of Gauls were killed while fighting against Caesar.
8. Caesar levied an annual tribute on the conquered Gauls.
9. Caesar attacked even the Germans who lived across the Rhine.
10. Pompey and many senators, who intended to fight against Caesar, crossed into Greece.

7. Review: Ablative Absolutes

a. If students have a decent grasp of participles, the ablative absolute construction is usually not too difficult.

b. Exercise 54c: Answers:
  M. Tulliō Cicerōne ōrātōre et C. Antōniō cōnsulibus (A:1), type 2
  obsidibus acceptīs (A:19), type 1
  dīmissīs exercitibus (B:7), type 1
  Pompeiō duce (B:12), type 2.

c. Exercise 54d: Again, only one possible translation (generally not the most literal one) is given. Suggested translations:

1. During the consulship of Cicero, Catiline was defeated and killed.
2. After Catiline's death, the state seemed to be safe.
3. While Caesar waged war in Gaul, Pompey remained in Rome.
4. After all of Gaul had been conquered, Caesar wanted another consulship.
5. Because Caesar was demanding a second consulship, civil war broke out.
6. Caesar, having received the Senate's answer, set out for Rome with his army.
7. After Caesar had returned to Italy, the Senate fled to Greece.
8. While the senators were fleeing with Pompey to Greece, Caesar made himself dictator.
9. In the Senate's absence, Caesar made himself dictator with no fixed term.
10. After Pompey's army in Spain had been defeated, Caesar crossed over into Greece.
11. When the first battle was finished, Caesar escaped because Pompey did not want to follow at night.
12. Since Pompey did not want to follow at night, Caesar escaped.
13. While Caesar and Pompey were fighting in Greece, the citizens in the city [Rome] did not know who would be the winner.

8. Review: Infinitives

a. Future infinitives of deponent verbs have the same form as those of regular verbs (e.g., **veritūrus esse** from **vereor**, similar to **habi-**

tūrus esse from **habeō**). Compare present participles, which are also the same for both regular and deponent verbs (e.g., **verēns, verentis,** similar to **habēns, habentis**).

b. Exercise 54e: Make sure students understand that deponent verbs (and the verb **sum**) will have only three infinitives. Answers:

dīmicāre, dīmicārī, dīmicāvisse, dīmicātus esse, dīmicātūrus esse

cognōscere, cognōscī, cognōvisse, cognitus esse, cognitūrus esse

dēlēre, dēlērī, dēlēvisse, dēlētus esse, dēlētūrus esse

aggredī, aggressus esse, aggressūrus esse

interficere, interficī, interfēcisse, interfectus esse, interfectūrus esse

audīre, audīrī, audīvisse, audītus esse, audītūrus esse

cōnārī, cōnātus esse, cōnātūrus esse

esse, fuisse, futūrus esse or **fore**

9. Review: Indirect Statement

a. This is an absolutely essential construction for students to master. Make sure they know their infinitive forms thoroughly before continuing with indirect statement.

b. Exercise 54f: Suggested translations:
1. Caesar wanted a second consulship, but he understood that Pompey would not help him.
2. Caesar knew that the Senate favored Pompey more than him.
3. Eutropius says that the armies at Pharsalus were very large.
4. The Roman citizens heard that Pompey had been put to flight and his camp ransacked.
5. Pompey believed that King Ptolemy would be friendly to him, and would give him reinforcements; therefore he went to Alexandria.
6. It is agreed that Caesar wept when he looked at Pompey's head.
7. Eutropius says that Caesar was killed in the Senate House, but we know in fact that the dictator died in Pompey's theater.
8. It is said that sixty senators conspired against Caesar.
9. After Caesar's death, Antony did not believe that the young Octavian could rule.
10. Everyone knows that Octavian was adopted by Caesar's will.

10. Other Review Material

Many teachers will wish to do additional review work beyond what is specifically provided in Part I, especially if students are beginning *From Republic to Empire* after a summer vacation.

A. Forms

One can begin by requiring students to review the five declensions of nouns and the four regular conjugations of verbs. We suggest the use of synopsis (an exercise where students conjugate a given verb in one form, such as third person plural, in all tenses) as an excellent way to review verbs. Students can begin with the indicative, add the participles and infinitives after completing the corresponding review sections, and add the subjunctive after Chapter 55. A synopsis blank is provided on page 93 of the Appendix to this handbook. (Note that this blank contains a line for the Future Passive Participle; you may wish to cover this when making copies for use with Part I, since the gerundive or future passive participle, which goes on this line, will not be taught until Chapter 58.) The blank can be used for deponent verbs too; if students have trouble remembering which forms to leave out, you may want to make a copy of the blank and draw a line through those spaces that will not be used for deponents (active indicative, active subjunctive, and present and perfect infinitives active) and reproduce this for the class.

As part of their review of verb forms, teachers will undoubtedly want to review principal parts—what they are and how they are formed for the regular verbs of the 1st, 2nd, and 4th conjugations (originally taught in Chapter 19). To help students deal with principal parts that do not follow the regular patterns, we have provided the supplementary activity *Irregular Third Principal Parts* (page 94), which could be done either now or in conjunction with Chapter 55. See page 16 for answers and additional discussion.

B. Syntax

Review of syntax should be based, as much as possible, on the readings. After the text has been read and understood, the teacher can pick out particular nouns and ask students what case they are in and why. For a more formal review, make up a sheet listing each case with its various uses, and have students find examples in the texts they have read. Teachers may wish to refer to the Syntax sections of the first four student's books, which outline all the syntax taught in those books.

Here are examples of some constructions from the reading that may be used as points of departure for review (this list is by no means exhaustive):
1. Nominative case: subject of verb (**Catilīna,** A:3); predicate nominative (**Sēquanī,** A:12, **hostis,** D:17)
2. Genitive case: equivalent to an adjective, describing a noun (genitive of description) (**nōbilissimī generis,** A:3); showing

possession (**tantī virī . . . generī . . . suī,** C:19)

3. Dative case: indirect object (**eī,** A:11); object of special intransitive verbs (**percussōribus . . . favēbat,** D:14–15, **ūnī Caesarī Augustō pāruērunt,** D:24–25)

4. Accusative case: direct object of a verb (**Helvētiōs,** A:12); object of prepositions (**per bella gravissima,** A:13, **inter Alpēs . . . ,** A:15, **ante eum,** A:18, **trāns Rhēnum,** A:21, **ad urbem,** B:7, **propter quam iniūriam,** B:8, **in Graeciam,** B:11, **apud Ēpirum,** B:11, **contrā Caesarem,** B:12); showing place to which, with no preposition (**Alexandrīam,** C:14, **Rōmam,** D:2)

5. Ablative case: object of prepositions (**cum quibusdam clārīs . . . virīs,** A:4–5, **ā Cicerōne,** A:5, **in carcere,** A:6, **ex urbe,** B:10–11); means (**proeliō,** A:7); time when (**annō . . . nōnō,** A:1–2, **illō . . . diē,** B:21), time within which (**annīs novem,** A:14–15), respect or specification (**tribūtī nōmine,** A:20)

6. Relative pronoun/clause: (**quae . . . est et . . . patet,** A:15–16, **quibus . . . cognitum erat,** A:18–19, **cui . . . datus fuerat,** C:14–15, **quem . . . relīquerat et . . . iusserat,** D:20–21); linking **quī,** (**Quī,** C:16, **Quō,** C:18)

7. Passive voice: (**expulsus est,** A:5, **strangulātī sunt,** A:6)

8. Deponent verbs (**sequī,** B:20, **cōnābātur,** D:16)

9. Comparison of adjectives and adverbs (**nōbilissimī,** A:3, **validissimōs et fortissimōs,** B:15–16, **īnsolentius,** D:2).

The notes for subsequent chapters will point out other opportunities for review.

11. In the right-hand coin on page 30, EID(IBUS) is an earlier spelling for IDIBUS; in inscriptions from the Republican period a long *i* is often spelled *ei.*

12. Supplementary Materials

a. *Exercises for the Introduction* (page 91): This set of exercises to check and reinforce students' understanding of the material may be followed up by the quiz on the Introduction that is found in the Test Masters. It should be emphasized that a time line gives a broad chronological framework rather than precise data, partly because only the years, not the months, are indicated. To No. 7, students will presumably give the answer "one year," but the time between the assassination of Caesar (March, 44 B.C.) and that of Cicero (December, 43 B.C.) was actually almost two years (21 months).

Answers for Exercise 2:
1. Twenty-one years old.
2. Seventy-seven years.
3. They were the same age.
4. Nineteen.
5. Approximately eighteen.
6. Augustus.
7. One year (actually, 21 months).
8. Ovid.
9. His date of birth is unknown.
10. Martial was older by about twenty-one years.
11. Twelve.
12. Forty-three.

b. *Political Jokes about Caesar* (page 92): This may be used any time after Reading 54D has been completed; it provides a nice change of pace and shows a different side of the Romans. Suggested translations:

1. *Not a thing happened recently during the consulship of Bibulus, but during that of Caesar; for I remember nothing taking place during Bibulus' consulship.* This jibe is cast as an elegiac couplet, a verse form that students have seen frequently in the *Versiculi* (although it has probably not been discussed formally).

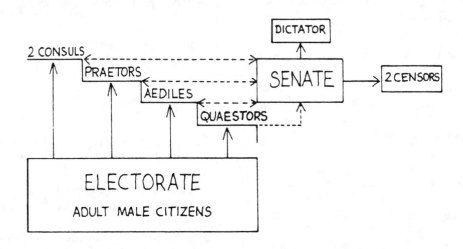

Chart of Republican Government

2. *Caesar led the Gauls in his triumph; the same [man] [led them] to the Senate House; the Gauls have put aside their trousers, and taken on the broad [purple] stripe.* **Brācae**, trousers or leggings worn by Gauls, were considered effeminate by the Romans. The archer in the illustration at the bottom is wearing **brācae**. For another allusion to this "exotic" garment, see the supplementary reading *Two Inscriptions from Britain* (page 111). This and the following item (No. 3) might be used as a springboard for discussion of ethnic prejudice and stereotyping.

3. *A good action: let no one point out the Senate House to a new senator!* This is a parody of an official decree; the "new senator" would be a provincial, appointed by Caesar, who had never been in Rome before. The prohibition **Nē quis . . . mōnstrāre velit** is similar to the negative imperative construction with which students are familiar (**nōlī** or **nōlīte** plus infinitive).

4. *Brutus, because he drove out the kings, became the first consul; this man [Caesar], because he drove out the consuls, in the end became king.* This is the same Brutus mentioned in D:8–9.

c. *Synopsis Blank* (page 93): See discussion on page 12 above. This blank may be used throughout the course to review verb forms.

CHAPTER 55: THE FALL OF THE REPUBLIC

1. The aims of this chapter are:

   a. to continue the narrative
   b. to review the forms of the subjunctive mood, and to review the sequence of tenses.

2. Translations

A. When Antony was put to flight, with his army lost, he took refuge with Lepidus, who had been [Julius] Caesar's second-in-command [master of horse] and who at that time had large troops of soldiers, by whom he [Antony] was protected. Soon, through the efforts of Lepidus [with Lepidus making efforts], Caesar made peace with Antony and, as if to avenge the death of his father, by whom he had been adopted in his will, he set out for Rome with an army and compelled a consulship to be given to him in his twentieth year. He outlawed the Senate, and he began to hold the government with Antony and Lepidus through force. By these men even Cicero the orator was killed and many other nobles.

Meanwhile Brutus and Cassius, Caesar's murderers, stirred up a huge war. For there were through-

out Macedonia and the East many armies that they had seized. Therefore, Caesar Octavian Augustus and M. Antony set out against them; for Lepidus had remained behind to defend Italy. At Philippi, a city in Macedonia, they fought against them. In the first battle Antony and Caesar were defeated, but Cassius, the leader of the nobles, perished; in the second [battle] they [Antony and Caesar] defeated and killed Brutus and countless nobles, who had waged war with them. And so the state was divided among them, so that Augustus held Spain, Gaul, and Italy, Antony [held] Asia, Pontus, and the East. But in Italy L. Antonius the consul stirred up a civil war, the brother of that one who had fought with Caesar against Brutus and Cassius. He was defeated and captured at Perugia, a city in Etruria, but he was not killed.

B. At this time M. Agrippa managed the situation in Aquitania efficiently, and L. Ventidius Bassus defeated the Parthians, who were breaking into Syria, in three battles. He killed Pacorus, son of King Orodes, on that very day on which once Orodes, the Perisan King, had killed Crassus through his general Surena. He [Bassus] was the first to celebrate a most justified triumph over the Parthians in Rome.

Antony, who held Asia and the East, after divorcing the sister of Caesar Augustus Octavian, took as his wife Cleopatra, the Queen of Egypt. He himself also fought against the Parthians. He defeated them in the first battles; however, on his return he suffered from hunger and disease and, when the Parthians pursued him as he fled, he himself went away as the defeated one.

He also stirred up a huge civil war, since his wife Cleopatra, the Queen of Egypt, forced him to, while she with a woman's greed wished to rule even in the city. He was defeated by Augustus in a famous and well-known naval battle at Actium, which is a place in Epirus, from which he fled into Egypt and, having given up hope for the situation, since everyone was going over to Augustus, killed himself. Cleopatra allowed an asp to reach her and was killed by its poison. Egypt was added by Octavian Augustus to the Roman empire and C. Cornelius Gallus was put in charge of it. Egypt had him as its first Roman governor.

3. Teaching the Text

The Latin text continues to be relatively straightforward. A potential source of confusion is the large number of new names, both of people and of places, which students encounter as they proceed. Teachers may ask students to keep lists of people and places, with short notes as to what they did or why they are important, to make time lines (showing the sequence of events if not exact dates for everything), and to refer frequently to the map on page 31 of the student's book. Students will need help from teachers in sorting out those individuals and places that are important and worth memorizing from those that are mentioned only in passing.

4. Reading Notes

A.

a. Words to be deduced: **grandēs** (3), **nōbilēs** (10).

b. **magister equitum** (2): The original role of the dictator was as a military leader in times of crisis. The dictator chose a second-in-command, who in early times did in fact command the cavalry. The title was retained, although by Caesar's time he was not limited to that role.

c. **prōscrīpsit** (8): Proscription was a practice first introduced by Sulla after his victory over Marius. Lists were posted of those who had fought on the losing side and were declared to be "outside the protection of the law." These men were then killed by agents of the winning side and their property was confiscated. Antony and Octavian did not, of course, proscribe the entire Senate, but only those who were active in opposing them—a large number nevertheless.

d. **Lepidō** (8): Lepidus received Africa to govern but he was soon shoved aside by Octavian. He lived in relative obscurity until his death.

e. **Philippōs** (16): Before this battle, Octavian took a vow to build a temple to **Mars Ultor** (Mars the Avenger) if he were victorious. He later made this temple the centerpiece of his forum, illustrated on page 46 of the student's book.

f. **Augustus** (21): The title is an anachronism at this point, since it was not granted by the Senate until 27 B.C.

g. **Asiam** (22): Students may remember from previous books that Sextus' father was on assignment in Asia (e.g., 38:2); remind them, if necessary, that this term in Latin refers to part of what is now Turkey (see the map on page 31).

h. Notice that the use of word **cīvitās** (25) to mean "city" prefigures both medieval Latin and the Romance langauges—cf. Spanish *ciudad*, Italian *cività*, and French *cité*. In classical Latin **cīvitās** normally means "state" or "citizenship." Remember that Eutropius wrote during the late fourth century, by which time Latin had undergone many changes as it evolved toward the Romance languages; the classical dialect, however, was still preserved for literary purposes.

B.

a. Words to be deduced: **nāvālī** (15), **pugnā** (15), and **exstincta est** (19).

b. **Agrippa** (1): Augustus' close friend and supporter, who served at one point as governor of Gaul. During Agrippa's tenure, the Aquitanians revolted, but the rebellion was crushed by Agrippa.

c. **Persās** (2), **Parthīs** (5): The Parthians and the Persians were actually two distinct peoples. The Parthians were a semi-nomadic people who migrated south into Persia and eventually acquired a large empire, but they remained a landowning, feudal aristocracy. The Persians, and the other peoples who made up their empire, remained ethnically separate, a distinction that Roman historians do not always make. King Orodes I of Parthia is shown on the tetradrachm shown on page 35 of the student's book.

d. **cōgente uxōre Cleopatrā** (13–14): Notice that Eutropius blames Cleopatra, not Antony's ambition to be sole ruler of the Roman world, for the civil war. Augustus himself used this tactic in the propaganda he spread while preparing for the civil war; he preferred to play on Roman prejudices against foreigners, especially those from the East, rather than denigrate a fellow Roman. That Cleopatra had seduced and corrupted Antony became almost the standard version among Roman historians. Teachers may wish to have students read in translation Horace, *Odes* I.37, the famous song of triumph over Cleopatra; notice the terms used to describe Cleopatra and that Antony is totally ignored.

Students who are intrigued by the story of Antony and Cleopatra may wish to read selections from Plutarch's *Life of Antony*. This is the source that has exercised the greatest influence on later treatments of the story, such as Shakespeare's *Antony and Cleopatra* and the movie *Cleopatra* (1963). The life of Antony is included among those translated by Rex Warner under the title *Fall of the Roman Republic: Six Lives of Plutarch*. For another view of Antony, see Seneca, *Epistulae Morales* 83, which discusses Antony as one of those who were corrupted by alcohol. A version of this letter is included in *The Romans Speak for Themselves*, Book II, pp. 23–31.

e. **C. Cornēlius Gallus** (21) was a friend of both Augustus and the poet Vergil. He served Augustus in various capacities during the civil wars, and, after playing a significant part in the capture of Egypt, was made its first governor. Because of Egypt's wealth and importance as a source of grain, Augustus never made it into a regular province but kept it under his personal control, governed by his appointees. Gallus fell from favor and was recalled for reasons now unclear; he committed suicide in 26 B.C. to avoid prosecution. He was a highly regarded love poet, author of four books of elegies of which only a few lines survive.

5. Review: The Subjunctive Mood

a. Remind students that **ferō** and **eō** are like 3rd conjugation verbs (subjunctive in -a-), while the other irregular verbs (**esse** and its compounds, **volō**, **nōlō**, and **mālō**) have the -i- subjunctive. Some students find the mnemonic "We eat caviar" helpful for remembering the vowels of the present subjunctive.

b. Exercise 55a: Call students' attention to the directions or they will do all of the items in the active. This exercise is a mini-synopsis; after completing it, you may want to assign one or more complete synopses (discussed above, page 12) so that students will compare and contrast the indicative with the subjunctive forms. See the sample blank on page 93. Answers:
1. **āmittat, āmitteret, āmīserit, āmīsisset.**
2. **vindicēmus, vindicārēmus, vindicāve-rimus, vindicāvissēmus.**
3. **possint, possent, potuerint, potuissent.**
4. **impediās, impedīrēs, impedīveris, impedīvissēs.**
5. **commoveam, commovērem, com-mōverim, commōvissem.**
6. **velītis, vellētis, volueritis, voluissētis.**
7. **suscipiant, susciperent, suscēperint, suscēpissent.**
8. **cōner, cōnārer, cōnātus (-a) sim, cōnātus (-a) essem.**
9. **ferātur, ferrētur, lātus (-a, -um) sit, lātus (-a, -um) esset.**
10. **cōgāmur, cōgerēmur, coāctī (-ae) sīmus, coāctī (-ae) essēmus.**
11. **iubēminī, iubērēminī, iussī (-ae) sītis, iussī (-ae) essētis.**
12. **regrediantur, regrederentur, regressī (-ae) sint, regressī (-ae) essent.**

6. Review: Sequence of Tenses

a. This is a prelude to the review of all the subjunctive constructions that comes in Chapter 56. It is probably best not to discuss the uses of the subjunctive now; exercise 55b does contain, however, examples of most of the constructions. It should be stressed that the subjunctive is mostly found in subordinate clauses (independent subjunctives are not formally discussed until Chapter 65).

b. Exercise 55b: Answers and suggested translations:
1. **(daret)** Because Lepidus intervened (made efforts), Antony and Octavian made peace with each other.
2. **(fūgerit)** Everyone knows why Antony fled to Egypt.
3. **(habēret)** Antony wanted to know how many soldiers Octavian had.

4. **(victus esset)** Because (After) Antony had been defeated at Actium, many of his soldiers went over to Octavian.
5. **(mortua sit)** We know how Cleopatra died.
6. **(esset)** The teacher taught us who the first Roman governor in Egypt was.
7. **(adiēcisset)** Octavian returned to Rome after he had added Egypt to the Roman Empire.
8. **(interfēcerit)** Everyone knows when [where] Cleopatra killed herself.

7. Octavia, shown on the coin at the bottom of page 32 in the student's book, became widely respected for her nobility, selflessness, and sense of duty. She made considerable efforts to prevent the rupture between her brother and Antony and was instrumental in arranging the Pact of Tarentum in 37, through which the Second Triumvirate was renewed. After Antony's death she brought up all of his surviving children, those he had by Fulvia (his first wife, widow of P. Clodius) and by Cleopatra, as well as her own. The legend above Antony's head reads M. ANTO-NIVS IMP(erator) III VIR (= triumvir) R(ei) P(ubli-cae) C(onstituendae), the same title mentioned by Augustus at 62A:10. Students who are interested in Roman women could research Octavia's life in more detail, and also those of the two Julias, daughters of Julius Caesar and Augustus, each of whom entered into a series of political marriages. Another woman, Fannia, will be featured in Chapter 66.

The coin on page 39 shows on the reverse a crocodile, which often appears on Roman coins to symbolize Egypt, with the legend AEGYPTO CAPTA (an ablative absolute). The obverse shows Caesar with a **lituus** or sacred staff and commemorates his sixth consulship (28 B.C.). The standard abbreviation COS for **cōnsul** will occur again in Chapter 62A:9.

8. Supplementary Materials

a. *Irregular Third Principal Parts* (page 94): We feel that it is easier for students at this level to learn principal parts if they understand the methods of lengthening, reduplication, and sigmatic formation; after doing this exercise, students should be asked to identify how the third principal parts of the new verbs they learn in future chapters are formed. Answers:
1. **poposcī**, reduplicative
2. **dūxī**, sigmatic
3. **fēcī**, lengthened
4. **discessī**, sigmatic
5. **clausī**, sigmatic
6. **dedī**, reduplicative
7. **lēgī**, lengthened
8. **scrīpsī**, sigmatic
9. **vēnī**, lengthened
10. **iūnxī**, sigmatic

11. **sēdī**, lengthened
12. **strīnxī**, sigmatic
13. **pepercī**, reduplicative
14. **adiūvī**, lengthened
15. **praestitī**, reduplicative

All these verbs have occurred in previous chapters; you may wish to ask for meanings, and/or for the other principal parts, as additional review. Notice that number 15, **praestitī**, is a compound verb; when reduplicative verbs are compounded the prefix comes first, then the reduplication (cf. **trādidī** and **condidī**, from **dō**). Note also the vowel weakening (**e** to **i** in compounds of both **dō** and **stō**). It would be an excellent idea to review the processes by which compound verbs are formed (first presented in Chapters 26 and 27), since so many of the new verbs that students will meet in *From Republic to Empire* will be compounds of verbs they already know.

CHAPTER 56: AUGUSTUS AND THE ESTABLISHMENT OF THE PRINCIPATE

1. The aims of this chapter are:

   a. to continue the narrative
   b. to review the uses of the subjunctive mood.

2. Translations

   A. When wars had been settled throughout the whole world in this way, Octavian Augustus returned to Rome, in the twelfth year after he had [first] been consul. From that time, he held the state alone for forty-four years. For previously he had held it with Antony and Lepidus for twelve years. Thus from the beginning of his principate up to its end there were fifty-six years. Moreover, he died in his seventy-sixth year of a natural death in the Campanian town of Atella. He was buried in Rome in the Campus Martius, a man who not undeservedly was considered, for the most part, like a god. For not easily was anyone more fortunate than he in wars, or more restrained in peacetime. During the forty-four years, in which he held the power alone, he lived very politely, very generous to all, [and] very loyal to his friends, whom he raised up with such great honors that he almost made [them] equal to his own greatness.

   At no time before him did Rome's condition flourish more. For, in addition to the civil wars [literally, the civil wars being excepted], in which he was undefeated, he added to the Empire Egypt, Cantabria, Dalmatia which had often been conquered before but at this time was thoroughly subdued, Pannonia, Aquitania, Illyricum, Raetia, the Vindelici and Salassi

in the Alps, [and] all the states on the shore of the Black Sea, among these the most noble Panticapaeum and the [kingdom of] Bosporus. Further, he overcame the Dacians in many battles.

B. He killed great numbers of Germans, and he moved [the tribes] themselves across the Elbe river, which is in foreign territory far beyond the Rhine. However, he conducted this war through Drusus, his stepson, just as he conducted the Pannonian war through Tiberius, his other stepson. In this war he brought 40,000 captives from Germany and settled them in Gaul above the bank of the Rhine. He recovered Armenia from the Parthians. The Persians gave him hostages, a thing which [they had done] for no one previously. They also gave back the Roman standards, which they had taken from the defeated Crassus.

The Scythians and Indians, to whom previously the Roman name had been unknown, sent gifts and ambassadors to him. Galatia also became a province under him, although it previously had been an [independent] kingdom, and M. Lollius was the first to govern it as propraetor. Moreover, he was so beloved even among foreigners that kings friendly to the Roman people founded cities in his honor, which they called Caesareas. Moreover, many kings came from their realms to honor him, and in Roman dress — wearing togas, of course — ran beside his vehicle or his horse. At his death he was named deified.

3. Background

Eutropius expresses unqualified admiration for Augustus. It is certainly true that Augustus had a long and generally prosperous reign. However, some aspects of his career were not so positive, such as his use of proscriptions during the Second Triumvirate. He also did have some military reverses, notably against the Germans. Students can get an idea of the condition of the Empire at Augustus' death by examining the map on page 31. It should be remembered that conditions during Eutropius' own time (fourth century A.D.) were not so good; there were periodic struggles for the throne, the economy was declining, and the Empire was threatened with foreign invasions; all this may have contributed to Eutropius' tendency to idealize earlier rulers, such as Augustus and Trajan. Students will return to Augustus in Part IV.

4. Reading Notes

   A.
   a. Words to be deduced: **quīnquāgintā** (6), **septuāgēsimō** (6), **moderātior** (11), **rēs Rōmāna** (15), and **exceptīs** (16).
   b. **sepultus est** (8): Augustus' tomb is important not only as a sign of the respect in which Augus-

tus was held, but also as the pattern for the better-known tomb of Hadrian, now referred to as the Castel Sant' Angelo. Augustus' tomb served as the burial place for all members of the Julio-Claudian dynasty (except Claudius and Nero). It was also outside this tomb that the original copy of the *Res gestae divi Augusti*, which students will read in Part IV, was set up. We print a reconstruction, rather than a photo of what appears today, because the visible remains (excavated under Mussolini) would give students little idea of how the tomb originally looked. A picture of its current state can be found in *The Mute Stones Speak*, p. 198. The numbers on the plan are identified as follows: (1) entrance; (2) pillars with *Res gestae* tablets; (3) entrance corridor; (4) remains of walls supporting the second level, with two entrance passages into the interior; (5) entrance passage; (6, 7, 8) niches for ashes of other family members; and (9) Augustus' own tomb. The other photo on page 46 shows Augustus' forum, with its centerpiece, the temple of Mars Ultor (Mars the Avenger), built in fulfillment of a vow made at the battle of Philippi. See also the plan on page 110 of the student's book.

c. The word **imperium** is often used by Eutropius in the sense of "empire," but sometimes has its original meaning of "power" (cf. lines 12 and 17). A similar distinction must be observed with the word **imperātor**, which means "victorious general" in Republican contexts and "emperor" in imperial ones.

d. **omnēs . . . Panticapaeum** (20–21): Eutropius' phrasing is slightly confusing when he discusses Augustus' settlement of the Black Sea area. First, teachers should be aware that Bosporus can refer to the straits of Kertch (between the Sea of Azov and the Black Sea) as well as to the passage between the Black and Aegean Seas, which is the more familiar usage. The Crimea had been settled with a number of Greek colonies, which during the Hellenistic period were united under a single monarchy. These cities later came under the control of Mithridates VI of Pontus; after his defeat by Pompey, the entire area became a client kingdom of Rome, referred to as the Kingdom of Bosporus. Augustus did not "add it" to the Empire, as Eutropius claims; it had been a client kingdom since Pompey's time, and it retained that status. Augustus did, however, intervene twice to ensure a stable local government. For more details see "Bosporus (2)," *The Oxford Classical Dictionary*, p. 176.

B

a. Words to be deduced: **administrāvit** (4), **prōvincia** (12), **barbarōs** (14), and **nōminārent** (16).

b. **Germānōrum** (1): One of Augustus' main objectives was to stabilize the northern frontier. He began by securing control of the south bank of the Danube and organizing the provinces of Rhaetia, Noricum, Pannonia, and Moesia. He then intended to push Roman control as far west as the Elbe River, which he considered a more defensible arrangement than simply holding the Rhine. Augustus' troops did in fact take control of this territory (this is probably what Eutropius is referring to when he says **ipsōs . . . trāns Albim fluvium summōvit** [1–2]), but the task of building forts, pacifying the tribes, and turning the area into a province still remained. Both the Danube and the German campaigns were conducted for Augustus by his stepsons, Drusus and Tiberius (mentioned in lines 3 and 4 below), sons of his second wife Livia by her first marriage to Ti. Claudius Nero. However, Drusus, one of Augustus' best generals, was killed in 9 B.C., and Tiberius was recalled to Rome shortly thereafter. This stopped the forward momentum of Augustus' plan. In A.D. 6, Tiberius was again on the German front, preparing to renew the war, when he was forced to take charge in Pannonia, where a serious revolt had broken out. Then, in A.D. 9, three Roman legions under the command of Quinctilius Varus were wiped out by the Germans under Arminius (see the supplementary reading *A Casualty of War*, page 106). Augustus then lost heart and decided to accept the Rhine as the permanent frontier—a decision that ultimately had momentous consequences for the Empire.

c. **Tiberium** (4): After the deaths of Lucius and Gaius, Augustus' grandsons, Tiberius was accepted as Augustus' heir (A.D. 4) and ultimately became the second Roman emperor.

d. Students may be confused by the various meanings of **mūnus** given in the gloss (11). Explain that the Etruscans held fights to the death at funerals to placate the spirits of the dead. The Romans took over this custom, which eventually turned into a form of mass entertainment. In this book, the notes sometimes give more than one meaning of a word, especially if it is a basic word or one that students have already encountered; the basic meaning is usually listed first, followed by more abstract or tranferred meanings.

e. The use of **prīmus** (13) is similar to that found in 55B:5. Translate "and M. Lollius was the first to administer it as propraetor." It takes a while for students to become comfortable with this construction.

f. **Caesarēās** (16): For one of the Caesareas founded by friendly foreign kings, see the *National Geographic* article on Caesarea in Palestine, in the February 1987 issue.

g. nōminārent (16) is subjunctive in a relative clause of characteristic, which will be presented in Chapter 64. This construction need not be discussed yet.

6. Review: The Subjunctive in Subordinate Clauses

a. One of the most important topics taught in *Pastimes and Ceremonies* was the subjunctive; it will also loom large in *From Republic to Empire*. It is essential for students to be thoroughly familiar with the various types of clauses that require the subjunctive. When doing exercises such as 56a and b, one student should not answer all parts of a question; vary the class routine by having one student choose, another translate, and a third identify the usage involved; one can also ask the student who answers first to pick the next student to answer. Teachers who have strong classes and want to do some Latin composition may duplicate the English translations to some of the exercise sentences and have students reconstruct the Latin (perhaps not the whole sentence) as a review exercise. You may also wish to have students review Building Up the Meaning VIII (*Pastimes and Ceremonies*, pages 61–62), which is designed to help students deal with verbs that can be followed by a direct object, an indirect statement, or an indirect question.

b. Exercise 56a: Answers and suggested translations:
1. (**cum** circumstantial) After Augustus had died, the Senate named him Deified.
2. (purpose) Augustus waged many wars so that there would be peace throughout the whole world.
3. (result) Augustus was such a great ruler that Eutropius praised him highly in his *Breviarium*.
4. (indirect question) Everyone knows why the Roman people loved Augustus.
5. (**cum** circumstantial) The Senate gave Octavian the title Augustus when he had gotten control of affairs.
6. (purpose) Many kings came to Rome to honor Augustus.
7. (result) Julius Caesar was so arrogant that the senators killed him.
8. (indirect command) The Emperor is asking the Senate to help him.
9. (indirect question) I do not know how many wars Augustus waged.
10. (result) Augustus behaved in such a way that no one wanted to kill him.

c. Exercise 56b: You may want to ask for translation and/or identification of the type of clause in

addition to choosing the correct verb form. Answers and suggested translations:
1. (**vellet**) Antony started a war against Octavian because he wanted to rule the whole world.
2. (**commōverit**) Everyone knows why Antony started the war.
3. (**irrumperent**) Antony fought against the Persians so that they would not break into Syria often.
4. (**vincant**) Cleopatra and Antony will go to Actium to defeat Octavian.
5. (**victī essent**) Because (After) they had been defeated, Antony and Cleopatra killed themselves.
6. (**fēcerit**) Egypt was such an important province that Augustus made his friend C. Cornelius Gallus governor.
7. (**vellet**) Cleopatra loved Antony so much that she wanted to die with him.

7. Supplementary Materials

a. *Practice with Subjunctive Clauses* (page 95): this activity provides additional reinforcement of the subjunctive usages. Answers and suggested translations:
1. (**laudāret**) Eutropius wrote these things in order to praise Augustus. (purpose)
2. (**esset**) When/Since Octavian was about to get control of Egypt, Cleopatra killed herself. (**cum** circumstantial or causal)
3. (**vīcisset**) After the battle at Actium took place, Antony understood why Octavian had beaten him. (indirect question)
4. (**possent**) The ships of Antony and Cleopatra were so large that they could not be steered easily. (result)
5. (**dēserant**) Antony, who was defeated at Actium, is begging his soldiers not to desert him. (indirect command)
6. (**esset**) Antony and Octavian fought each other to decide who would rule the world. (purpose, indirect question)
7. (**adiecta esset**) When Egypt had been added to the Roman Empire, Octavian returned to Rome.
8. (**laudāret**) Augustus was an emperor of such great excellence that Eutropius praised him very highly. (result)
9. (**commoveant**) Many senators are warning Octavian and Antony not to start a civil war. (indirect command)
10. (**pugnāvissent**) All the students knew where Antony and Octavian had fought each other. (indirect question)

PART II
Political Violence in the Late Republic

CHAPTER 57: A POLITICAL MURDER (ASCONIUS' ACCOUNT)

1. The aims of this chapter are:

    a. to introduce the incident of Clodius and Milo (53–52 B.C.) as an example of the political forces and personalities at work during the late Republic
    b. to introduce the gerund formally.

2. Translation

    A. On 20 January [52 B.C.] Milo set out for Lanuvium, from which town he was and where he was chief magistrate at that time, in order to appoint a priest on the following day. At about the ninth hour Clodius, while returning from Aricia [where] he had addressed the town council of the citizens of Aricia, met him a little beyond Bovillae. Clodius was riding on horseback; nearly thirty lightly-armed slaves equipped with swords, as was the custom at that time for those making a journey, were following along. There were with Clodius, furthermore, three of his comrades, of whom one was a Roman knight [and] two well-known men from the plebeians. Milo was riding in a carriage with his wife Fausta, daughter of L. [Cornelius] Sulla, the dictator, and his close friend Marcus Fufius. A long column of slaves followed them, among whom there were also gladiators, two of whom, Eudamus and Birria, [were] well-known. These latter, going rather slowly at the rear of the column, began a skirmish with P. Clodius' slaves.

    B. When Clodius had looked back menacingly at this commotion, Birria pierced his arm with a lance. Thereupon, when a pitched battle had arisen, more of Milo's men ran up. Clodius, wounded, was carried into the nearest inn in the area of Bovillae. When Milo learned that Clodius had been wounded, [and] when he realized that it [the wounding of Clodius] would be more dangerous for him with Clodius alive but that with Clodius dead he would have a great consolation even if he had to undergo punishment, Milo ordered [him] to be dragged from the tavern. And so Clodius, in hiding, was dragged out and finished off with many wounds. His body was left in the road, since Clodius' slaves had either been killed or were in hiding, seriously wounded, [and] Sextus Teidius the senator, who by chance was returning to Rome from the country, picked [it] up and ordered it to be brought to Rome in his litter.

    C. The body of Clodius was brought in just before nightfall, and a huge mob of the most vile common people and slaves stood with great mourning around the body placed in the atrium of his house. Moreover, Fulvia, Clodius' wife, who was pointing out his wounds with unrestrained weeping, magnified [their] outrage at the deed. At dawn the next day a greater crowd of the same type flocked together, and several distinguished men were seen [there]. With their encouragement, the ignorant mob carried the naked and crushed body, just as it had been placed on the bier, into the Forum so that the wounds could be viewed, and they placed it on the Rostra. There, before a public meeting, [T. Munatius] Plancus and Pompeius [Rufus], who were supporting Milo's political rivals, brought hatred down upon Milo. The people, under the leadership of Sextus Clodius the scribe, brought the body of P. Clodius into the Senate House and burned it with benches, platforms, tables, and the ledgers of the secretaries; because of this fire, the Senate House itself also was burned, and likewise the Basilica Porcia, which had been joined to it, was burned.

3. Background

    a. Parts II and III, which should be treated as a unit, provide a look at the political disturbances and resulting civil strife characteristic of the late Republic. Part II centers on a political murder and the ensuing trial in which Cicero defends Milo, who had been charged with killing Clodius, his political opponent during the elections for 52 B.C. Cicero's speech of defense, the *Pro Milone* (Chapter 58) is prefaced in Chapter 57 by selections from Asconius (9 B.C–A.D. 76), who wrote a commentary to explain for his children the difficulties of the speech. By carefully orchestrating the readings and activities of Part II, the teacher can exploit the "murder mystery" atmosphere by gradually building suspense until the verdict of the trial is announced at the end of Chapter 58. Students will be able to compare the account of Asconius, who had access to senatorial transcripts of the events surrounding the murder (through the ācta diūrna or ācta pūblica, daily records of the business of the Senate, ordered to be made public in the Forum by Julius Caesar during his consulship of 59) with that given by Cicero, who had both a professional and an ideological bias in favor of Milo's version of what happened. In making this comparison, students will gain insight into what made Cicero the most successful barrister of his day.

    For more on Asconius, consult "Asconius Pedianus" in *The Oxford Classical Dictionary*, p.

130. For further details from the account of Asconius, see the paraphrase-translation of his commentary found in the Loeb edition of the *Pro Milone*, pp. 124–136, and for a scholarly treatment of the events surrounding the murder and trial, see "The Trial of Milo in 52 B.C.: A Chronological Study."

b. In Part I, students became familiar with the general historical context of the readings to be presented in Chapters 57 and 58. Before beginning the reading, it would be useful for the teacher to review these events with students, making use of the introduction to Part I and the time line at the front of the student's book. Especially recommended are 54A:1–7 on the Catilinarian conspiracy, to reintroduce Cicero and to reinforce in students' minds the political intrigue that so characterized the time of the late Republic. For further information on the complex events of this period, see: "Roman Politics in the 1st Century B.C.: A Basic Bibliography;" "Pompey and Caesar," *From the Gracchi to Nero*, pp. 109–128; "Cicero and Rome," *The Oxford History of the Classical World*, pp. 454–478; and *Pompey and Caesar*. An excellent videotape series, "History of Roman Civilization," offers an overview of the Roman Republic (available from Educational Filmstrips, Huntsville, Texas). The supplementary reading *Politics in the Late Republic* (found on page 97 of this handbook) will also be useful in helping students gain some understanding of Roman politics.

c. P. Clodius Pulcher and T. Annius Milo had a long history of political enmity, dating from 57 B.C., when Milo had prosecuted Clodius for public violence (the latter escaped by being elected aedile). Cicero's alliance with Milo had begun in 61 B.C. when Cicero gave evidence against Clodius, who had been involved in the Bona Dea scandal. Clodius then moved a bill as tribune of 58 to banish from Rome anyone who executed a Roman citizen without trial, which Cicero had done to the Catilinarian conspirators in 63. Cicero fled to Greece, but was recalled in 57, with the support of Pompey and Milo. For the general historical context of the conflict between Clodius and Milo, see *From the Gracchi to Nero*, "Clodius," pp. 120–125 and see also *The Oxford Classical Dictionary*, "Publius Clodius Pulcher," p. 154, and "Titus Annius Milo," p. 687.

d. The historical events of 53/52 are outlined as follows:
1. Milo and Clodius run for office (Milo for consul, Clodius for praetor) for 52 B.C. It is the hope of each to establish a constitutionally legal power base from which to continue factional warfare.
2. The elections in 53 for the year 52 are postponed, due to the violence of the candidates.
3. The election of an **interrēx** (for which, see *The Oxford Classical Dictionary*, p. 549) is vetoed in the Senate, perhaps with the deliberate intent of prolonging the postponement.
4. Milo murders Clodius along the Appian Way (20 January 52 B.C.).
5. The Senate House in Rome is burned (19 January).
6. **Interrēgēs** are appointed, but violence continues; the **senātūs cōnsultum ultimum** (for which, see *The Oxford Classical Dictionary*, p. 975) is invoked, and Pompey is called upon by the Senate to protect the state.
7. Pompey is appointed sole consul by an **interrēx**.
8. Milo is tried for Clodius' murder (early April).

e. Notes on the architectural structures mentioned in Reading C (see the plan on page 56 of the student's book):
rostrīs (37): Of the rostra that existed in front of the Curia in Cicero's day, little remains. Caesar's move of the rostra to the west end of the Forum was completed in 44 B.C. (For a hauntingly beautiful view of the Forum from this vantage point, see the photograph in *Greece and Rome*, pp. 340–341.) Coins indicate that Augustus built the marble hemicycle and flight of steps that formed the back of the Julian rostra. See the picture on page 51 of the student's book, the plan on page 78 of the second student's book, and additional photographs of the existing remains of the Julian rostra in *Forum Romanum*, p. 18. The section devoted to the rostra in the *Pictorial Dictionary of Ancient Rome*, Vol. 2, pp. 272–283, includes several views of the remains of the Republican structure. Acquaintance with the rostra will prove useful to students as an introduction to the speech presented in the next chapter. For some excellent suggestions on how to build learning units around the study of political monuments in the Roman Forum, see the second teacher's handbook, Chapter 23, note 7.
Cūriam (40): Students have already learned something of the history of the Senate House (see the second teacher's handbook, Chapter 23, student's book, note 6d). The present remains of the Curia Julia, rebuilt by Caesar after the fire described in this chapter, are from a restoration by Diocletian in A.D. 283, which itself was restored in the 1930's (see the picture on page 51 of the student's book). For more information, see *Forum Romanum*, pp. 13–14, and *Pictorial Dictionary of Ancient Rome*, Vol. 1, pp. 301-303, both with excellent views of the restored interior.
Porcia Basilica (42): Of this basilica, nothing now exists. For M. Porcius Cato (great-grandfather of the Cato who opposed Caesar, mentioned in 54B:7), see the **sententia** on page 68 of the student's book and "Marcus Porcius Cato

'Censorius' " in *The Oxford Classical Dictionary*, pp. 215–216. For basilicas in general, see "Basilica," *The Oxford Classical Dictionary,* p. 162.

4. Teaching the Text

a. Students should be guided to an appreciation of Asconius' narrative style as straightforward and matter-of-fact, almost as if he were presenting at the trial the deposition of an unbiased observer. His rather methodical presentation of facts should be compared with the more rhetorical and less impartial account by Cicero, Milo's defense attorney, provided in the next chapter. The teacher may wish to observe the following sequence of activities for this chapter:

1. As mentioned, before beginning the reading the teacher should review with students the general political context of the murder using Part I, supplemented by assigned readings from the books mentioned above, by individual or team reports, and/or by presentations from the teacher.

2. The teacher may wish to preview the vocabulary for these readings by asking students either to glance through the facing vocabulary and notes, paying particular attention to vocabulary marked with an asterisk or bullet, or to highlight or underline difficult words and phrases in the text as they are treated in the notes.

3. Students should then be guided through the reading and analysis of the text, with meaning progressively elicited through oral recitation in Latin (with careful attention to vocal identification of clauses and other "sense units"), use of the comprehension questions provided (or others designed and delivered orally by the teacher), literal translation (either by the class or by small groups, teams, or reading partners) and, finally, by explication and discussion of the text. In general, the teacher should first guide students toward a comprehensive understanding of the text before requiring a literal translation. Expectation of a polished (written) translation as a product of the students' initial contact with the text is both unrealistic and destructive of students' confidence in reading a text written by an ancient Roman.

4. Chapter 57 consists of three sections (lines 1–14, 15–27, and 28–43), which can be taught in three days, one section each day.

5. For assigned homework, students may be asked to produce a written "transcript" of Asconius' "testimony" for comparison with Cicero's account in the next chapter. Students may also be asked to produce an "eyewitness" account of the events along the Appian Way or in the Forum. This writing assignment could be varied by having half the class write from the point of view of Clodius and half from that of Milo, or by acting out Asconius' description of the scene. The facts according to Asconius should be firmly established in students' minds through reading, writing, staging, and discussion.

6. Review grammar and syntax: These readings are particularly rich in ablatives and provide a suitable context for review: ablative of place from which (1–2), place from which with the name of a city (4; note that Asconius uses a preposition here), means (5, 7, 9, 16, 23, 26–27, and 40–41), time when (3, 32, and 33), accompaniment (7 and 9–13), place where (13, 18, 24, 30, and 35), absolute (20, 34, and 39), manner (29–30 and 31–32), and cause (41).

   Additional grammar and syntax that may be reviewed include dative object of special verb (3 and 38), deponent verb (2, 4–5, 7, 11, 17, 26, and 34), irregular verb (1, 4, 6, 7, 12, 13, 18, 20, 21, 22, 27, 28, 36, and 40), present participle (4, 6–7, 13, 23, and 34), past participle (7, 18, 20, 24, 30, and 35), **ut** + indicative (6 and 19), **cum** circumstantial (16–17 and 19–21), **ut** purpose clause (36), indirect statement (20), and active periphrastic, **esset habitūrus** (21), first met in Chapter 45:5–6.

   The gerundive (3) and passive periphrastic (22) will be presented in the next chapter; for present contrary to fact conditions (21–22), see Chapter 66.

5. Reading Notes

a. **A.d. XIII Kal. Febr.** (1): Students should be asked to produce this date in modern terms. For a review of the Roman system of dating, see Chapter 34, pp. 59–60.

b. **dictātor** (2): This word, from **dīcere** "to speak," does not have the same meaning as that encountered in 54B:14 or in line 10 below. With respect to Milo, the word has a meaning equivalent to "mayor." For the precise constitutional meaning of the term, see above, page 8, note 3c2, and *The Oxford Classical Dictionary*, p. 339.

c. **ab Arīciā** (4): This town still exists and is called Arricia.

d. **ut illō tempore mōs erat iter facientibus** (6–7): Students should be asked to recall the hazards of traveling along the Appian Way, for which, see the second student's book. Undoubtedly conditions were more unsettled at this time than during the first century A.D.

e. **eques** (8): This word has previously had the meaning "horse soldier" or "cavalryman"

(54C:3). The **equitēs** were originally the second rank of nobility in Rome, drawn from those who could afford a horse. With the common people, or **plēbs** (9), and the nobility, or **patriciī**, the equitēs ranked as one of the permanent classes of the **populus Rōmānus**, equivalent to our "middle class." For additional information, see "Equites," *The Oxford Classical Dictionary*, pp. 403–404.

f. **L. Sullae dictātōris** (10): L. Cornelius Sulla (138–78 B.C.), mentioned in the introduction to Part I, page 8, was a man who contributed mightily to the autocratic tendencies of politicians during the late Republic, through his ruthless dictatorship after winning the civil war against C. Marius.

g. **rixam commīsērunt** (14): Students may be reminded of the idiom **pugnam committere** (Exercise 46C:10).

h. **minitābundus** (15): Students should be reminded that Latin adjectives are sometimes best translated as English adverbs.

i. **Milō . . . iussit** (19–22): Students may need guidance through this complex sentence. The interplay of the pronouns **sibi** and **eō**, as well as that of the ablative absolutes **vīvō eo** and **occīsō (eō)** should be noted, in recognition of the deliberations taking place in Milo's mind. He apparently believed that the removal of his political enemy was worth the risk of his indictment for murder. Points of grammar to be noted here:

    ut + indicative, **ut cognōvit** (19)

    use of ellipsis, **vulnerātum (esse)** (19) and **futūrum (esse)** (20)

    cum circumstantial clause, **cum . . . intellegeret** (19–20)

    active periphrastic (future active participle + esse), **esset habitūrus** (21)

The passive periphrastic, **subeunda esset** (22) and the present contrary to fact condition **etiam sī subeunda esset** (21–22) should not be discussed formally yet.

j. **uxor Clōdiī Fulvia** (31): Clodius' wife Fulvia played an active part in later political events as the wife of Marc Antony.

k. **prō cōntiōne** (37): The word **contiō** is a contraction of **conventiō**, "assembly."

7. *VERBS: The Gerund or Verbal Noun*: Students were exposed to the gerund as a vocabulary item in Chapter 32 (**arbiter bibendī**). The teacher may wish to refer, at this time, to the gerund phrases commonly used in English, which are found on page 55 of the student's book. The examples of the function of the gerund in the various cases of nouns should be studied carefully, as these usages apply as well to the presentation of the gerundive in the next chapter.

8. Exercise 57a: suggested translations:
1. Milo's gladiators were desirous of fighting.

2. Having seen the gladiators, the slaves of Clodius ran forward to help (literally, for the sake of helping).
3. Clodius' slaves fought bravely for the purpose of resisting.
4. Clodius' comrades had fled into the nearest inn to hide.
5. The gladiators, when they had caught sight of the approaching senator, made an end of the fighting.
6. Several knights caused commotion by speaking out against Milo in the Forum.
7. Do you think that Milo was a man fit to govern (literally, fit for governing)?
8. Cicero wrote that man was born for two purposes, for thinking and for acting.

9. Exercise 57b: Answers and suggested translations:
1. (**proficīscendum**) Fulvia, Clodius' wife, had prepared everything for departure.
2. (**fugiendō**) Clodius was hoping that he could save himself from danger by running away.
3. (**vincendī**) Aren't all gladiators desirous of winning?
4. (**gubernandum**) New magistrates will be elected by the Roman people for the purpose of governing.
5. (**loquendī**) The orator climbs (climbed) onto the rostra for the sake of speaking (to speak).

10. Supplementary Materials

a. *Practice with Gerunds*, page 96. This is simply an additional exercise to reinforce the new grammar. The figure in the margin is a **flāmen**, a priest assigned to the cults of Jupiter, Mars, or Quirinus, among others. The **flāmen** wore a special cap and a purple cloak over his toga. Answers for section I:

    cōnspiciendum, monendum, collocandum, veniendum, vehendum, redeundum, arripiendum, oriendum, cōnandum, pellendum.

Answers for section II:
1. Milo set out from Rome in order to go to Lanuvium.
2. Cicero hoped that he could help Milo by speaking in the Forum.
3. Cicero went to the Forum to speak.
4. After the attack was made against Milo, several slaves ran to the carriage in order to help.
5. The teacher helped the students by explaining everything.
6. Octavian was eager to rule (desirous of ruling).
7. Octavian and Antony went to Greece to fight.

b. *Politics in the Late Republic*, page 97: Students began to acquire some understanding of Roman politics in Part I; this reading is designed to develop the topic further. Notice the very pragmatic tone of Quintus Cicero's advice—to flatter people, and to never say no to anyone; many comparisons can be made with contemporary American politics on such points. Ask students to decide whether the opinion expressed by Cicero in his speech *Pro Plancio* (printed at the bottom of the page) corresponded to reality, as shown by Quintus Cicero's advice above. For a lengthy excerpt from Quintus Cicero's *On Being a Candidate for the Consulship*, see "Campaigning for Office," *Roman Civilization Sourcebook I*, pp. 394–399. For an interesting discussion of Roman politics as compared to modern, see "And Never Say No—Politics as Usual in Ancient Rome."

The right-hand picture at the bottom of the sheet is a side view of a **sella curūlis**, the ivory folding seat used by consuls and praetors and symbolic of their **imperium** or supreme administrative power. The left-hand illustration represents a **līctor** or attendant who accompanied holders of the **imperium** and who carried the **fascēs**, a bundle of rods and an axe, which symbolized the authority of the magistrate to beat or execute offenders. Compare the painting *Magistrates and Lictors* in the second student's book, page 62.

CHAPTER 58: A POLITICAL MURDER (CICERO'S ACCOUNT)

1. The aims of this chapter are:

   a. to continue the story of Clodius and Milo as an example of the nature of public life during the late Republic
   b. to provide students with an opportunity to assess the relative value of ancient sources
   c. to introduce the gerundive, the gerundive of obligation (passive periphrastic), and the dative of agent.

2. Translations

   A. Meanwhile, since Clodius knew (for it wasn't difficult to know) that on 20 January Milo had a customary, legitimate, [and] necessary journey [to make] to Lanuvium for the purpose of appointing a priest, because Milo was chief magistrate of Lanuvium, he [Clodius] suddenly set out from Rome the day before, to arrange an ambush for Milo in front of his farm (as subsequent events proved); and his departure was so timed that he left a rowdy public meeting, in which

his mad frenzy was in demand [and] which was being held on that very day, and which he never would have left, unless he had wanted to appear at the time and place of the foul deed.

B. Milo, however, since he had been in a Senate meeting that day until the Senate was adjourned, came home, changed his shoes and clothing, waited a bit, as usual, while his wife made ready, then departed at the time when Clodius could have already returned, if, indeed, he was going to return to Rome that day. Clodius, who was lightly-armed, on horseback, with no carriage, no baggage, [and] no Greek companions, contrary to his usual custom, and without his wife, which he almost never was, met him [Milo]; while this [so-called] highwayman, who had prepared that expedition for the purpose of committing a murder, was wearing a **paenula** [and] riding in a carriage with his wife and with a large, cumbersome, womanly, and delicate company of handmaids and youths.

C. Milo meets Clodius in front of his [Clodius'] farm at about the eleventh hour or not much later; at once, several men make an attack on him with weapons from a higher position; those standing in the way [of the carriage] kill the driver; when, however, Milo had jumped down from the carriage after throwing off his cloak and was defending himself with a stout heart, some of those who were with Clodius, having drawn their swords, begin to run back to the carriage in order to attack Milo from behind, and others, because they believed that Milo had already been killed, begin to kill his slaves, who were at the rear.

D. Of those slaves who were loyal and steadfast toward their master [Milo], some were killed and some, when they saw the fighting at the carriage and were prevented from aiding their master and heard from Clodius himself that Milo had been killed and actually believed [it], Milo's slaves—and I will say this openly, not with any intent of diverting the accusation, but [just] as it happened—without the order, the knowledge, or the presence of their master, did what everyone would have wanted his own slaves to do in such a situation.

E. Twelve senators found him guilty, six innocent; thirteen knights found him guilty, four innocent; thirteen treasury officials found him guilty, three innocent. The members of the jury seemed not to have been unaware that Clodius had been wounded without Milo's knowledge initially, but had found out for certain that after Clodius had been wounded, he had been killed at Milo's order. Milo set out for exile in Massilia within a very few days. His property was sold for one twenty-fourth [of its value] because of the magnitude of his debts.

Background

a. Readings A–D present excerpts from the **partī-tiō**, or outline, of Cicero's speech on behalf of Milo. To assist students with their comprehension and appreciation of the text, the teacher is encouraged to provide background readings from the *Pro Milone* in translation, for which, see the Loeb edition or *Selected Political Speeches of Cicero*. Reading E comes full circle back to Asconius and presents the verdict of Milo's trial, which concludes Part II. Students should be cautioned not to peek at the verdict ahead of time!

b. Before beginning the text, the teacher may wish to review with students what they know about Roman oratory, for which, see Chapter 37 and the notes and cultural background readings for that chapter in the third teacher's handbook, and the supplementary activity *Oratory in Republican Politics* (page 99 in this handbook). For further information on rhetoric, see:

1. "Rhetoric," *The Oxford Classical Dictionary*, pp. 921–922.

2. An interesting excerpt from Tacitus' *Dialogus de oratoribus* is given in "Why Oratory Flourished in the Late Republic," *Roman Civilization Sourcebook I*, pp. 498–501.

3. For an entertaining photograph of a young Roman student declaiming, see *Roman Life*, p. 157.

4. For the famous fresco by Cesare Maccari (1888) of Cicero attacking Catiline in the Senate House, see *Greece and Rome*, pp. 342–343. This painting is found in Rome's Palazzo Madama, seat of the Italian Senate.

c. The platform of the Republican rostra (for which, see background note 3e of the previous chapter) was, presumably like its successor, wide enough for a speaker to move about. The present ruins of the Julian rostra are 11 feet (3 meters) high, 78 feet (24 meters) long, and 39 feet (12 meters) deep. It was here that Marc Antony, in macabre tribute, placed the head and hands of Cicero after murdering him in 43 B.C. (For the historical account of this incident, see the supplementary readings on page 105 at the end of this handbook.) In discussing Roman oratory and the rostra, reference should be made to the photographs on page 61 of the student's book.

d. Cicero, who had been allotted three hours to speak, attempted to deliver the *Pro Milone* in the face of Clodius' hecklers (see 57C:29 and 32–33), who were not intimidated even by the sergeants-at-arms, whom Pompey, appointed as sole consul to deal with the crisis surrounding the elections, had stationed around the Forum (and who precipitated a famous **sententia**: **Silent lēgēs inter arma**, *Amid arms, laws grow silent, Pro Milone* 11). Speaking with far less than his usual confidence, Cicero failed to complete the speech, which he later published and sent to Milo in exile. Given the accounts of witnesses provided by Asconius, it is improbable that Cicero's complete speech would have saved Milo. Some four years after returning from exile, Milo was captured and executed for insurrection.

e. With respect to Milo's trial, the jury composed an extraordinary *ad hoc* court, called by Pompey specifically to hear the case, which, because of the circumstances, lay outside the regular jurisdiction of the **quaestiōnēs**, or permanent courts. For details of normal Roman court procedures, see the articles "Quaestiones," pp. 905–906, "Law and Procedure, Roman," pp. 583–590, and "Iudex," pp. 558–559, in *The Oxford Classical Dictionary*; "A Simple Account of Legal Procedure in a Roman Court"; and "Law," *Rome, Its People, Life and Customs*, pp. 191–206, which makes some thought-provoking comparisons between ancient and modern legal professions.

4. Teaching the Text

a. As this reading is the students' first encounter with Ciceronian prose, the teacher should progress slowly and carefully with the Latin, in order to win them over to the style of Cicero's writing. Familiarity with the general circumstances of the murder as presented by Asconius in the previous chapter should assist students with comprehension. Therefore, it is advisable for the teacher to review, in detail, the events surrounding Asconius' account of Clodius' murder, in order that students may be able to be critical of Cicero's version. As an alternative to assigning preparation of a written translation, the teacher may approach the reading first by using the comprehension questions provided in the student's book or by having students make up their own. The organization of the reading into five- to eight-line passages lends itself to class preparation of the answers to these questions in small groups, to be followed by sharing and discussion. As with the passage from Asconius, the teacher may pull together the entire reading by having students act out the murder according to the account of Cicero. After the facts as Cicero presents them have been established, his account should be compared with that of Asconius.

b. Discussion and debate might center on Cicero's claims, which are as follows:

1. Clodius had no legitimate justification for his presence on the Appian Way (lines 4–10; cf. Asconius, 57:5–9).

2. The nature of Clodius' traveling party was much more suspicious than was that of Milo (15–18; cf. 57:5–9).

3. The attack was an ambush, deliberately planned and precipitated in the vicinity of Clodius' own estate (5–6 and 22; cf. 57:13–14).
4. Milo had no knowledge of, or complicity in, the actual killing of Clodius (36–37; cf. 57:19–24).

The teacher may wish to format presentation of the evidence as a debate in the Senate by dividing the class in half and assigning opposite positions of the debate to each half. The debate could then be organized as a simulated meeting of the Roman Senate and formalities of senatorial procedure observed (and, furthermore, practical application of the elements of good speechmaking could be brought into play). For debate in the Senate, see "Senatus, Procedure," *The Oxford Classical Dictionary*, p. 973; "Parliamentary Practices of the Senate," *Roman Civilization Sourcebook I*, pp. 399–400; and "A Meeting of the Senate."

c. Students should be required to read aloud portions, or the entirety, of the Latin text of the passages from the *Pro Milone* provided, in order to appreciate fully the power of Cicero's words and sentence structure. Such an exercise, which will sharpen pronunciation skills, could be extended to include a selection from the Catilinarian orations, e.g., *In Catilinam* I.1. For cassette recordings of dramatic readings from these orations, both in Latin and in English, see "Selections from Cicero," "Classics of Latin Prose and Poetry," and "Cicero versus Catiline." State and national conventions of the National Junior Classical League often provide competitions in Latin and English oratory. The teacher might establish contact with the school's debate coach or speech teacher to serve as a resource person or judge.

5. Reading Notes

A.
a. **ad flāminem prōdendum** (3–4): Asconius uses this very same gerundive phrase (57:2–3).
b. **contiōnem turbulentam** (7): For **contiō**, see the note on 57:37, above.
c. In reading this passage, the teacher should give attention to the following clauses and constructions:
  cum causal clause: **cum scīret** (1)
  indirect statement: **scīret . . . iter . . . esse** (1–3)
  purpose clause: **ut . . . collocāret** (5–6)
  result clause: **ut . . . relinqueret** (7–8)
  relative clauses: **quod . . . intellēctum est** (5–6), **in quā . . . dēsīderātus est** (7–8), **quae . . . habita est** (8), and **quam . . . relīquisset** (9–10)

past contrary to fact condition: **nisi . . voluisset . . . relīquisset** (9–10), a type of clause to be introduced in Chapter 66.

B.
a. Attention may be given to the following:
  cum causal clause: **cum . . . fuisset** (11)
  cum circumstantial clause: **cum . . . potuisset** (14–15)
  gerundive phrase: **ad caedem faciendam** (18–19)
  relative clause of characteristic: **quī . . . appārāsset** (18–19), a construction not formally introduced until Chapter 64
  contracted verb: **appārā(vi)sset** (19), the meaning of which is to be deduced.
b. As students read, they should be asked to observe the effect of the use of asyndeton (11–13, 16–17, and 19–20), the balance and symmetry of the phrases used to compare the traveling parties of Clodius and Milo (16–21), the irony presented in **cum hic īnsidiātor** (18), the sarcasm in **quī . . . appārāsset** (18–19), and the ways in which Cicero exaggerates the size and nature of Milo's party (20–21).

C.
a. **faciunt . . . occīdunt . . . incipiunt** (24–29): Students should be asked to observe how effectively Cicero draws the reader into the action through the use of the historical present tense, for which, see Chapter 27 of the third student's book.
b. Students may need assistance with the condensed use of the main verb **incipiunt** (29), the subject of which is **illī** (26, Clodius' men) and which governs the infinitives **recurrere** (27) and **caedere** (29).
c. The first three passages of this chapter provide convenient examples for review of time and place constructions: time (2–3, 5, 8, 11, 14–15, and 22–23) and place (3, 4, 12, and 15). The distinction between **hic** and **ille** may also be reviewed using this passage (**hunc**, 24, **hic**, 25, **illī**, 26, and **hunc**, 28).
d. **partim . . . partim** (27–28): The sequencing of the action using this adverb will be continued into the next passage (D).
e. Note the following clauses and constructions:
  cum circumstantial clauses: **cum . . . dēsiluisset . . . (cum) dēfenderet** (25–26)
  ablative absolutes: **reiectā paenulā** (25–26) and **gladiīs ēductīs** (27)
  purpose clause: **ut . . . adorīrentur** (28)
  causal clause with a subjunctive verb: **quod . . . putārent** (28–29)
  elliptical infinitive: **interfectum (esse)** (29)

D.
a. **Ex quibus servīs** (31): These slaves are those who were following Milo's carriage (29–30).

b. **partim . . . partim** (27–28 and 32): The repetition of **partim** reveals the fragmented, yet continuous action of the battle. Cicero's description achieves a certain balance, with Clodius' men, who had the upper hand, described first, followed by a picture of Milo's slaves as they fought back.

c. The following clauses and constructions should be given attention:

ablative of description: **animō fidēlī** (31)

    cum circumstantial clauses: **cum . . . vidērent . . . (cum) . . . prohibērentur, (cum) . . . audīrent . . . (cum) . . . putārent** (32–35)

    elliptical infinitive: **occīsum (esse)** (34)

    gerundive phrase: **dērivandī crīminis causā** (36)

    ut + indicative: **ut factum est** (36)

    ablative absolute: **imperante . . . dominō** (36–37)

    relative clause of characteristic: **(id) quod . . . voluisset** (37–38), a type of clause to be introduced in Chapter 64.

E.

a. This reading from Asconius concludes Part II by resolving the uncertainty about Milo's guilt. In so doing, something of Roman judicial process is illustrated. The Latin is simple enough and could be used for sight reading, especially since students will be eager to learn what finally happened to Milo. In discussion, students should be guided to an appreciation of the fact that even in a crisis the machinery of the Roman judiciary could operate effectively.

b. **tribūnī aerāriī** (2): About these, little is known. They were officials who had financial duties associated with the military and who, during the first century B.C., had become a class intermediate between the **equitēs** and the **plēbs**.

c. Attention should be given to the following:

    indirect statement: **ignōrāvisse . . . vulnerātum esse Clōdium** (4–5)

    ablative absolute: **īnsciō Milōne** (4)

    temporal clause introduced by **postquam**: **postquam vulnerātus esset** (5). **Postquam** is usually followed by the indicative but introduces a subjunctive clause here because it is a subordinate clause within an indirect statement.

    elliptical infinitive: **occīsum (esse)** (6)

    ablative of price: **sēmiūnciā** (8)

VERBS: The Gerundive or Verbal Adjective: Students have seen the gerundive form in the passive periphrastic construction since Chapter 45, and examples have appeared in the two chapters in this Part (57A:3 and 58A:4, B:19, and D:36). The identity of the gerundive as an *adjective* should be stressed and the boxed summaries on page 66 of the student's book studied carefully. The various uses of the

gerund, presented on pages 54–55 of the student's book, should also be reviewed, since they are applicable also to the gerundive. For the gerundive as future passive participle, see the next chapter (59A:7).

7. Exercise 58a: suggested translations:
   1. The political rivals were making plans for the sake of obtaining power.
   2. It was necessary for the candidates to be prepared to undergo many dangers.
   3. And so, to Pompey asking why (Cicero) himself had become consul, Cicero replied, "For the sake of protecting the Republic."
   4. Surely Clodius was not a man suitable for governing the state?
   5. Was Milo attempting to preserve the Republic by killing Clodius?
   6. Wicked men burned the Senate House for the purpose of cremating the body of Clodius.
   7. Surely the Senate House was not an appropriate place for burning Clodius' corpse?
   8. Cicero hoped that by giving speeches he would persuade the senators.

8. Exercise 58b: answers and suggested translations:
   1. (Gerundive) It was necessary for Clodius to be present at the public meeting in order to deliver speeches.
   2. (Gerundive) With Milo as consul, Clodius knew that he could not make plans to destroy the state.
   3. (Gerundive) Do you believe that Clodius laid an ambush for the sake of killing his rival?
   4. (Gerund) When his slaves had been killed, Clodius tried to save himself by running away.
   5. (Gerund) Several men tried to increase the hatred of the common people by speaking out against Milo.
   6. (Gerundive) Cicero thought that he could save Milo by giving a speech.
   7. (Gerund) To Milo's question, Cicero replied, "You will be freed by telling the truth."

9. Exercise 58c: Answers and suggested translations:
   1. (**creandī**) The electoral assembly ought to be held for the sake of electing a consul.
   2. (**custōdiendam**) Dictators were appointed by the consuls for the purpose of protecting the state.
   3. (**iūdicandīs**) Praetors spend much time judging criminals.
   4. (**habendās**) The orators were assembled for the purpose of giving speeches.
   5. (**faciendō**) Will gangs destroy the Republic by attacking the citizens?

10. *VERBS: Gerundive of Obligation (Passive Periphrastic)*: The term *gerundive of obligation*, which emphasizes the identity of the form as a gerundive, is presented here as an alternative to the more traditional

and unwieldy term *passive periphrastic*. The teacher should select one of these terms and remain consistent in its usage. The term *passive periphrastic* may be introduced by way of the *active periphrastic* (future active participle + a form of **esse**, which was introduced in Chapter 45 and seen mostly recently in 57B:21), in an attempt to bring students to an understanding of the word "periphrastic," from a Greek word meaning "to speak around." The gerundive of obligation has been seen a number of times since Chapter 45. For reference, the ablative of agent was first presented in Chapter 29 of the third student's book.

11. In connection with the **sententia** on page 60, the teacher might introduce such common phrases as **vōx populī, rēgnat populus,** and **prō bonō pūblicō. SALUS POPULI** is the motto of the state of Missouri.

12. Exercise 58d: suggested translations:
    1. All citizens must obey the laws.
    2. Pompey asked Cicero what plans had to be made regarding Milo.
    3. Who will deny that Milo must be sent away from Rome?
    4. Candidates will always have to avoid many pitfalls.
    5. Everyone must avoid the urge to kill.
    6. The consul Pompey ordered that everyone who had participated in the murder of Clodius had to be punished.
    7. Surely Rome has not been abandoned by all good men, has it?
    8. Since Clodius had been killed, Milo knew that he would have to pay the penalty (i.e., to be punished).
    9. Cicero is trying to persuade the jury that they must not send Milo into exile.
    10. I had to do this.

13. Supplementary Materials

    a. *Practice with Gerunds and Gerundives* (page 98) provides additional practice with the structures introduced in this chapter. Sentence no. 8 is in-

cluded to remind students that purpose can be expressed by a subjunctive clause as well as a gerund or gerundive construction. Answers and suggested translations:
1. (**Milōnī**) Milo had to go to Lanuvium.
2. Did Clodius leave Rome to address the town council in Aricia or to set up an ambush for Milo?
3. (**ā Pompeiō**) Soldiers were stationed in the Forum by Pompey to protect the jury and the lawyers.
4. Milo believed that he had to kill the wounded Clodius.
5. Cicero is telling the jury that Milo should be set free; but others are there to convict Milo.
6. (**explicandam**) Asconius wrote a commentary to explain the speech; by reading this commentary, we can understand the speech much better.
7. Milo will have to leave Rome for Massilia immediately.
8. Milo will leave so that he won't be killed by Clodius' friends.
9. Cicero said that Milo's slaves killed Clodius to avenge their master.

b. *Oratory in Republican Politics* (page 99) attempts to provide some insight into this subject which is so very important for any understanding of Roman political and judicial processes. It is hard for students nowadays to understand the importance of oral argument in ancient life. The passage from Tacitus (part of a longer extract from the *Dialogus* found in *Roman Civilization Sourcebook I*, pp. 498–499) gives a good sense of the influence of the orator in the waning days of the Republic. You may wish to ask students to rephrase the main points of the passage in their own words to be sure they have understood it. You may also wish to refer to the sections on Roman education in *Home and School*, and to the various discussions of rhetoric from Quintilian, Tacitus, Petronius, and Cicero printed at the end of the third teacher's handbook (pages 44–48).

PART III

Warfare in the Late Republic

CHAPTER 59: EYEWITNESS TO CIVIL WAR

1. The aims of this chapter are:
   a. to explore the character of Cicero as a private citizen and statesman
   b. to establish a connection between politics and warfare during the late Republic
   c. to present the substantive clause following words of fearing (clause of fearing).

2. Translations

   A. Tullius sends heartiest greetings to [his wife] Terentia, to [his daughter] little Tullia, his two darlings, and to his best mother and sweetest sister.

   If you are well, so am I. It is now of concern to you, [and] not only to me, as to what you must do. If he [Caesar] is going to come to Rome in civilized fashion, it is all right for you to stay at home for the present; but if, [as] a madman, he is going to hand the city over to be plundered, I am afraid that Dolabella himself cannot help us enough. Furthermore, I also fear this, that we may at any moment be cut off, so that you cannot leave [Rome] when you wish. There remains [a matter] that you will do very well to consider, [the question] whether or not there are women like you [left] in Rome. For if there are not, you must consider whether or not you can be [there] with respectability. Indeed, as things stand now, provided that we are allowed to hold onto these places, you will be able to be very comfortable either with me or on [one of] our estates. Also, it is to be feared that there may be famine in the city in a short time. I wish you would make plans about these matters with Pomponius, Camillus, [and] with whomever else it seems [advisable] to you, [and], in short, I would like you to be stout-hearted. Write to me as often as you can, my dearest darlings, and [tell me] how you are doing and how it's going over there [in Rome]. Farewell.

   B. Cicero sends greetings to Atticus.

   I observe that there is not one [square] foot of Italy that is not in that man's [Caesar's] control. Of Pompey I know nothing, and I think he will be captured, unless he boards a ship. As for me, what should I do? By what land or sea should I follow him, when I don't know where he is? Should I, then, hand myself over to that man [Caesar]? Suppose that I can [surrender] safely (for many are advising it), it wouldn't be with honor, would it? By no means. I

will certainly seek out your advice, as I always do. The situation cannot be resolved.

   C. Gnaeus [Pompeius] Magnus, Proconsul, sends greetings to Marcus Cicero, Commander.

   It is good if you are well. I read your letter eagerly, for I recognized [in it] your previous courage even with regard to the common welfare. The consuls have reached the army that I had in Apulia. I seriously urge, because of your extraordinary and continuous zeal in [support of] the Republic, that you should come to me in order that, with mutual planning, we may bring help and aid to [our] stricken state. I think that you should travel by way of the Via Appia, and arrive quickly in Brundisium.

   D. Caesar, Commander, sends greetings to Cicero, Commander.

   Although I am in a rush and on the march, having already sent the army ahead, nevertheless I did not hesitate to write and thank you, although I have done this often and it seems to me that I will do [so] more often. You deserve this [i.e., thanks] from me. First of all, since I trust that I will arrive quickly in the city [Rome], I ask to see you there so that I can take advantage of your advice, your influence, your good name, and the help of all your resources. You will pardon my haste and the brevity of [my] letter.

3. Background

   a. Part III concludes the two-part unit on the late Republic by presenting four letters from Cicero's correspondence and a scene from Caesar's *Commentarii de bello civili* describing the battle of Pharsalus. The intent is to show that the events of the late fifties, illustrated in Part II, escalated into civil war between Caesar and Pompey. This civil war, which ended, in reality, with Pompey's death soon after Pharsalus, was to precipitate events which were ultimately to lead to the dissolution of the Republic and the establishment of the Principate, which will be explored in Part IV. For an entertaining look at this period of history and the personal relationship between Caesar and Cicero, the teacher should read Taylor Caldwell's historical novel *A Pillar of Iron*.

   b. Success in Roman public life during the late Republic required not only wealth and family connections, followed by the proper education, but also a glorious military career, if not the outright support of the army. This use of the army to meet political objectives, begun by Marius and Sulla (see the introduction to Part I, pages 9–10), is described by Plutarch as follows:

   > The generals of this period were men who had risen to the top by violence rather than by merit.

They needed armies to fight against one another rather than against a common public enemy. And so they were forced to combine the arts of the politician and the authority of the general. They spent money making life easy for their soldiers, and then, after purchasing their labor in this way, failed to observe that they had made their whole country a thing for sale and had put themselves in a position where they had to be slaves of the worst sort of people in order to become masters of the better.

—*Lysander and Sulla*
trans. Rex Warner

c. As to the events immediately preceding Cicero's letters in Chapter 59, in 52 B.C. Caesar put down the revolt of Vercingetorix, bringing the Gallic campaigns to a conclusion and incurring the jealousy of his political ally, Pompey. Although the historical events of 52 to 49 B.C. are much debated, it is clear that both Caesar and Pompey, the former through his new agent in Rome, C. Scribonius Curio, attempted to manipulate these events, each in his own interest. When Caesar refused to abandon his army until his election as consul, which Pompey blocked, the Senate passed a **senātūs cōnsultum ultimum**, asking Pompey to save the Republic and assume command of all forces in Italy. On the night of 11 January 49 B.C., Caesar illegally led his army out of his province of Cisalpine Gaul and into Italy by crossing the Rubicon River. For a beautifully-illustrated presentation of this moment in history, see "Across the Rubicon," in Isenberg's *Caesar*, pp. 100–107, out of print but worth the search. See also *From the Gracchi to Nero*, pp. 125–127. For translations of Caesar's commentaries, consult the Loeb or Penguin editions.

d. Cicero's letters provide an intimate look at the emotional atmosphere in Rome before and during the civil war. Students should be informed that a vast collection of his correspondence survives, having been gathered together and published by his esteemed secretary, Tiro. These letters were written throughout a twenty-five year public career to Cicero's friends and family, his adviser and confidant T. Pomponius Atticus, and his younger brother, Quintus. Cicero's more than 800 epistles, written for the most part in a colloquial and uninhibited style, are not only our best primary source for the final days of the Republic, but also provide a glimpse inside the mind and personality of the man himself. For these letters, see the Loeb editions cited in the bibliography.

For an excellent appreciation of Cicero's involvement in the political events of the late Republic, see Miriam Griffin's article "Cicero and

Rome" in *The Oxford History of the Classical World*, pp. 454–478, with notes for further reading. Also valuable is "Civil War: The 'Irrepressible Conflict'," a collection of Cicero's letters in translation on the civil war, found in *Roman Civilization Sourcebook I*, pp. 279–285.

e. Cicero, although a **novus homō**, was a member of the senatorial aristocracy and devoted to the Optimate interest in maintaining the stability of the Republic through the dominance of the Senate.

Caesar was a general and member of the First Triumvirate; he had fought in Gaul to develop a military and financial power base for his future political ambitions. His interests in Rome had been maintained through agents such as Clodius and Curio.

Pompey was a general and member of the First Triumvirate; he had established a political power base by gaining the support of the Senate in resolving the crisis of 52 B.C. as sole consul.

The pictures on page 73 of the student's book give faces to these important men who provide the linkage of personality between politics and warfare, which are the general themes of Parts II and III. The relative positions of these photographs illustrate what Cicero's own words in the chapter reveal: that he was caught in the middle between Caesar and Pompey. The bust of Cicero during his mature years is believed to be an early copy of one executed during his lifetime. Although it is uncertain whether any of the busts of Caesar that have survived were contemporary portraits, the one pictured here is generally believed to be the best of those extant, which differ widely in their representations. Pompey was 57 at the beginning of the civil war, and the face of the bust pictured shows something of the weight of those years.

The readings in Part III are designed to provide students with an opportunity to observe Cicero, Caesar, and Pompey as they touched one another's lives during the years between the outbreak of the civil war and their deaths, which were roughly contemporary (see the historical accounts on page 105 of this handbook). Chapter 59 presents not only a perspective on the public personality of Cicero, who was courted as a man of influence by both Pompey and Caesar, but also provides Cicero with an opportunity to reveal himself, in his own words, as an intensely human figure, with fears and doubts of the type that all people share.

The following resources will be of special value in helping the teacher to establish the historical context of the readings in Part III: "Parallel Chronological Table for the Lives of Caesar, Cicero, and Pompey" and "A List of Consuls from 77 B.C. to 43 B.C. and Some Important Events in Each Consulship." Another valuable resource for a comparative study is *Pompey and Caesar*.

4. Teaching the Text

   a. The teacher should begin with a review of the historical context for the readings in this chapter. This should include reference to the introduction to Part I, pages 9–11, the Latin reading in Chapter 54B, and discussion of how the events of 52 B.C., as presented in Part II, contributed to the development of the rift between Caesar and Pompey.

   b. The readings in this chapter should provoke discussion about the subject of civil war in general. The teacher may wish to use this opportunity to encourage students to read about or discuss the War Between the States or to simulate, in writing, their own involvement in such a conflict, ancient or modern. An opportunity for imaginative writing is provided in Exercise 59c of the student's book, which may be assigned (or offered for extra credit) as an immediate follow-up either to the reading and translation of Letter A or to discussion generated by the content of all the letters. Students may become interested in the historical events of this chapter by writing and staging a playlet describing Caesar's crossing of the Rubicon. In this regard, the teacher may wish to review the **sententia, Ālea iacta est**, found in the third student's book, page 30. For classes interested in debate, the question of the need for subordination of the military to the civil in government could be argued (**Cēdant arma togae**, Cicero, *De consulatu suo*).

   c. This chapter also provides opportunity for reviewing Roman epistolary conventions (there are nine letters in *From Republic to Empire*), which were first presented in Chapters 34 and 38 of the third student's book. In this regard, see also Word Study XIV on page 100 of this handbook.

   d. The teacher should make every effort to assist students in gaining a picture of Cicero as a man devoted to and fearful for his family (Letter A), while being torn between his allegiance to the Republic, as represented by Pompey, and fears for his personal safety, as represented by Caesar (Letter B). Together with Letters A and B, Letters C and D, in which Pompey and Caesar both state and imply that Cicero is a man of considerable position and influence, provide students with a balanced perspective of Cicero as private and public man.

   e. Letters A and B may be taught in a single assignment (24 lines), or Letter A assigned and Letter B presented for sight-reading in class. Letters C and D (16 lines), together with Exercise 59d,

may be presented as a unit; comparison of these two letters lends itself to work in small groups. For more able classes, Letter C might be assigned for preparation outside of class and Letter D given in class as a sight-reading. The analysis called for in Exercise 59d may be requested in writing or orally, either by individuals or teams.

   f. The following new grammar and syntax is introduced in this chapter and not treated further in the course. Additional information will be provided in the reading notes below.

   Double indirect question, **sintne** (A:11)
   Clause of proviso, **modo ut . . . liceat** (A:13)
   Potential subjunctive, **velim** (A:16)
   Optative subjunctive, **cōnsīderētis . . . sītis** (A:17–18)
   Ablative of description, **animō fortī** (A:17–18)
   Deliberative subjunctive, **Ego quid agam?**, etc. (B:4)
   Concessive clause, **cum properārem** (D:2)
   Clause of doubt, **dubitāvī quīn . . . scrīberem . . . agerem** (D:3–4)

   g. The teacher should be especially alert to the fearing clauses found in Letter A, as this new subjunctive usage is formally introduced in this chapter:

   vereor ut . . . possit (8)
   metuō nē . . . interclūdāmur (9)
   verendum est, nē . . . sit (15–16)

   h. The following uses of the subjunctive are found in these letters and may be presented for review: indirect question (A:5 and 19 and B:5); **cum** circumstantial (A:9); result (A:12), indirect command (C:6 and D:6–7), and purpose (C:6–7 and D:7–8).

5. Reading Notes

   A.

   a. Cicero wrote this from Minturnae, a town on the Via Appia just south of Formiae, en route to his duties in Campania, where he was levying troops for Pompey's army. Caesar had crossed the Rubicon and, unknown to Cicero, was bypassing Rome in pursuit of Pompey, who had abandoned the city.

   b. **TERENTIAE . . . S.P.D.** (1–3): Cicero was shortly to divorce Terentia after a marriage of nearly 30 years. Cicero's son Marcus, about whom students read in Chapter 50, was serving as a cavalry officer in Pompey's army at the time of this letter.

   c. **TULLIOLAE**: A diminutive. Diminutives were presented in Word Study XI (*Pastimes and Ceremonies*, page 28); this might be an appropriate time to review them.

d. **Sī vōs valētis, nōs valēmus** (4): Cicero's greeting is a variation of the more usual formula **Sī valēs, bene (est)**, found in Letter C.

e. **vereor ut . . . possit** (8): Students should be asked to comment on how the use of fearing clauses contributes to the anxious tone of this letter.

f. **illud . . . nē . . . interclūdāmur** (9): The demonstrative pronoun is commonly used in Cicero's letters in anticipation of a clause: "(I fear) this, (the fact) that we may be cut off." Cf. **illud verendum est, nē . . . sit** (15–16).

g. **modo ut . . . liceat** (13): **modo**, "provided that," is regularly followed by an **ut** clause with the subjunctive expressing a proviso.

h. **loca** (13): The noun **locus** becomes neuter in the plural when referring to places in the same area. In addition to Formiae, Cicero owned estates at Arpinum and Tusculum in Campania.

i. **velim** (16): Cicero uses the potential subjunctive **velim**, "I should like . . . ," to express in a polite but firm way one of the possibilities he would like his family to consider.

j. Several days after this letter was written, Cicero's family left Rome for their villa at Formiae.

B.

a. This excerpt is from a letter written in early February, 49 B.C., from Formiae, where Cicero had retreated after giving up his duties as recruiting officer. It reveals the terrible mental struggle through which he was passing in the early months of 49. He admired Caesar's resourcefulness and was financially in his debt. But an alliance with Caesar would force a rejection of all the principles he had defended as a statesman, and, in addition, would alienate Pompey, to whom he owed a debt of gratitude for assisting in his recall from exile in 57 B.C. Cicero, however, was disillusioned by Pompey's failure to take a stand against Caesar and questioned Pompey's decisions regularly, perhaps reflecting frustration at his own indecision.

b. **explicārī rēs** (8): The phrase **rem explicāre** occurred in Chapter 18. During these trying months, Cicero wrote to Atticus almost daily, in search of a decision. Atticus sympathized with the position of the Senate but refused to engage in politics himself.

C.

a. Pompey wrote this letter in late February, 49 B.C., from Canusium, near Brundisium, where he was marshaling his forces shortly before abandoning Italy for Greece. Pompey and Cicero corresponded often, and it was customary for Cicero to forward to Atticus copies of his letters to and from both Pompey and Caesar.

b. As students read, they should be asked to appreciate Pompey's conciliatory tone toward Cicero. His repetition of the word **commūnis** (3 and 6),

his use of the first person plural **ferāmus** (7), supported by his excessive flattery (**pristinam virtūtem**, 3, and **singulārī perpetuōque studiō**, 5) all suggest that Cicero shares with him the common purpose of saving the Republic.

D.

a. Caesar wrote this letter in March, 49 B.C., while approaching Brundisium by forced marches (an example of his famous **celeritās**) in an attempt to cut Pompey off from Greece.

b. **Cum properārem** (2): **Cum** here means "although," and the clause with the subjunctive, often followed by the word **tamen**, as here, grants or concedes the truth of what is being maintained. This use of **cum** with the subjunctive is called a *concessive clause*.

c. Students should be encouraged to use the present tense in translating this letter. Often in Roman letters a past tense (usually imperfect) can be translated as present in English because the writer is describing an action which will be perceived by the reader as already past. Hence **Cum properārem** may mean, "Although I am in a rush."

d. **grātiās tibi agerem** (4): Cicero tried several times, unsuccessfully, to mediate Caesar's conflict with Pompey (see especially *Ad Atticum* IX.11a), and it is perhaps for this reason that Caesar is thanking him.

e. After vacillating for several months, Cicero finally decided to join Pompey in Greece. In a subsequent letter, Caesar replied:

> **Quod nē faciās, prō iūre nostrae amīcitiae ā tē petō. Postrēmō quid virō bonō et quiētō et bonō cīvī magis convenit quam abesse ā cīvīlibus controversiīs?**
> —quoted by Cicero, *Ad Atticum* X.8b
> *I ask you not to do this [i.e., join Pompey], by right of our friendship. After all, what is more appropriate for a distinguished and peaceful man, and a good citizen, than to refrain from civil conflict?*

6. *VERBS: Clauses of Fearing*: A noun clause with its verb in the subjunctive regularly follows words of fearing. Students will initially feel confused, and even betrayed, by the turnabout in the meanings of **ut** and **nē**. The self-discovery of working this out in the reading, plus additional practice in Exercise 59a, rather than attempts at explanation by the teacher, will rebuild confidence.

7. Exercise 59a: Suggested translations:

1. Pompey was afraid that Caesar already had all of Italy in his control.
2. Terentia and Tullia were afraid to remain in Rome any longer.
3. Surely Caesar did not fear that he would not overcome Pompey.
4. Cicero seems to be afraid that Caesar will harm Roman citizens.

5. Does Cicero fear that Dolabella cannot protect Tullia?

6. Atticus was always afraid that Caesar wanted to become dictator.

7. There was the greatest concern that Cicero had already been cut off from Terentia.

8. Cicero is afraid that Terentia may not receive his letter.

9. Every Roman feared that civil war would break out.

10. Caesar feared that Cicero would go over to Pompey.

Note: additional practice with fear clauses will be found in the supplementary activity *Practice with Fear Clauses and Impersonals* (page 104) which may be done after Chapter 61.

8. Exercise 59b: Answers and suggested translations:

1. (Indirect Command) Certain friends of Cicero were encouraging him to hand himself over to Caesar.

2. (Purpose) Cicero is leaving for Capua to levy soldiers for the purpose of helping Pompey.

3. (Fearing) Was Pompey afraid that Cicero was going to bring help to Caesar?

4. (Result) There was so much famine in Rome that no one had enough food.

5. (Indicative with **ut**) Pompey, as you all know, had more soldiers than Caesar.

6. (Purpose) Pompey wrote to Caesar for the purpose of obtaining help.

7. (Fearing) Cicero feared that his household would not be safe in Rome.

8. (Indirect Command) Cicero warned his family that they had to leave Rome.

9. (Result) Caesar wanted to win Cicero over so much that he sent him a flattering letter.

10. (Purpose) Pompey will send Cicero to Campania in order to enlist soldiers.

9. Exercise 59d: Suggested Answers:

1. Each general asks Cicero to ally himself with him (**hortor**, C:5, and **petō**, D:5) by giving the impression of having the upper hand militarily (**exercitum**, C:4, and **legiōnibus**, D:3), by using flattery (C:3 and 5, and D:4−5), and by appealing specifically to Cicero's resources (**opem**, C:7 and D:7) and influence. Pompey asks Cicero to join him in Brundisium, whereas Caesar declares that he will be joining Cicero in Rome soon.

2. Each general hopes to gain Cicero as a political ally. Pompey seeks help on behalf of the Republic (C:6 and 7), whereas Caesar appeals on the grounds of their personal relationship (D:4−5).

3. Caesar, confident in the fact that he will make short work of Pompey (D:6), betrays a self-assurance bordering on arrogance. His words focus on himself, while those of Pompey focus on the common purpose (**commūnī**, C:3 and 6, **nōs**, 6, and **ferāmus**, 7). Pompey legitimizes his plea by referring to consuls (C:3) and to the Republic (C:6 and 7).

4. Cicero is a loving family man and devoted to the Republic. Although he possesses intelligence enough to weigh his options, he seems too hesitant and indecisive to act, despite Pompey's and Caesar's deference to him as a man of counsel (**cōnsiliō**, C:6 and D:7). He seems to be conscious of social station (A:11), to have influential friends (A:8 and 16), and to have a sense of honor (B:6−7).

10. Supplementary Materials

a. *Word Study XIV* (page 100): The Word Study sections in *From Republic to Empire* all focus on how Latin words have influenced the development of Romance languages, a study begun in *Pastimes and Ceremonies*, pages 96–97. The various letters which students have read in Chapter 59 make it logical to begin with salutations and greetings. The second half of this worksheet will help consolidate the gerund and provide opportunity for a quick review of the present participle. Answers to the Exercise: **dēsīderandō, faciendō, praeparandō, scrībendō, videndō.**

CHAPTER 60: THE BATTLE OF PHARSALUS (PART I)

1. The aims of this chapter are:

   a. to introduce Caesar as a writer and man of war
   b. to introduce some conventions of Roman warfare
   c. to present the use of the ablative case with special deponent verbs.

2. Translations

   A. When [Caesar] was exhorting his army to the fight, according to the custom of war, and was setting forth his constant services toward them, he recalled especially that he could use his soldiers as witnesses [to the fact that] with how much zeal he had sought peace and that he had never wished to waste the blood of his soldiers nor had he wished to deprive the Republic of either army [i.e., his own or Pompey's]. When he had given this speech, he gave the signal by war horn to his men, [who were] insistent and afire with enthusiasm for the fight.

   There was in Caesar's army a re-enlisted soldier, Gaius Crastinus, a man of remarkable courage, who in the previous year had led the **prīmus pīlus** in the Tenth Legion under him [Caesar]. When the signal had been given, this [man] said, "Follow me, [those of you] who were my comrades-in-arms, and give to your commander the service that you pledged. This one battle remains; after it is finished, he will regain his prestige and we our liberty." At the same time, looking back at Caesar, he said, "Today, general, I will see to it that you thank me, whether living or dead." When he had spoken this, he was the first to run forward from the right wing, and about 120 picked troops, volunteers from the same century, followed.

   B. But when our soldiers, after the signal had been given, had run forward with spears prepared [to attack] and when they had noticed that Pompey's men were not attacking, skilled through practice and trained in previous battles, they stopped their charge on their own and took a stand at about half the distance, so as not to approach with their strength drained; after a brief amount of time had passed, having again renewed their charge, they threw [their] javelins and quickly drew their swords, as it had been instructed by Caesar. Nor indeed did Pompey's men fail [to meet] this situation. For they withstood the thrown weapons and endured the attack of the legionaries, kept their ranks and, having cast [their own] javelins, resorted to their swords.

   At the same time the cavalry from Pompey's left wing, as it had been commanded, rushed forward all together, and the whole mass of archers poured forth. Our cavalry did not withstand their attack, but, dislodged from [their] position, gradually retreated, and

Pompey's horsemen began to press on all the more fiercely, to deploy themselves by squadrons, and to surround our battle line on the exposed flank.

   C. When Caesar noticed this, he gave the signal to the fourth line, which he had arranged from six cohorts. These ran forward quickly and, in attack formation, made an attack on Pompey's horsemen with such force that none of them stood fast, and all turned tail and not only withdrew from the place, but headed immediately in headlong flight for the highest mountains. When these had been driven off, all the slingers and archers, deserted and unarmed, without protection, were killed. In the same attack the cohorts surrounded the left wing, [where] Pompey's men even then were still fighting and resisting in formation, and attacked them from the rear.

3. Background

   a. The selections in this and the next chapter are taken from the *De bello civili*, Caesar's three books of commentaries, or memoirs, describing the events of the civil conflict from its outbreak early in 49 B.C. until Caesar's arrival in Alexandria, Egypt, in late 48. Caesar is believed to have composed the *De bello civili* during the course of the conflict for the purposes of propaganda, perhaps to win over opponents to his anticipated regime. Like his earlier and more famous commentaries on the Gallic wars, which established a new literary genre, these are written in a straightforward and lucid style and have been studied as handbooks of military science by generals such as Napoleon. The episodes presented in Chapters 60 and 61 are intended not only to illustrate something of Caesar's masterful generalship, but also to reveal his more human side as an observer of human nature.

   b. Further information on various aspects of Roman military science may be found in the following:
   1. *The Military Institutions of the Romans*, a translation of a fourth century A.D. treatise on Roman military science by Flavius Renatus Vegetius, includes much anecdotal information about the recruitment and training of a legionary soldier.
   2. "The Roman Army," *Roman Civilization Sourcebook II*, pp. 490–531, provides ancient sources in translation.
   3. *The Roman Army* includes illustrations and ancient sources describing the individual soldier, life in camp, the army in battle, and the life of the soldier after discharge.
   4. *Warfare in the Classical World*, especially pp. 144–187 on the wars of the Republic, is a wonderfully illustrated history, which covers all aspects of Greek and Roman warfare and includes many battle plans and artist's recon-

structions of the weaponry of individual soldiers and of warships and artillery.

Additional resources include the following:

1. Students may enjoy reading translations of Caesar's dramatic accounts of the sieges of the Gallic strongholds Avaricum and Alesia in Book VII of the *De bello Gallico*. Excellent reconstructions of the siege of Avaricum can be found in *Imperial Rome*, pp. 89–97. "Conqueror's Path to Mighty Empire," *Greece and Rome*, pp. 372–434, presents a beautifully illustrated account of Caesar's conquest of Gaul, including a colorful artist's rendering of the siege of Alesia, pp. 412–414.

2. Those teachers who wish to construct a Roman catapult or ballista or who have students who are fascinated by the engineering design of Roman artillery are directed to *Catapult Design, Construction, and Competition*, and to the illustrated article "Ancient Catapults" in *Scientific American*, March 1979.

c. The Romans experienced the fratricidal horror of civil war three times in the final years of the Republic. The civil war between Caesar and Pompey (49–45 B.C.) was so stirring that the imperial poet Lucan devoted to it an entire epic, the *De bello civili (Pharsalia)*. Feeling the oppression of Nero's regime, Lucan saw in the battle of Pharsalus and Caesar's subsequent dictatorship the final loss of freedom and the triumph of military rule. Lucan summarized the power struggle between Caesar and Pompey with this **sententia**:

Nec quemquam iam ferre potest Caesarve priōrem, Pompeius parem.
Caesar cannot tolerate a superior, nor Pompey an equal.
— *De bello civili* I.125–126

d. After defeating Pompey's armies in Spain and accepting the surrender of Massilia, Caesar determined to pursue Pompey in Greece. The engagement of the two armies at Dyrrachium (modern Durazzo), a town on the west coast of Macedonia, ended in a stalemate, with Pompey pursuing Caesar to Pharsalus in Thessaly (for which, see the map on page 18 of the student's book). The actual site of the battle is uncertain; Caesar himself never mentions Pharsalus. The battle was probably fought on the northern bank of the Enipeus river, with Pompey's camp to the west of the plain, which was encircled by hills (see the battle plan on page 83 of the student's book). For details about the battle and subsequent events, see, "Pharsalus," *The Oxford Classical Dictionary*, pp. 810–811, and "War in Greece, Egypt, and Asia (48–47 B.C.)," *From the Gracchi to Nero*, pp. 142–144. For Lucan's compelling description of the battle itself, see the Loeb translation.

e. **Aciēs** (B:17, C:1 and 9) was the front line of an army drawn up in battle formation and conceived by the Romans as the edge of a knife or sword (the literal meaning of the word). For the technical military terms presented in this reading, see the reading notes. Here is a list, for reference, with the location of each word's first appearance:

   aciēs (54C:7)
   centūria (A:18)
   cohors (C:2)
   cornū (54C:3)
   equitātus (B:15)
   equitēs (54C:3)
   exercitus (54B:7)
   funditor (C:7)
   gladius (25:32)
   imperātor (59C:1)
   legiō (54A:11)
   manipulāris (A:11)
   ordō (B:10)
   pīlum (B:1)
   prīmus pīlus (A:9)
   proelium (54A:7)
   sagittārius (B:14)
   signum (56B:8)
   tēlum (B:9)
   tuba (A:7)

For further information on matters pertaining to the organization of the Roman army, see *The Roman Army*, "Soldiers of the Emperor," pp. 3–20, "Life in Camp," pp. 21–35, and "Open Battle," pp. 42–43, and the sound filmstrip "Caesar's Army" published by Educational Audio Visual Inc.

4. Teaching the Text

a. It is, of course, important to "set the stage" for the readings in these two chapters by reviewing what the students already know about the historical context of the battle of Pharsalus. Especially useful for this purpose are Chapter 54, readings B and C. It would also be useful for the teacher, if time allows, to provide the student with readings in translation from Caesar's *De bello civili* as historical background for the text, especially the chapters describing the stalemate at Dyrrachium (III.39–57), the scene in Pompey's camp just prior to the battle (III.82–84), and the preliminaries to the fighting (III.85–89).

b. A gold mine of creative ideas and materials for teaching Caesar will be found in Fred Mench's article "Caesar in the Curriculum — Some New Approaches." This article contains a valuable annotated bibliography of current books and historical novels, a list of audio-visual aids, and suggestions for historical, thematic, and literary approaches to teaching Caesar. Also, the American Classical League Teaching Materials and Resource Center makes available to the teacher a packet of mimeographed items written by teachers, scholars, and students on subjects relevant to the study of Caesar (Mimeograph Packet M1). See also "A Selected Bibliography of Recent Work on C. Julius Caesar."

c. Rather than dwelling on details of the fighting, the teacher should use the readings to build an appreciation of Caesar as both writer and soldier. (Mench's article is especially useful for this purpose.) Class or individual biographical study of Caesar could precede reading and discussion of these chapters or could be left until the end of Part III and introduced in connection with the supplementary reading that describes Caesar's death (page 105 in the Appendix). The readings given in these chapters provide vignettes that will allow the teacher to guide students toward an appreciation of Caesar's propagandistic style, e.g., his interesting digression on the vainglory of Pompey's men at Pharsalus in the next chapter (Reading C:1–10).

d. The teacher may ask students to underline or highlight the technical military terms listed above in note 3e or to discuss the vocabulary of the reading prior to translation. The following words appear frequently during the six readings in these two chapters and should be learned by the student (first appearance in parentheses): **cohortor** (A:1), **procurrō** (A:17), **conficiō** (A:13), **animadvertō** (B:2), **cōnsistō** (B:4), **cēdō** (B:15) and its compounds, **circumeō** (B:17), and **adorior** (C:10).

e. For a fine example, on film, of the tactics of Roman legions on the battlefield during the late Republic, see the feature length movie *Spartacus* (1962). The movie *Fall of the Roman Empire* (1964) also has some lively battle scenes of the Romans against the barbarians in the 2nd century A.D. Students should become aware of Caesar's tendency to focus on a particular individual amidst all the maneuvering of units and the heat of battle (in the manner, again, of film-making). The episode of Crastinus presented in Reading A:8–18 may be followed up at the end of the battle in the next chapter with an epitaph celebrating the life and death of a centurion in the Roman army (printed in the Appendix, page 106). A photograph of a model of a legionary soldier of the late Republic is provided on page 85 of the student's book. For a well-illustrated appreciation of the individual Roman soldier, see *The Roman Legionary*, and see also "Directions for Making a Costume of a Roman Legionary." For an interesting look at the life of a soldier, see the translation from Livy "Career of a Humble Citizen-Soldier (200 B.C.)," *Roman Civilization*

Sourcebook I, pp. 452–454, and the various historical novels available through the American Classical League Teaching Materials and Resource Center. Available for the younger student (although the Latin is difficult) is the *Asterix in Latin* series (seven different stories) by Goscinny and Uderzo, cartoon stories about the misadventures of the Gallic "hero" Asterix and company, a sort of whimsical counterpoint to Caesar's commentaries.

f. The following subjunctive clauses are available for review: **cum** circumstantial (A:1 and 16 and B:1–2), indirect question (A:4), substantive result (A:15), negative purpose (B:5), and result (C:4–6). Caesar makes frequent use of participles and ablative absolutes, which provides opportunity for further review. These readings are particularly rich in various uses of the ablative case: with special verbs (A:3 and 4–5), means (A:4 and 7, B:3, C:6 and 8), absolute (A:6, 10, and 13, B:1, 5, 5–6, and 10, C:3, 6, and 9–10), separation (A:5 and C:5), place where (A:8 and 9), time (A:8–9 and B:12), description (A:10), place from which (A:16–17, B:12 and 17, C:10), manner (B:1 and C:3), agent (B:2), specification or respect (B:3), and with a preposition (C:7).

5. Reading Notes

A.

a. **in eum ... officia praedicāret** (2): The meaning of these words might be unclear. Be sure students understand that the **officia**, "services," are those of Caesar and that **eum** refers to the army, **exercitum**.

b. **testibus ... mīlitibus** (3): Ablative after **ūtī**; cf. **sanguine** after **abūtī** (4–5).

c. **commemorāvit ... voluisse** (3–6): Students should note that comprehension of this sentence depends upon observing that there are three infinitive phrases in indirect statement after **commemorāvit**: **sē .. posse** (3), **sē ... abūtī** (4), and **(sē) ... voluisse** (6).

d. **alterutrō exercitū** (5): Ablative of separation after **prīvāre** (6), "to deprive" X (*acc.*) of Y (*abl.*).

e. **exposcentibus mīlitibus ... ardentibus** (6–7): This is better taken as a dative indirect object after **dedit** than as an ablative absolute. These telling words follow upon Caesar's claim in the previous line that he always looked after his men. Caesar goes on to illustrate the eagerness of his men with the story of Crastinus.

f. **in exercitū Caesaris** (8): Students should be asked to note that Caesar writes in the third person and to speculate on the reasons why he does so. Caesar's use of the third person gives the reader the illusion that the writer is someone other than Caesar himself and is, therefore, objective and unbiased.

g. prīmum pīlum in legiōne X (9): **Prīmus pīlus** was the term both for the top-ranking century (unit of 60 men) of the 60 centuries in each legion and the title of the senior centurion of the **prīmus pīlus**. Crastinus had commanded the **prīmus pīlus** of the first cohort of the 10th Legion, Caesar's favorite.

h. superiōre annō (8–9): Crastinus had probably served against Pompey's armies in Spain and during the campaign at Massilia (see *De bello civili* II.1–22 and Chapter 54B:15–17).

i. Sequiminī (10): This word provides an opportunity for review of the imperative of deponent verbs.

j. manipulārēs (11): A maniple (**manipulāris**) was a military unit intermediate between century and cohort and consisted of 120 men (= two centuries). Thus: 1 legion (= 3,600 soldiers) = 10 cohorts (360 men per cohort or three maniples) = 30 maniples (120 men per maniple or two centuries) = 60 centuries (60 men per century). A century, originally, had been 100 men.

k. dignitātem (13): For this term, see the introduction to Part I, page 9 and Chapter 59:D7 in the student's book, and page 9, note 3c3, in this handbook. Caesar wanted to stand for a second consulship *in absentia* while still commanding in Gaul; after lengthy legal maneuvering, his opponents in Rome had passed legislation requiring him to give up command and return to Rome as a private citizen. By doing so, he would have been finished as a political force, and perhaps even put on trial by his enemies; consequently he would have suffered a great loss of **dignitās**.

l. ut . . . grātiās agās (15–16): Substantive (noun) clauses of result with **ut** (negative **ut nōn**) are used as the objects of verbs such as **faciō** and its compounds and **accidit**. Thus, **faciam . . . ut** = "I will bring it about that."

m. ex dextrō cornū (16–17): The 10th Legion was stationed on the right wing of Caesar's line, opposite Pompey's left wing and his cavalry, and was led by Titus Labienus, Caesar's **lēgātus** and second-in-command during the Gallic Wars. See the battle plan on page 83 of the student's book.

n. sunt prōsecūtī (18): Note the inverted word order of this verb, a common occurrence in Caesar.

B.

a. īnfestīs pīlīs (1): This was a position where the lances (**pīla**) were leveled for attack. Cf. **īnfestīs signīs** (C:3).

b. nōn concurrī ā Pompeiānīs (2): The impersonal passive will be discussed in Chapter 61, page 92, of the student's book.

c. ūsū perītī ac superiōribus pugnīs exercitātī (3): **ūsū** and **superiōribus pugnīs** are ablatives of means.

d. spatium (4): This word can mean an interval of space, as here, or of time, as in line 6.

e. ut erat praeceptum (7): Note the use of **ut** + indicative; also in lines 12–13, below.

f. huic reī (8): Dative after the compound verb **dēsum**.

g. equitēs . . . Pompeiī . . . noster equitātus . . . equitēsque Pompeiī (12–16): Note the back and forth nature of the description, to illustrate the action of the battle.

h. Quōrum impetum (14): Students should be asked to note Caesar's frequent use of linking **quī** (cf. A:13). Pompey's cavalry outnumbered Caesar's (see *De bello civili* III.88–89 and Chapter 54C:2–8 for the relative strength of the two armies).

i. locō mōtus cessit (15): In Caesar, the verb **cēdō** and its compounds may be found with the ablative without a preposition denoting place from which.

j. ā latere apertō (17): I.e., in the space left open by Caesar's retreating cavalry. See the battle plan on page 83.

C.

a. quārtae aciēī . . . sex cohortium (1–2): Caesar had drawn up a fourth battle line of six cohorts and stationed it behind his right wing (see the battle plan), to oppose Pompey's superior cavalry. This was an unusual tactic, because Caesar normally attacked with three battle lines (**aciēs triplex**).

b. īnfestīsque signīs (3): For military **signa**, see the illustration on page 43 of the student's book.

c. The break in the Latin text was designed to provoke curiosity about what will happen next in the battle and to generate anticipation for the readings in the next chapter.

6. *Roman Bullets*: For a photograph of a lead sling bullet, see *The Roman Army*, p. 18. The illustration on page 84 of the student's book is about actual size. It may be of interest that the English word "bullet" derives from **bulla**, which literally means "a round swelling," such as a ball or bubble (cf. a child's **bulla**, as shown on page 14 of the second student's book).

Here are suggested translations of the bullet inscriptions, all found at Asculum (modern Ascoli Piceno), near the Adriatic, and all products of the so-called Social War of 90–89 B.C.:

Hit Pompeius!
A "gift" for the Asculans
Runaways, you've had it!
Here's some hell for you, devil!

Em in the fourth inscription is an interjection used when handing or pointing out something to someone. It is derived from the verb **emere**, the original meaning of which was "to take."

7. *VERBS: Ablative with Special Verbs*: Two examples of this new usage are found in the reading: **testibus . . . mīlitibus ūtī** (A:3) and **abūtī . . . sanguine**

(A:4–5). Students should be asked to memorize the deponents listed on page 85 of the student's book; they should also be told that the compounds of these verbs take the ablative also (examples of this occur in Exercise 60a). It is appropriate at this time to review the forms and translations of deponent verbs with students, perhaps using the format of a synopsis (for which, see section 10A on page 12 of this handbook).

8. Exercise 60a: suggested translations:
   1. When the signal had been given, Crastinus called out, "Hurl your spears and use your swords!"
   2. When they had completed their very great labors, the centurions were praised by Caesar.
   3. When they had driven off the cavalry, Caesar's cohorts took control of the camp.
   4. In the battle of Pharsalus, Caesar made use of four battle lines.
   5. Were Roman soldiers ever allowed to enjoy holidays?
   6. The fourth battle line, which Caesar was hoping to use against Pompey's cavalry, consisted of six cohorts.
   7. Crastinus will do his duty, won't he?
   8. Caesar's army attempted to get possession of the plain of Pharsalus.

9. Supplementary Materials: The activity *Genitive and Dative with Special Verbs* (pages 101–103) may be done either now or after Chapter 61. See pages 41–42 for discussion and suggested answers.

CHAPTER 61: THE BATTLE OF PHARSALUS (PART II)

1. The aims of this chapter are:

   a. to conclude Caesar's narrative of the battle of Pharsalus
   b. to complete the picture of Caesar as writer and soldier
   c. to present passive verbs used impersonally.

2. Translations

A. At the same time, Caesar ordered the third line, which had been inactive and had held itself in position up to this time, to charge. And so, when fresh and intact troops had aided the weary [and] others moreover were attacking from the rear, the Pompeians could not hold out and they all together turned tail [i.e., retreated]. Nor, indeed, was Caesar wrong [in thinking] that the origin of victory would derive from those cohorts that had been stationed in a fourth line against the cavalry, as he himself had declared in exhorting his men. For the cavalry was driven away by these, first of all, by these same [cohorts] the massacre of the archers and slingers was done, [and] it was by these that the Pompeian line was surrounded on the left side and the beginning of flight was made.

But Pompey, when he saw his cavalry driven away and noticed that part [of his army] on which he most relied in a state of panic, having no confidence in the others, left the battle and rode straight into the camp and, to those centurions whom he had placed on duty at the praetorian gate, he said loudly, so that the soldiers could hear, "Watch over the camp and guard it attentively, in case anything worse happens [will have happened]. I am going around to the remaining gates and [will] encourage the guards of the camp." When he had said this, he went into the general's tent, having no confidence in the outcome, nevertheless awaiting it.

B. Caesar, thinking that he ought to give no respite to the terrified Pompeians who had been driven in flight inside [their] stockade, encouraged his soldiers to take advantage of fortune's generosity and storm the camp. His men, even though the heat was intense (for the action had been prolonged until midday), nevertheless, ready in spirit for every challenge, obeyed his command.

The camp was being defended zealously by the cohorts that had been left there on guard and even more fiercely by Thracian and [other] foreign auxiliary troops. For the soldiers who had deserted the line, both broken in spirit and overcome by exhaustion and very many having thrown away their weapons and military standards, were thinking more about continuing their flight than about defense of the camp. Nor, indeed, could those who had stood fast on the rampart withstand the volley of weapons any longer, but, done in by wounds, all left their posts and, under the leadership of [their] centurions and military tribunes, fled immediately into the very high mountains which bordered [reached] the camp.

C. In Pompey's camp it was possible to see [artificial] tree-arbors set up, a great weight of silver laid out, tents paved with fresh sod, even the tents of Lucius Lentulus and several others covered with ivy, and, furthermore, many things that indicated excessive self-indulgence and [over]-confidence in victory, so that it could easily be thought that those who were procuring unnecessary comforts had no fears regarding the outcome of that day. But [ironically] these [were the very ones who] were throwing [the charge of] self-indulgence at the very wretched and long-suffering army of Caesar, which had always lacked every necessity.

Pompey, since our men were now situated inside the stockade, obtained a horse [and], having torn away the insignia of command, threw himself out of the camp by way of the main gate and, spurring on his horse, immediately galloped to Larisa. He did not stop there, but, having picked up a few of his men in retreat, with the same haste and having traveled through the night without stopping, with a company of thirty cavalrymen, he reached the sea and boarded a grain ship, complaining frequently, as it was said, that he had been so terribly mistaken that, by the very class of men [i.e., cavalry] from whom he had hoped for victory, by that [very class], once the beginning of flight took place, he seemed almost [to have been] betrayed.

3. Background

a. For information about the context of the readings in this chapter, see the background section of the previous chapter on pages 34–35 of this handbook. The three readings in this chapter conclude Caesar's six-part narrative of the battle of Pharsalus.

b. At the end of each day's march, a Roman army constructed a camp (castra) for protection and as a place of refuge in a battle zone. The location, established by forward scouts, was determined by the availability of wood and water and was often on the slope of a hill. The camp, shaped as a rectangle, contained two main streets (viae prīncipālēs) at right angles to each other and terminating in four gates (portae). The porta praetōria (61A:17) was the gate in the center of the front face of the camp; the porta decumāna (61C:12–13) was at the opposite end of the camp, in the center of the rear face. The following terms, several of which appear in the chapter

readings, are used with reference to the castra (see the plan on page 89 of the student's book):

1. fossa: a 10' (3 meter) ditch or trench, 12–18' (4–6 meters) wide, dug around the camp
2. agger: an embankment, 10' high and 10' wide, and consisting of the earth excavated from the fossa, encircling the camp
3. vāllum: a rampart or defensive wall comprised of sturdy wooden stakes driven in at the outer edge of the agger (in the manner of the military forts of the early American West). See 61B:1.
4. praetōrium: the commanding general's headquarters
5. tabernācula: soldiers' tents, made of hide, and pitched by unit. Each tabernāculum held ten soldiers. See 61C:3–4.

For additional information on Roman camps, see "Camps," *The Oxford Classical Dictionary*, pp. 199–200 and "Life in Camp," *The Roman Army*, pp. 21–35, which contains scenes from Trajan's column of soldiers constructing a fortification. See also the Loeb edition of Caesar's *De bello Gallico*, pp. 601–602.

4. Teaching the Text

a. With the presumption that students will move quickly from the readings in Chapter 60 to those in Chapter 61, there is little need for extensive review. It is best that Reading 60C and Reading 61A be treated, as far as possible, as a continuous whole.

b. The text provides an opportunity for an appreciation of Caesar as general, man, and writer. After Caesar's narrative has been read and discussed, using the comprehension questions and the battle plan on page 83, the teacher may wish to use all six readings in the two chapters to make the following points about Caesar.

Caesar as general: Caesar's resourcefulness as general is demonstrated in 60C:1–10, where he anticipates and neutralizes Pompey's advantage in cavalry by adjusting his aciēs triplex to form a fourth line on his open flank.

Caesar as man: In describing the over-confidence of the Pompeian forces (61C:1–10), Caesar provides an example of his psychological insight in dealing with the enemy. The picture of the luxuries of Pompey's camp, coupled with his description of the arguments of Pompey's men over the anticipated spoils of victory (for which, see III.82–84, some of which is quoted below), and Pompey's ignominious desertion of his camp (61C:11–20), seem a propandistic attempt to illustrate the moral that "pride goeth before a fall." The question of Caesar's bias should be discussed with students.

Caesar as writer: As students read, they should form a general impression of Caesar's style of writing, which, because of its lack of rhetorical ornament, Cicero compared to a simple and unadorned statue. Students may be asked to explain why such words as "direct," "terse," and "restrained" have been used to describe Caesar's style.

c. The appearance of the word **castra** in 61A:16 (first seen in 54C:13), provides the opportunity for discussion of English derivatives. Permanent forts constructed on the frontiers of the Roman Empire often developed into communities that have lasted into modern times. The word **castra** survives today in such place names as Chester, Lancaster, Manchester, and Worcester in Britain, and these names were, of course, brought to America by English settlers.

d. New and review grammar and syntax: The following examples of the relative clause of characteristic will be found (this use of the subjunctive will be presented in Chapter 64): C:4–5, 7, and 9–10. Examples of items introduced in recent chapters include the gerundive (A:8) and the ablative with special deponent verbs (B:3 and 15). The following may also be used for review: present participle (A:21 and 21–22, B:2, and C:17), past participle (A:15, B:5, 10, and 14, C:1–4, 12, and 15), ablative absolute (B:10–11, C:12, 13, 15, and 19), indirect statement (A:13–14, B:1–2, C:6–7 and 17–18), dative with special verbs (A:3, 14, B:6, and C:8–9), **ut** + indicative (A:8, 13, and C:17), and uses of the subjunctive: **cum** circumstantial (A:3–4 and 20 and C:11), purpose (A:17), indirect command (B:3–4), and result (C:5–6).

5. Reading Notes

A.

a. **tertiam aciem** (1): Students should be asked to note Caesar's tendency toward emphasizing words by placing them first in phrases or clauses, e.g., **impetum** (60B:14), **sinistrum cornū** (60C:8), **sustinēre** (61:A:4), and **missīs** (61B:10). Here, it is the **tertiam aciem** that Caesar wishes to emphasize. The point may now be made, or reiterated, that in Latin word order, the most emphatic place is first, next in importance is last, with the weakest point in the middle.

b. **recentēs atque integrī dēfessīs successissent** (3): These substantive adjectives serve as nouns: "fresh, intact (troops) had come to the aid of (the troops that were) exhausted."

c. **terga vertērunt** (5): This military phrase may be rendered by the English idiom "they turned tail." Other such phrases appear, e.g., **locō mōtus cessit** (60B:15), "gave ground," (cf. **nēmō cōnsisteret**, 60C:4, and **locō excēderent**,

60C:5), and **sē . . . locō tenuerat** (61A:2), "had held its ground."

d. **Caesarem fefellit . . . orīrētur** (5–7): Impersonal verbs may be followed by the subjunctive; see Chapter 63, pages 110–111, of the student's book.

e. **ut ipse in cohortandīs mīlitibus prōnūntiāverat** (8): This refers to Caesar's speech given in 60A:1–6.

f. **Ab hīs . . . ab eīsdem . . . ab eīsdem** (8–10): Note the use of anaphora for emphasis, and the ellipses **factae (sunt)**, **circumita (est)**, and **factum (est)**.

g. **equitātum suum pulsum vīdit atque eam partem . . . perterritam animadvertit** (13–15): Supply **esse** to complete the infinitives (**pulsum esse** and **perterritam esse**) in indirect statement after **vīdit** and **animadvertit**, respectively.

h. **cui . . . cōnfīdēbat** (14), **aliīs . . . diffīsus** (15), and **summae reī diffīdēns** (21): Note the use of these "trust" verbs with the dative.

i. **aciē excessit** (15): See the reading note 5B:i for Chapter 60 on page 37 of this handbook.

j. **sē . . . contulit** (15–16): Cf. 59B:4 for this idiom, used again in lines 20–21 of the text here.

k. **Tuēminī** (18): another opportunity to review the imperative of deponent verbs; cf. 60A:10.

l. **si quid . . . acciderit** (18–19): This use of the indefinite **sī quid** will be explained in the next chapter. The future more vivid condition **sī** + future (perfect) tense will be presented in Chapter 66.

m. **praesidia** (20): This word (**prae** + **sedeō**) can mean "garrison," as here, or it can have a more generalized meaning of "defense" or "protection," as in 60C:7.

B.

a. **Pompeiānīs . . . compulsīs . . . perterritīs** (1–2): Take as dative indirect objects of **dare** (2); the direct object is **nūllum spatium** (1–2).

b. **oportēre exīstimāns** (2): Supply the reflexive pronoun **sē** (= Caesar) as subject of the infinitive in indirect statement.

c. **beneficiō . . . ūterentur** (3): Here is an opportunity for immediate followup to the grammar presented in the previous chapter (ablative with special verbs). See also **ducibus ūsī** (15, below).

d. **Quī . . . erat perducta** (4–5): Note the characteristic Caesarian features of linking **quī** and inverted perfect passive here.

e. **praesidiō** (7): This is dative of purpose, first seen in 47:2.

f. **ā Thrācibus barbarīsque auxiliīs** (8–9): The Thracians were well-known in antiquity for their ferocity as warriors. For more on **auxilia** in the Roman army, see the reading note on 54C:4 in the student's book.

g. **aciē refūgerant . . . et animō perterritī et lassitūdine cōnfectī** (9–10): These phrases provide opportunity for reviewing respectively ablative of separation, ablative of respect, and ablative of cause.

h. **missīs . . . armīs signīsque mīlitāribus** (10–11): This is another example of emphatic placement. In the case of **missīs**, it is the fact of the abandonment, rather than the weapons themselves, that is emphasized. See Reading note A:a above.

i. Reading B provides an excellent opportunity for review of relative clauses: 4–6, 7, 9, 13, and 16.

C.

a. **strūctās . . . expositum, . . . cōnstrāta . . . prōtēcta** (1–4): Note the repeated use of the perfect passive participle in the description of Pompey's camp.

b. **trichilās strūctās . . . recentibus caespitibus tabernācula cōnstrāta** (1–3): Given the heat in August on the plains of Macedonia (cf. **magnō aestū**, B:4), arbors for shade and fresh sod on the floors must, indeed, have been luxuries. The ivy might also have been used to provide shade, as well as a decorative appearance. The silver (eating utensils) were probably plunder.

c. **Lūcī . . . Lentulī** (3): Lucius Cornelius Lentulus Crus, praetor in 58 B.C. and consul of 49, was a determined anti-Caesarian. He had brought two legions to Dyrrachium for Pompey and fought at Pharsalus, but he fled to Egypt after the battle and lost his life one day after Pompey.

d. **quae . . . dēsignārent** (4–5): The relative clause of characteristic will be presented in Chapter 64. Cf. **quī . . . conquīrerent** (7), and **cui . . . dēfuissent** (9–10).

e. **victōriae fīdūciam** (5): In an earlier chapter of Book III, Caesar wrote of the eve of the battle of Pharsalus, "They (Pompey's men) were already starting to squabble openly among themselves about rewards and priesthoods and were assigning the consulships for years to come, while some were claiming the houses and property of people in Caesar's camp" (Chapter 82).

f. **ut . . . posset** (5–6): This is a result clause after **nimiam**.

g. **exīstimārī posset** (6): "It could be thought," an impersonal passive infinitive, for which, see page 92 of the student's book. **Exīstimārī** governs the indirect statement **eōs . . . timuisse** (6–7).

h. **miserrimō ac patientissimō** (8): This description may be exaggerated and somewhat propagandistic, although Caesar was, no doubt, short of supplies.

i. Note the use of the ablative absolute in the final paragraph: 12, 13, 15, and 19. Note also the use of words and phrases suggesting or stating the haste with which Pompey fled: **sē ex castrīs ēiēcit, prōtinus, citātō** (13), **contendit** and **celeritāte** (14), and **nocturnō . . . intermissō** (15), all emphasizing the magnitude of Caesar's victory and the humiliation of Pompey's defeat.

j. **Lārīsam** (13): This town still exists; it is some 65 miles (40 kilometers) from Pharsalus (modern Farsala) and just a short distance from the sea.

k. **querēns tantum sē opīniōnem fefellisse, ut . . . prōditus (esse) vidērētur** (17–19): "Complaining that he had been so wrong that . . . he seemed to have been betrayed." **Ut . . . vidērētur** is a result clause.

6. *VERBS: Passive Verbs Used Impersonally*: Students have seen the impersonal use of passive verbs in previous chapters of this book (this usage was first presented in 46:22–23). Students often find the English translation of impersonal verbs difficult, but patience on the part of the teacher will help them gain confidence. The sentences in Exercise 61a may first be translated literally and then idiomatically, to develop the contrast between the Latin and the English. Impersonal verbs will be consolidated in Chapter 63. Previous appearances of the impersonal passive in *From Republic to Empire*, in addition to those provided as examples in the student's book, include **contrādictum est** (54B:6) and **pugnātum est** (54C:12). The worksheet entitled *Practice wtih Fear Clauses and Impersonals* (page 104) may be used after completing the exercises in the text.

7. Exercise 61a: suggested translations:
   1. He persuaded (was persuading) me.
   2. We are running to the Forum in order to see Caesar.
   3. All the judges had to be persuaded.
   4. The fighting with the Pompeians was fierce until nightfall.
   5. All those who burned the Senate House will have to leave Rome.
   6. Was there excessive grief after Caesar had been killed?
   7. The top of the hill was soon reached.
   8. Which centurions will the commander favor?
   9. The Caesarians will have to be persuaded to make peace.
   10. Caesar wrote that all his men did not charge forward.

8. Supplementary Materials

A. *Genitive and Dative with Special Verbs* (pages 101–103): This activity, which continues the theme of special verbs (those with the ablative were introduced in Chapter 60) may be done in connection with either Chapter 60 or 61.

   Section 1 (Genitive with Special Verbs) will be new to students, although they have seen **potior** before (54D:22); **potior** takes the ablative more often than the genitive, but the genitive is always used in the expression **potīrī rērum**, "to get control of affairs." **Oblīvīscor** will occur frequently in Chapter 65. Students will almost certainly need help with the tense usages of **meminī**.

Section 2 (Dative with Special Verbs) is mostly a review and consolidation activity, since students were first introduced to these verbs in Chapter 21 (**appropinquāre**), and a number of them occurred throughout the third and fourth students' books. In connection with the verb **dēesse**, we have also introduced its "opposite," the *dative of possession*; students met one example of this in Chapter 29:5–6, but it has not been formally taught.

The illustration at the bottom of page 102 shows a **funditor** (slinger); cf. 60C:7 and "Roman Bullets" on page 84 of the student's book. The slinger in this picture appears to be using stones rather than **glandēs**, the acorn-shaped bullets shown on page 84 of the student's book.

Answers and suggested translations:

1. (**meī, tuī**) He remembers me, but he forgets you. Note: the genitive of these pronouns was not taught in the first four books of ECCE ROMANI, but the forms are given in the charts at the end of this book; this would be a good time to review the declension of the personal pronouns.
2. (**imperātōrī**) The centurions always obey the general.
3. (**multīs mīlitibus**) Caesar put Marc Antony in charge of many soldiers.
4. (**hominum**) You feel sorry for the men who died in battle.
5. (**omnibus suīs, tribūnīs**) Pompey ordered all his men to obey the tribunes.
6. (**nōminum** or **nōmina**) Can Caesar remember the names of each of all the centurions?
7. (**eīs**) Although Pompey's men had fought very fiercely, Caesar's soldiers wished to spare them.
8. (**nōbīs, Caesaris**) We are not allowed to forget Caesar.
9. (**hostibus, eīs**) The Pompeians were resisting the enemy bravely; they were not yet persuaded to lay down their arms.
10. (**castrīs, mihi**) Caesar approached Pompey's camp and said "I like this" (literally, "This pleases me").

B. *Practice with Fear Clauses and Impersonals* (page 104): This sheet is designed to provide practice with two important (but sometimes difficult) new structures taught in Part III. Sentence 10 also contains a gerundive for review. Suggested translations (note that impersonal verbs can often be translated in many different ways):

1. Caesar feared that Pompey's cavalry would throw his line into confusion.
2. A charge was made by Pompey's cavalry; there was no resistance from Caesar's infantry.
3. Pompey fears that he may not defeat Caesar in battle.
4. Pompey was afraid to remain in Greece after his defeat; for he greatly feared that he would not be able to escape from Caesar's soldiers.
5. There was heavy fighting around Pompey's camp.
6. After Pompey's cavalry was put to flight, Caesar rejoiced greatly (there was great rejoicing on Caesar's part).
7. Pompey's supporters very quickly made their escape to the sea.
8. Many Romans feared that Caesar would make himself dictator and that the Senate could not stop him.
9. Caesar was afraid that the king of Egypt would help Pompey.
10. In Rome there was great anxiety that Caesar's soldiers might come to plunder the city.

C. *The Deaths of Caesar and Cicero* (page 105): These readings are provided to round out Part III, which has focused on the three leading characters of Caesar, Cicero, and Pompey. They may be used at any time after the completion of the main readings of this chapter. Pompey's death at the hands of King Ptolemy's agents has already been mentioned in 54C:13–19; a version of these events taken from Book III of Caesar's *De bello civili* will be found in the Test Masters which accompany this book. Teachers who do not plan to use the Test Masters may want to supply students with an English account of Pompey's death; that of Plutarch, contained in *Fall of the Roman Republic*, is convenient.

D. *A Casualty of War* (page 106): This inscription is particularly appropriate for use after Chapter 61, although it might be used at other points.
1. Translation
   [Dedicated] to Marcus Caelius, son of Titus, of the Lemonian tribe, [whose] home was Bononia [Bologna], centurion of the 18th Legion, fifty-three-and-one-half years old. He fell in the Varian campaign. It will be allowed to bring in [bury] his bones [here]. Publius Caelius, son of Titus, of the Lemonian tribe, [Marcus's] brother, made [this monument].
2. Background
   a. In A.D. 9, three Roman legions under the command of Quinctilius Varus were annihilated by the Germans. This was one of Augustus' most serious military reverses and gave rise to the famous **sententia** which is printed at the bottom of the student's sheet. This should be explained to students prior to reading the inscription. It is interesting that Eutropius (Chapter 54B:1–7), perhaps out of a desire to portray Augustus in a purely positive way, makes no mention of this disaster.

b. For a photograph of the Caelius tombstone, see *The Ancient Romans*, p. 93. In the illustration provided with the text, the figures on either side are two of Caelius' freedmen (freedmen are often shown or mentioned on their master's tombs). The medallions (**phalerae**) on the centurion's breastplate and the circlets on his shoulders (**torquēs**) are medals of valor. On his head is a **corōna cīvica**, a wreath of honor indicating that Caelius had risked his life to save that of a fellow soldier. The rod in his hand is a swagger-stick (**vītis**) used for enforcing discipline. Tacitus tells of one centurion nicknamed **Cede Alteram** ("Gimme another!") because he broke his rod so often over his men's backs (*Annales* I.23). Centurions were grizzled veterans, equivalents of modern sergeants, who often supplied the heroics in Roman war stories, e.g., the story of Pullo and Vorenus (*De bello Gallico* V.44). For more information on centurions, see *The Roman Army*, pp. 10–12.

c. For the historical context of Varus' ambush, see "Publius Quinctilius Varo," *The Oxford Classical Dictionary*, pp. 1108–1109, and "The Northern Frontier," *From the Gracchi to Nero*, p. 267. Part IV of the B.B.C. film "I, Claudius" does a nice job of portraying the effects of this disaster on Augustus. The arch of Tiberius, about which students read in Chapter 23, commemorated the recovery of the eagles of Varus by Germanicus. Tacitus gives a moving account of the discovery by Germanicus' legions of the ambush site in the Teutoberg forest, ending his account with the words "So a Roman army, six years after the disaster, came to this place and buried the bones of the men of three legions" (*Annales* I.62, tr. Donald R. Dudley).

3. Teaching the Text
This funerary epitaph is designed to focus on the individual soldier within the larger context of the battle described in Chapters 60 and 61. This reading will, perhaps, provide students with an opportunity to reflect on the inhumanity of war and to develop a sense of sympathy towards the victims of war.

4. Reading Notes
Students should note that the inscription makes provision for the inclusion of Caelius' remains in the tomb, should they be recovered (**ossa īnferre licēbit**).

PART IV

Emperor and Empire:
The Rise of the Roman Principate

CHAPTER 62: AUGUSTUS

1. The aims of this chapter are:

   a. to present primary source materials for the study of Augustus and the Augustan Principate

   b. to present indefinite pronouns and adjectives in the context of interrogative and relative pronouns.

2. Translations

   A. At the age of nineteen on my own responsibility and at my own expense I raised an army, through which I emancipated the Republic, which had been oppressed by the tyranny of a faction. On that account the Senate, by honorary decrees, enrolled me in its order during the consulship of Gaius Pansa and Aulus Hirtius, granting me the consular right [of precedence] of giving my opinion [in debate], and it give me **imperium**. [The Senate also] ordered me, as propraetor together with the consuls, to see to it that the state should come to no harm. Moreover, in the same year, since both consuls had fallen in battle, the people elected me consul and triumvir for the organization of the Republic.

   Those who murdered my father I drove into exile, having avenged their crime by due process of law, and later, when they were waging war on the state, I defeated them twice in battle.

   The whole of Italy swore allegiance to me of its own free will and demanded me as leader of the war in which I was victorious at Actium; the Gallic and Spanish provinces, [and] Africa, Sicily, and Sardinia swore the same oath.

   B. In [my] sixth and seventh consulships, after I had exstinguished civil wars, having gotten control of all affairs by universal consent, I transferred the Republic from my own power to the authority of the Senate and People of Rome. For this service of mine I was named Augustus by senatorial decree, and the door-posts of my house were publicly adorned with laurel, and a civic crown was fixed above my door, and a golden shield was placed in the Curia Julia which, as attested by the inscription thereon, the Senate and People of Rome presented to me because of my courage, clemency, justice, and sense of duty. After that time I surpassed all in influence, although I had no more [official] power than the others who were my colleagues in office.

   C. I waged wars often, both civil and foreign, on land and sea throughout the whole world and as victor I spared [the lives of] all citizens seeking pardon. I preferred to preserve rather than exterminate the foreign nations who could safely be pardoned. I increased the territory of all those provinces of the Roman people on the borders of which there were nations who were not yet subject to our control.

   When I returned to Rome from Spain and Gaul, after having successfully managed affairs in those provinces, during the consulship of Tiberius Nero and Publius Quintilius, the Senate decreed that an Altar of Augustan Peace should be consecrated in the Campus Martius in honor of my return, [an altar] on which it ordered that the magistrates, priests, and Vestal Virgins make an annual sacrifice.

   [The gateway of] Janus Quirinus, which our ancestors wanted closed when throughout the whole Roman Empire, on land and sea, peace had been secured through victory, although from the foundation of the city tradition records that it had been closed twice altogether before I was born, the Senate decreed should be shut three times during my principate.

   D. I restored the Capitol and theater of Pompey, both works at enormous expense [to myself], without any inscription of my name on either. I rebuilt the channels of aqueducts, falling into disrepair through old age, in several places, and I doubled the [volume of the] aqueduct which is called the [Aqua] Marcia by diverting a new spring into its channel. I completed the Forum Julium and the basilica which was between the temples of Castor and Saturn, works begun and almost completed by my father, and began [to rebuild] that same basilica when it was destroyed by fire, having enlarged its foundation, [dedicated] under the name of my sons, and in case I had not finished it during my lifetime, I ordered it completed by my heirs. In my sixth consulship and with the authority of the Senate, I restored eighty-two temples of the gods in the city, omitting none that ought to be restored at that time. In my seventh consulship I rebuilt the Via Flaminia from Rome to Ariminum and all the bridges save the Mulvian and the Minucian.

3. Background for Part IV

   a. The chapters in this Part will offer three perspectives on Roman imperial rule: the historical transition from Republic to Empire, the role of the Emperor, and the nature of the Roman Empire as a world state. The readings and activities of this part are also designed to introduce the main sources for the study of the Roman Empire—literature, coins, inscriptions, and monuments—with emphasis on the reigns of Augustus and Trajan.

b. The names and historical dates of the imperial rules between Augustus and Trajan are given on the time line at the front of the student's book. The age of Augustus (27 B.C.–A.D. 14) was followed by the rule of the Julio-Claudian emperors (A.D. 14–68), so called because they were all related either to Augustus (grand-nephew and adopted son of Julius Caesar) or to his second wife Livia (daughter of M. Livius Drusus Claudianus). Following the year of the four emperors in A.D. 68/69, the Flavian emperors ruled (A.D. 69–96), so called because they were all related to T. Flavius Vespasianus. Nerva, Trajan, and Hadrian, who were known as the "adoptive emperors" (A.D. 96–138), because their succession was determined by adoption, were followed by the Antonine dynasty (A.D. 138–192). The rulers Nerva, Trajan, Hadrian, (A.D. 117–138), Antoninus Pius (A.D. 138–161), and Marcus Aurelius (A.D. 161–180) have been called the "Good Emperors" because they ruled with the good will of the Senate. For additional information about the history of the Roman Empire with emphasis on the emperors, see the following:

1. For literary sources, see Suetonius' *Lives* of the first twelve Caesars and the *Historia Augusta*, a collection of biographies of the emperors from Hadrian to Numerian (A.D. 283–284). Both of these are available in Loeb and Penguin translations.

2. For readable paraphrases of Suetonius, see Michael Grant's *The Roman Emperors* and also Ivar Lissner's *The Caesars: Might and Madness*, now out of print but worth the search.

3. For a general introduction to the history of the Roman Empire, see *The Romans and their Empire* and *The Ancient Romans*, with excellent chapters on Augustus and Hadrian.

4. Invaluable for a study of imperial court life from Augustus through Claudius is the thirteen-part B.B.C. series "I, Claudius," (available for rental from Budget Films in Los Angeles), after the novel by Robert Graves.

5. For an illustrated discussion about how various archaeological and written sources are used by the historian, see *How We Know about Antiquity* (available from the American Classical League).

4. Background for Chapter 62

a. This chapter is designed to provide linkage between the readings of the previous five chapters, covering the late Republic, and the succeeding five chapters, covering the early Empire. The passages in this chapter are taken from the *Res gestae* of Augustus and present, in the Emperor's own words, the transition from Republic to Em-pire that took place during the final quarter of the first century B.C. This chapter is intended to provide more detailed information about this important time in Roman history than that presented in Eutropius' summary, found in Chapters 55 and 56.

b. The photograph on page 94 of the student's book depicts the famous Prima Porta statue of Augustus, found in the villa of Livia at Prima Porta on the outskirts of Rome and now in the Vatican (the statue recently toured the United States as part of an exhibit entitled "Treasures of the Vatican"). Augustus' breastplate shows the restoration by Parthia of the legionary eagles lost in the defeat of Crassus (see 54B:1–6 and 56B:8–9). The cupid on the dolphin at Augustus' feet suggests his descent from the goddess Venus (back through the Julian **gēns** to Iulus [Ascanius], son of Aeneas and grandson of Venus). The statue of Trajan pictured on the same page can be found opposite the remains of Trajan's Forum in Rome, on the Via dei Fori Imperiali, built by Mussolini. The ceremonial armor of both Augustus and Trajan reveals their status as soldier-emperors.

After completing the texts in this chapter, the teacher may wish to return to the statue of Augustus, since some of the same propagandistic devices that Augustus used in his *Res gestae* also appear in the statue. It is an excellent teaching tool for showing how art can be used to create the desired image in the observer's mind. To help students get at the essence of this statue, it is useful to compare it with the Greek statue that served as its model, the Doryphorus (Spearbearer). Photos of the latter statue can be found in any standard general history of art (e.g., those of Janson or Gombrich) or in any text on Greco–Roman art. Susan Woodford draws the comparison thus:

> Polykleitos' Spear-bearer was the acme of classical sculpture, and the Romans deeply appreciated the air of serenity and dignity conferred on the figure by the carefully constructed pose. It was therefore chosen to provide the framework for a representation of Augustus that was meant to convey to his subjects both respect for his authority and admiration for his grace and control. But the Greek statue could hardly be taken over as a model just as it was, for it had several features that offended Roman taste.
>
> First of all, the Spear-bearer was an ideal figure—perhaps a representation of the Homeric hero Achilles, but certainly not any real person. This had to be changed, and so the head of the Spear-bearer was modified as much as was necessary to capture the actual features of Augustus, which were, nevertheless, made just beautiful

enough to reflect the Spear-bearer's purity of form.

Second, the Spear-bearer was nude. This was, of course, natural for a heroic Greek statue and furthermore essential to reveal the harmonious contrapposto. But it might have seemed improper for a Roman, especially for a Roman who posed as the guardian of ancient traditions of propriety and sobriety, as Augustus did. So the sculptor dressed his imperial subject in a suit of armour, and even gave him a cloak. The armour was, however, made so form-fitting that while decency was preserved, the modelling of the torso still remained clearly visible.

Third, the Spear-bearer lacked focus and direction. It was not felt right that the Roman emperor should stroll so dreamily through space. Rather, he should address his subjects directly and dominate the spectators who stood before him. Only slight modifications of the pose of the Spear-bearer were needed to bring this about: the head lifted and turned a little to look forward and outward, and the right arm raised to a commanding position. Thus Augustus, by gaze and by gesture, as if through the force of his personality, controls the space in front of him.

The statue was placed against a wall, as was often the case with Roman sculpture, and so all the emphasis is concentrated on the front view. The sides are less carefully thought out than in the Spear-bearer, and the back is not even finished. Perhaps this is why the accomplished sculptor who carved this statue did not mind destroying Polykleitos' contrapposto by raising the shoulder on the same side as the raised hip. The balance of the torso is somewhat obscured anyway by the armour and the cloak, and in the front view the curve of the raised arm responds handsomely to the curve of the relaxed leg on the opposite side. The internal balance and self-contained rhythm of the classical statue have been lost, but a new rhythm, one which captured the authority of the imperial subject, was created.

> —*Greece and Rome* (Cambridge Introduction to the History of Art), pp. 85–86.

The cover of this book shows a sculptor putting the finishing touches on this statue of Augustus. We chose this cover illustration because it symbolizes the transition from Republic to Empire; Augustus created the imperial form of government, as well as an image of himself, and both lasted for centuries. The supplementary activity *Comparison of Sculptures* (page 107) will be helpful for those teachers who want to explore the meaning of this statue with their students, using the quotation from Woodford as a point of departure. This makes an excellent introduction to the critical viewing of art. See pages 50–51 for suggested answers.

c. The complete Latin text of the *Res gestae* may be found on the face of the street-side retaining wall of the structure currently housing the Ara Pacis Augustae in Rome, across from the Mausoleum of Augustus, where the original was located (see the picture on page 46 of the student's book). For photographs of the inscription of the *Res gestae*, also known as the *Monumentum Ancyranum* (Ancyra = Ankara, Turkey), see *Illustrated Introduction to Latin Epigraphy*, pp. 108–111 and plates 22 and 23. The best text edition, containing the Latin text, translation, and copious notes, is that edited by Brunt and Moore. The Greek and Latin texts, with translation, may be found in the Loeb edition of Velleius Paterculus.

d. For additional secondary sources, consult the following:
   1. "The Second Triumvirate," *From the Gracchi to Nero*, pp. 159–177, covering the years between Caesar's death and the battle of Actium.
   2. "Augustus," *The Oxford Classical Dictionary*, pp. 149–151.
   3. "Augustus, the First Emperor" and "The Augustan Age," *The Ancient Romans*, pp. 86–95 and 104–108.
   4. A good source of new ideas is *The Augustan Age*, an annual publication of the Vergilian Society.

e. The timing and legality of the powers assumed by Octavian (presented in Readings A and B) are much debated by scholars. For an excellent discussion, see Brunt and Moore, pp. 75–80. After his victory at Actium, Octavian claims to have laid aside all the extraordinary powers granted to him by the Senate "to see to it that the state should come to no harm" (A:7) during the civil crisis that followed Caesar's murder, but the oath of allegiance that the whole of Italy took to him (A:15–18) set a precedent for the ensuing assumption of imperial rule (cf. the oath to Caligula on pages 93–94 of the student's book).

f. For discussion of the Roman use of architecture as propaganda (Readings C and D), see *Art and the Romans* and "Augustus: Buildings as Propaganda," *The Mute Stones Speak*, pp. 145–171. During the 1930's, the Italian dictator Benito Mussolini used a program of reconstruction of Roman buildings and monuments to win popular approval of his fascist dictatorship.
   1. *Ara Pacis Augustae* (C:7–12): This monument was dedicated to the Emperor on 30 January 9 B.C., in honor of his return from a three-year absence in Gaul and Spain (16–13 B.C.). The altar, excavated in 1903 and called "the greatest artistic masterpiece of the Augustan age" (MacKendrick, *The Mute Stones*

Speak, p. 162), features a sculptural relief running around the altar, in the manner of the Parthenon frieze, and depicts the dedicatory procession, including the Emperor Augustus performing priestly duties, together with members of his family. These sculptures represent, as propaganda, the ideals of the Augustan regime: peace and prosperity, return to the old religion, and the dynastic hopes of the Emperor. For a good closeup of the relief of Mother Earth as the personification of the benefits of the Augustan **Pāx Rōmāna** (or a personification of Italy?), see *The Ancient Romans*, p. 122. There is an excellent presentation of both the Ara Pacis Augustae and Trajan's Column in "War and Peace," *Art and the Romans*, pp. 11–34 (superior photographs). See also "Ara Pacis," *The Oxford Classical Dictionary*, pp. 90–91, *The Mute Stones Speak*, pp. 156–170 (with illustrations), and *Pictorial Dictionary of Ancient Rome*, Vol. 1, pp. 63–73.

2. *Gateway of Janus Quirinus* (C:13–17): This structure is called **geminae bellī portae** by Vergil, who writes:

> There are twin gates of war–that is their name; the religion and indwelling presence of Mars have sanctified them. A hundred brazen bolts and bars of durable iron secure them; Janus keeps his perpetual watch by the entrance.
>
> —*Aeneid* VII.607–610, tr. C. Day Lewis

Ancient references to this structure are confusing; it is most probable that the monument was a free-standing arched gateway, having religious associations, and used for the formal departure of the army from Rome. See "Janus," *The Oxford Classical Dictionary*, p. 561; Brunt and Moore, pp. 54–55; and *Pictorial Dictionary of Ancient Rome*, Vol. I, pp. 502–503 (Janus Geminus). The universal peace brought about by the end of the civil wars was celebrated not only by the closing of the gates of Janus but also in the verses of the Augustan poets Vergil and Horace, among others. See especially Horace, *Odes* III.2 and IV.15 and *Epodes* 7 and 16.

Additional structures mentioned in the readings will be discussed in the reading notes found below. An excellent source of general information is *Rome and Environs* in the Blue Guide series.

5. Teaching the Text

a. The four selections from the *Res gestae* may be read in four classes, especially given the "head start" students have with the historical background from Chapters 55 and 56. The readings are arranged chronologically, with the first two presenting high points in the Emperor's rise to power (44–27 B.C.) and the last two presenting notable achievements of his subsequent principate.

b. The events between the death of Caesar (44 B.C.) and the battle of Actium (31 B.C.), for which see Chapter 55 in Part I, may be summarized in oral or written individual or team reports, which might focus on the fascinating character of Cleopatra. For this, the teacher may wish to give a dramatic reading of Horace's song of triumph over the Egyptian queen (*Odes* I.37) or show the film *Cleopatra* (1963, 180 minutes), with its exciting footage of the battle of Actium. For a coin with the head of Antony on the obverse and Cleopatra on the reverse (32 B.C.), see *Roman Coins*, p. 111 and plates 188 and 189. Students will always be interested in what the "real" Cleopatra looked like. For ideas along this line, see "Egypt versus Rome," *The Classical Companion*, pp. 124–140.

c. The four selections provided may be supplemented by additional readings in translation from the *Res gestae* or from Suetonius' *Life of Augustus*. In reading the Latin, attention should be paid to the overblown way in which Augustus represents himself, even while attempting to be restrained. His narrative in the first person might be contrasted with that of Caesar, who wrote in the third person. As students read, they should begin to develop an appreciation of the character and accomplishments of Augustus in preparation for comparison with Trajan in the next chapter. Additionally, students will be asked to compare Eutropius' assessment of Augustus with what the Emperor says about himself and, furthermore, to compare both written accounts with the visual portrayal in the Prima Porta statue.

d. With respect to the fact that Roman emperors customarily inscribed their names on public works (D:2 and 8–9), the following inscription may be taught. This inscription, placed on an Egyptian obelisk in the Circus Maximus in 10 B.C., is now in the Piazza del Popolo in Rome.

IMP(erator) CAESAR DIVI F(ilius)
AUGUSTUS
PONTIFEX MAXIMUS
IMP(erator) XII CO(n)S(ul) XI TRIB(unicia)
POT(estate) XIV
AEGYPTO IN POTESTATEM
POPULI ROMANI REDACTA
SOLI DONUM DEDIT

The Emperor Caesar Augustus, son of the deified [Julius], high priest, victorious general for the 12th time, consul for the 11th time, holding the power of tribune for the 14th time, having brought Egypt under the control of the Roman people, has dedicated this as a gift to the sun.

Additional examples of honorary inscriptions will be found in the supplementary activity entitled *Credit Where Credit Is Due*, printed on page 109 of this handbook (see complete discussion on page 51).

e. The following new grammar and syntax may be noted:

> **priusquam** + subjunctive (C:15)
> **cum** concessive clause (C:15–17)
> past contrary to fact condition (D:9–10)

The following may be reviewed in the context of this chapter: present participle (A:6 and 14, C:2, and D:3), past participle (A:1, 3, and 13, B:2, D:5, 6–7, and 8), ablative absolute (A:5, C:8–9 and 17, and D:8 and 12), gerundive (A:6 and 10), and passive periphrastic (C:10 and 17).

6. Reading Notes

A.

a. **Annōs ūndēvīgintī nātus** (1): This idiomatic use of the past participle of **nāscor** is the normal way of expressing age in Latin. Augustus was 19 in 44 B.C.

b. **dominātiōne factiōnis** (3): According to Caesar's will, Octavian had become his adoptive son and heir and had taken his name. This brought Octavian into conflict with Marc Antony, then consul, for leadership of the Caesarians. Augustus formed a temporary union with the Republican senators in order to deal with Antony.

c. **in lībertātem vindicāvī** (3): Octavian won the battle of Mutina against Antony in Cisalpine Gaul in January, 43 B.C.

d. **Eō nōmine . . . et imperium mihi dedit** (4–7): Octavian's position representing the Senate against Antony, whom it saw as a would–be tyrant, was legitimized by a motion of Cicero on 1 January 43 B.C. The **imperium** granted was that of a praetor and thus subordinate to that of the consuls Hirtius and Pansa.

e. **Rēs pūblica nē quid dētrīmentī caperet** (7): This was the formula used during the Republic for the **senātūs cōnsultum ultimum**, the so-called "final decree" of the Senate, granting in times of emergency extraordinary powers to the magistrates to override normal legal controls in order to protect the state (previously mentioned on page 21, note d in this handbook). It was this decree that granted **imperium** to Octavian. For more information, see "Senatus Consultum Ultimum," *The Oxford Classical Dictionary*, p. 975.

f. **Populus . . . mē cōnsulem . . . creāvit** (8–11): The consuls Hirtius and Pansa had been killed fighting Antony at Mutina. Far from receiving a popular mandate, Octavian had marched on Rome after the battle and forced the Senate to agree to his irregular election as consul (1 August, 43 B.C.). For this, see Chapter 55A:6–7.

g. **triumvirum reī pūblicae cōnstituendae** (10–11): For the Second Triumvirate of Octavian, Antony, and Lepidus, formed in November of 43, see 55A:7–9. The pact was made primarily to eliminate the true Republicans such as Brutus and Cassius and to enable the three to assume autocratic powers. Augustus held the **imperium** (the right to command soldiers) first as propraetor (8), then as consul (9), and finally as triumvir (10). It was his possession of **imperium** that provided the real, and legal, basis for his power. Note the use of the gerundive here and in line 6 in legal formulas.

h. **iūdiciīs lēgitimīs** (13): Caesar's assassins were condemned by a special court established after the triumvirs had made themselves masters of Rome. Brutus and Cassius were portrayed as murderers warring against the Republic (**bellum īnferentēs reī pūblicae**, 13–14).

i. **vīcī bis aciē** (14): These were the two battles at Philippi in Greece (42 B.C.), when Antony and Octavian defeated Brutus and Cassius, both of whom committed suicide in defeat. During this battle Augustus had vowed a temple to Mars Ultor (Mars the Avenger; cf. **ultus**, 13) in vengeance for the murder of Julius Caesar. This temple, which housed Caesar's sword as a relic, became the centerpiece of Augustus' new Forum, begun in 37 B.C. and dedicated in 2 B.C. See the picture on page 46 and the plan on page 110 of the student's book; see also "Augustus: Buildings as Propaganda," *The Mute Stones Speak*, pp. 146–150, and also Chapter 55A:11–20 for more on the battle of Philippi.

j. **prōvinciae Galliae, Hispāniae, Āfrica, Sicilia, Sardinia** (17–18): These areas comprised the western provinces, granted to Octavian during the division of the Empire among the triumvirs. Antony received the East (see Chapter 55A:20–22).

B.

a. **per cōnsēnsum ūniversōrum** (2): This statement is not really true, since many of Augustus' powers during the civil wars had been extorted by force via his **imperium**. Cf. the sentiment in A:15, **in mea verba tōta Italia sponte suā**.

b. **potītus rērum omnium** (2–3): With the word **rēs**, **potior** is regularly found with the genitive rather than the ablative (see also Chapter 54D:22). For the ablative with deponent verbs, see Chapter 60, pages 84–85, of the student's book.

c. **rem pūblicam ex meā potestāte in Senātūs populīque Rōmānī arbitrium trānstulī** (3–4): Augustus restored the Republic in form (Senate, magistrates, etc.) but, in substance, the real power (**potestās**) rested with him through his **tribūnicia potestās** (right of veto and the right to propose legislation) and **imperium** (right to command soldiers). In any event, what Augustus wishes posterity to believe is clear from these lines.

d. **laureīs . . . corōnaque cīvica** (5–6): Both the laurels and the wreath of oak leaves are represented on Augustan coinage, which often bears the inscription **ob cīvēs servātōs**. For the appearance of this crown, see the illustration on page 99 of the student's book, and see also the illustration of the tombstone of Marcus Caelius on page 106 and the accompanying note on pages 42–43 of this handbook.

e. **per eius clupeī īnscrīptiōnem** (10): Another inscription (*CIL* IX.5811) is found with two Victories holding a shield and the words "The Senate and People of Rome have given to Augustus a shield on account of his valor, clemency, justice, and piety." For illustrations of Augustus' valor in the passages provided, see A:2–3 and 13–14; for clemency, see below, C:2–4; for justice, see A:12–13; and for piety, A:12–13 and D:10–12.

f. **auctōritāte . . . potestātis** (11): Augustus here contrasts his personal influence with his legal power. See the introduction to Part I, page 9, and the introduction to Part IV, page 93.

C.

a. **Bella . . . cīvīlia externaque tōtō in orbe terrārum saepe gessī** (1): For the civil wars, see Chapters 55A and B, 56A:1–2 and 15–16, and 62B:1–2. For the foreign wars and the expansion of the empire under Augustus, see Chapter 56A:15–22 and 56B.

b. **omnibus veniam petentibus cīvibus pepercī** (2–3): Augustus refers here to the citizens who sought amnesty after the battle of Actium. His general pardon in 27 B.C. led to the award of the **corōna cīvica** for saving Roman lives. See Horace, *Odes* II.7, on the return of a friend under this amnesty. Augustus' claim of clemency (B:9) was not entirely factual, since he was said to have executed prisoners after both Philippi and Actium. Augustus' use of **veniam petentibus** here and **tūtō** (3) implies that pardons were granted only when it was to the benefit of Augustus or Rome. Cf. Vergil's assessment of Rome's mission, **parcere subiectīs et dēbellāre superbōs** (*Aeneid* VI.853).

c. **omnibus . . . petentibus cīvibus . . . quibus . . . imperiō nostrō** (2–6): Note these examples of dative objects of the special verbs **parcō**, **ignōscō**, and **pareō**.

d. **fīnēs auxī** (6): This resulted from campaigns in Gaul, Spain, Ethiopia, Arabia, Germany, and against the Alpine tribes north of Italy. Cf. the tombstone of Caelius and the accompanying **sententia** on page 106 of the Appendix to this hand-

book, with discussion on pages 42–43. The disaster of Varus halted Augustan expansion.

e. **cōnsecrandam** (10): Understand **esse** to complete the passive periphrastic in indirect statement after **cēnsuit** (cf. line 17 in the text below). **Cēnseō** is followed by an indirect command in Chapter 59C:8. Verbs of decreeing or voting are often followed by the passive periphrastic, as here.

f. **sacerdōtēs virginēsque Vestālēs** (11): for the state religion under Augustus, see *The Romans and Their Gods in the Age of Augustus*, pp. 112–123.

g. **cum . . . prōdātur memoriae** (15–17): This is a **cum** concessive clause: "Although tradition records . . . ." The phrase **prōdātur memoriae** governs an indirect statement, the subject of which is **Iānum Quirīnum** (13) and the infinitive of which is **clausum fuisse** (16).

h. **bis omnīnō clausum fuisse** (16): According to tradition, the gateway was first closed by Numa Pompilius, the second king of Rome, and then again after the first Punic War in 235 B.C.

i. **ter mē prīncipe** (17): During the Augustan era, the gateway was first closed in 29 B.C. after the end of the civil war and again, four years later, at the close of the Cantabrian war in Spain. The occasion of the third closing is unknown.

D.

a. **Capitōlium** (1): This was the great temple of Jupiter Optimus Maximus, Juno, and Minerva atop the Capitoline Hill. The temple was burned in 83 B.C. and repaired by Augustus in 26 and 9 B.C. Suetonius tells us that at one time Augustus made a donation of 16,000 pounds of gold to the temple (*Augustus*, 30). For more information, see "Capitol," *The Oxford Classical Dictionary*, pp. 202–203, and *Pictorial Dictionary of Ancient Rome*, Vol. I, pp. 530–533 and p. 637.

b. **Pompeium theātrum** (1): This was the first and most important stone theater in Rome, built in 55 B.C. The foundations of this great theater may still be seen in subterranean restaurants near the Piazzo Teatro Pompeo in central Rome. See *The Mute Stones Speak*, pp. 138–139, and *Pictorial Dictionary of Ancient Rome*, Vol. II, pp. 423–438.

c. **aquam quae Marcia appellātur** (4): Students may remember the Aqua Marcia from the second student's book, pages 57 and 58. This aqueduct had been built by Q. Marcius Rex (praetor, 144–143 B.C.). Its source was in the Sabine hills near Subiaco, east of Rome. The Augustan work was completed by 5/4 B.C. and may still be seen as the lowest course of the three-tiered aqueduct forming the Porta Tibertina. The dramatic increase in Rome's water supply was one of Augustus' greatest gifts to the city. See *Pictorial Dictionary of Ancient Rome*, Vol. I, pp. 48–51.

d. **Forum Iūlium** (5): The Julian Forum, also called the **Forum Caesaris**, was dedicated by Julius Caesar in 46 B.C. after the battle of Thapsus. It annexes the Forum Romanum at the northeast corner. See the plan on page 110 of the student's book; "Forum Caesaris," *The Oxford Classical Dictionary*, p. 446; *The Mute Stones Speak*, p. 139–144; and *Pictorial Dictionary of Ancient Rome*, Vol. I, pp. 424–432.

e. **basilicam quae fuit inter aedem Castōris et aedem Saturnī** (5–6): Students met the word **basilica** in 57C:42. The Basilica Julia was dedicated in 46 along with the Forum Julium, but burned soon thereafter. Augustus began reconstruction in A.D. 12 but probably died before it was completed. The Emperor's "sons" (9) were Gaius and Lucius, sons of his daughter Julia by Agrippa and adopted as his heirs. For more on this basilica, see *Forum Romanum*, pp. 23–24 and *Pictorial Dictionary of Ancient Rome*, Vol. I, pp. 186–189.

f. **aedem Castōris** (6): The temple of Castor and Pollux stood adjacent to the Basilica Julia and across from the Basilica Aemilia. Several columns have been re-erected. See "Castor and Pollux," *The Oxford Classical Dictionary*, p. 213, *Pictorial Dictionary of Ancient Rome*, Vol. I, pp. 210–213, and *Forum Romanum*, p. 25.

g. **aedem Saturnī** (6): For this temple, the ruins of which may still be seen and which served as a treasury (**aerārium Saturnī**), see "Saturnus," *The Oxford Classical Dictionary*, *Forum Romanum*, p. 23, and *Pictorial Dictionary of Ancient Rome*, Vol. II, pp. 294–298.

h. **sī vīvus nōn perfēcissem** (9–10): This type of condition, a past contrary to fact, will be introduced in Chapter 66.

i. **viam Flāminiam** (13): Students may recall from Chapter 53 that Titus was entombed along this road. This was the only Italian road of which the repairs were not paid for by the war-booty of Augustus' generals, but by Augustus himself, who may have used Cleopatra's treasure as financing. The Via Flaminia, built in 220 B.C. by C. Flaminius, served as the great northern highway of Italy and was over 200 miles long. Parts of Augustus' bridge (at Narnia) and his honorific arch at Ariminum survive. See "Via Flaminia," *The Oxford Classical Dictionary*, p. 1118.

j. **pontēs omnēs praeter Mulvium et Minūcium** (14): The **pōns Mulvius** over the Tiber is now the Ponte Milvio; the location of the Minucian bridge is unknown. The Via Flaminia (now the Via del Corso) crossed the Ponte Milvio in the northern part of Rome. It was at this bridge that Constantine defeated Maxentius in A.D. 312 to become emperor (the battle is celebrated in relief sculpture on the arch of Constantine).

7. *Indefinite Pronouns and Adjectives*: Students have seen forms of **quīdam** since Chapter 10, **aliquis** since Chapter 24, and **quisquam** since Chapter 55, all of which should make them generally comfortable with indefinites, once the regular forms of **quī, quae, quod** and **quis, quid** have been reviewed. The regular forms of these relative and interrogative pronouns have been printed in boldface type in the chart on page 105 of the student's book to ensure recognition by the student. They may be asked to write out the forms of **quisque** and **quisquam**, since these forms are not included in the reference charts at the end of the student's book.

8. Exercise 62a: suggested translations:
   1. Can justice ever harm anyone?
   2. "Is anyone at home?" exclaimed the robber.
   3. Augustus gave instructions that no one was to say that the emperor was a god.
   4. Certain of the senators wanted to address Octavian as "Romulus."
   5. There is no one who fights in battle without fear.
   6. Indeed, we obey someone asking more willingly than (someone) ordering.
   7. "There are as many opinions as there are people; to each his own," wrote Terence.
   8. There can be no just cause for anyone taking up arms against (his) country.
   9. We observe that there are certain (people) present who fought at Actium.
   10. Was Augustus, even though he wanted to be the best emperor, a tyrant?
   11. If anyone says "No" to the emperor, he will be punished.
   12. Was a crown of triumph also given to Augustus?

   Notes:
   1. Sentences 6 and 10 contain **quidem** and **quamquam**, respectively, words often confused with indefinites.
   2. Sentence 7 is quoted from Terence's *Phormio*, 454.
   3. Sentence 12: For an illustration of the **corōna triumphālis**, see page 99 of the student's book. For information about Roman triumphal parades, see "Triumphal Procession," *The Roman Army*, p. 44 and "Roman Triumphs," *Roman Civilization Sourcebook I*, pp. 216–220.

9. Supplementary Materials

   a. *Comparison of Sculptures* (page 107): Before doing this activity, the teacher should study carefully the quotation from Woodford's *Art of Greece and Rome* given above on pages 45–46. This activity should certainly be done in class, as a group undertaking; rather than simply lecturing, the teacher should try to get students to observe the similarities and differences for themselves. The various categories may need some explanation.

Suggested answers:

Clothing: The Doryphorus is nude, while Augustus has both armor and a cloak. (Discuss the fact that Greek heroic statues were normally nude.)

Pose: The Doryphorus exhibits a harmonious balance, which derives partly from the fact that the raised arm is on the opposite side of the body from the raised leg. The basic pose of the Doryphorus was used as the model for the Prima Porta statue, but the balance is less perfect because the raised arm is on the same side of the body as the raised leg.

Orientation: The Doryphorus may be viewed from any angle; you can walk around it. Augustus is meant to be viewed from the front only, like a Roman temple; the back is not even totally finished.

Focus: The Doryphorus is looking out into space, without any particular relationship to the viewer; he seems lost in his own thoughts. Augustus, on the other hands, gazes firmly out and dominates the viewer, much like the old Army recruiting posters with Uncle Sam pointing directly at the viewer and saying "I want you!" The raised arm contributes to this feeling of authority.

Specificity: The Doryphorus is not meant to portray any particular person; the Prima Porta statue, on the other hand, clearly shows a particular individual, Augustus. The Doryphorus has no reference to any particular historical event, while the statue of Augustus is placed in history by the carving depicting the recovery of the Roman standards from the Parthians and by the reference to the Julian **gēns** in the form of the Cupid at Augustus' feet.

Realism: The Doryphorus shows us an idealized human form and is not meant to refer to any individual. While the sculptor apparently made Augustus a bit more handsome than he actually was, it was nevertheless clearly his intent to produce a recognizable likeness; this fits into the tradition of realistic portrait sculpture in the Roman world (cf. the statue of L. Caecilius Jucundus, complete with warts, found in Pompeii).

Purpose: The Doryphorus was meant to be a beautiful work of art in its own right and to show an appreciation of the human form. The Prima Porta statue is meant to convey a sense of political power and adherence to Roman tradition.

b. *Credit Where Credit Is Due* (page 109): Two honorary inscriptions are reproduced for students to read. They may be read either now or after Chapter 63, for comparison with Trajan's building program. The first one is translated as follows:

> Numerius Popidius Celsinus, son of Numerius, with his own money restored from [its] foundations the temple of Isis, which had collapsed because of the earthquake. Because of his generosity, the town council elected this man to their membership, although he was [only] six years old, without any fee.

This inscription was found in 1765 near the entrance to the Temple of Isis, which had been destroyed by the earthquake in A.D. 62. The usual age for the decurionate was 30. At this point in imperial history, public benefaction was a privilege. **Decuriōnēs** were previously mentioned in 57A:5.

These inscriptions will help students to understand the Roman value system, based on **dignitās** and **auctōritās**, (cf. the Introduction to the student's book, pages 8–9). Civic-minded Romans fully expected their contributions to be recognized. Knowing this makes the actions of the emperors who claimed inscriptional credit for their benefactions (see above, note 5d, page 43) more comprehensible. This background will also help students understand why Trimalchio wants his generous acts depicted on his tomb (Chapter 65, Readings A and B). The second inscription, which records Pliny's life, is an excellent lead-in to the Pliny letters found in Chapters 63, 64, 66, and 67. The teacher may also wish to draw comparisons with the nature of philanthropy in modern civic life.

CHAPTER 63: EMPEROR AND EMPIRE

1. The aims of this chapter are:

   a. to present materials for a study of the life and achievements of the Emperor Trajan
   b. to provide a context for comparison between Augustus and Trajan
   c. to consolidate the forms and uses of impersonal verbs.

2. Translations

   A. Pliny to the Emperor Trajan

   Indeed, most august emperor, [because of] your devotion [you] had wished to succeed your father at the latest possible moment; but the immortal gods have hastened to bring your skills to the helm of state, which you had [already] assumed. And so, I pray that all may turn out successfully, that is, worthy of your reign, for you and, through you, for the human race. Both as a private citizen and a public servant, I wish you health and happiness, best of emperors.

   B. Marcus Ulpius Trajanus governed the state so [well] that he is deservedly placed foremost of all the emperors, a man of unusual courtesy and bravery. He expanded far and wide the boundaries of the Roman Empire, which, after Augustus, had been defended more than enlarged. His courtesy and temperance, however, surpassed [even] his military accomplishments, at Rome and throughout the provinces showing himself to be a man of the people, visiting friends often to say hello, either when they were ill or had a holiday, giving and attending dinner parties with these same friends without regard to [their] social status, often sitting in their carriages, bringing harm to no senator, doing nothing unethical for the purpose of increasing his private purse, building much throughout the world, granting exemptions [from public duties] to city-states, [and] doing nothing that was not calm and peaceful. For this reason, throughout the world, most like a god he earned nothing but veneration, both while alive and after death. He passed away in the sixty-third year, ninth month, [and] fourth day of his life; in the nineteenth year, sixth month, [and] fifteenth day of his reign. He was taken up among the gods and alone of all [the emperors] was buried within the city limits [of Rome]. His bones were gathered in a golden urn and placed at the foot of his column, which was 144 feet high, in the forum that he built. His memory was preserved to such an extent that to our own era emperors are acclaimed in the Senate by no other words than "More successful than Augustus, a better [ruler] than Trajan."

3. Background

   a. Chapter 63 contains two readings designed to introduce the Emperor Trajan, one written during Trajan's own life and the other two hundred years later. Students have already met Eutropius in Part I and will be familiar with Pliny through the Latin and English readings in *Pastimes and Ceremonies* and the introduction to Part IV of this text (more letters of Pliny will be found in Chapters 64, 66, and 67). Those found in Part IV present aspects of Pliny's official and public life, while those in Part V present his more private and personal side.

   b. Trajan succeeded his adoptive father Nerva on 23 January A.D. 98, while in Germany commanding armies along the Rhine. Pliny's letter presented in Reading A must have been written soon after Trajan learned of his accession, although it was more than a year before the new emperor actually entered Rome. For biographical information about Trajan, whose life is not included in either Suetonius or the *Historia Augusta*, see:
      1. "Trajan," *Lives of the Later Caesars*, pp. 38–53, a compilation of the ancient sources
      2. "Trajan," *The Oxford Classical Dictionary*, pp. 1088–1089
      3. "Nerva and Trajan," *Five Roman Emperors*, pp. 169–211
      4. "Trajan: Port, Forum, Market, Column," *The Mute Stones Speak*, pp. 251–272.

   For a reel-to-reel film covering the Trajanic period (available from the University of Illinois film bureau), see: "Old Soldiers Never Die" (1969), dramatizing the life of a typical Roman soldier in Trajan's army of A.D. 100 (filmed by the B.B.C. in Timgad, Algeria), 31 minutes.

   c. This chapter and the next provide students with an introduction to the range of source materials available for study of Roman imperial history: inscriptions (see below and page 118 of the student's book), art (page 94), coins (pages 106 and 119), and monuments (pages 110, 112, and 113). Teaching suggestions for these are provided below. These materials should be used to reinforce not only the impressions of Trajan given by Pliny and Eutropius, but also of Roman imperial rulers in general (see background note 3b, Part IV, for the previous chapter). For instance, the statue of Trajan on page 94 illustrates what Eutropius says about him as a soldier-emperor (B:3–5). The coin on page 106 reveals that Trajan, through his association with Jupiter, believed that he enjoyed divine patronage, a belief confirmed by the Emperor's subjects (A:3–5 and B:13–15 and 16–17). (The role of the emperor as god will be explored in the next chapter.) Monuments such as Trajan's column (B:18–20), pictured on page 113 of the student's book, reflect the imperial vision of

Rome as a city destined to rule the world. These readings and source materials state or imply the imperial virtues of size, power, and control and, at the same time, demonstrate that the Roman Empire was a world state whose people enjoyed the rule of law and prosperity brought by political stability (A:5–7 and B:6–7 and 11–13). In discussion, teachers should ask students to consider that Roman emperors could express genuine concern for their subjects, in order to correct the common misconception that all Roman imperial rulers were egomaniacal, perverted, or bloodthirsty.

1. On coin A, pictured on page 106 of the student's book, Trajan puts himself under the protection of Jupiter and is therefore in the company of, but subservient to, the gods. Pliny supports this perception in the following quotation from his *Panegyricus*, a speech thanking the Emperor for granting him the consulship of A.D. 100. In this speech, Pliny identifies Trajan as Jove on earth:

> This truly is the concern of an emperor and even of a god—to restore good feeling between rival cities, to restrain angry peoples not by force but by reason, to correct the injustices of government officials, and to undo what should never have been done—finally, like a shooting star, to see and hear all, and to be present and offer assistance whenever called upon. It is in this way that I believe that the father of the universe controls all with a nod of his head, whenever he looks down upon the earth and thinks it worthy to reckon the destinies of mortal men among the works of the gods. He is now free of this duty and can turn his full attention to the heavens, since he has given you to us to carry out his responsibility toward the human race. (80.3–5)

The globe pictured on coin B symbolizes the worldly dominion of Trajan's rule and portrays him, as Pliny puts it, "like a shooting star, seeing and hearing all." This symbolism reinforces Eutropius' statement regarding Trajan's expansionist aspirations (B:3–5). The "message" of this coin is one of power, stability, and control, with Trajan, as a "benevolent despot," serving as Jupiter's regent on earth. Students may become interested in exploring the names and titles found in the inscription on coin B. The expanded inscription reads:

> **Imp(erātōrī) Trāiānō Aug(ustō)**
> **Ger(mānicō) Dāc(icō) P(ontificī)**
> **M(aximō) Tr(ibuniciā) P(otestāte)**
> **Cō(n)s(ulī) VI, P(atrī) P(atriae)**

(Dedicated) to the Emperor Trajan Augustus Germanicus Dacicus, Pontifex Maximus, holding the tribunician power, consul six times, Father of his Country.

The complete text and translation of the *Panegyricus* may be found at the end of Volume II of the revised Loeb edition of Pliny's letters. For more on coins, see *Roman History from Coins* and *Roman Coins*, plus "Roman Coins for the Latin Class," all useful as background for the study of coins as propaganda by the Roman emperors. Excellent replicas of imperial **dēnāriī** are available from the American Classical League Teaching Materials and Resource Center. For photographs of Roman emperors as they appear on coins, see *Rome and her Empire*, pp. 194–199 (Augustus to Antoninus Pius) and pp. 272–301 (Marcus Aurelius to Romulus Augustulus). Good closeups of imperial coins are also available on plates 4 and 64 of *Rome: Its People, Life, and Customs*.

2. The Arch of Trajan at Beneventum (modern Benevento) was erected in A.D. 114 in honor of Rome's prosperity under the Emperor's rule. In that very same year, the Senate had bestowed on Trajan the title of **Optimus** (see A:7 and the note). The sculptural reliefs facing Rome represent Trajan's domestic policy, and those on the side facing outward represent his provincial policy (for which, see the readings in the next chapter). On the vaulting of the arch are scenes from the Emperor's coronation. The arch, built at the northern terminus of the Trajanic extension of the Via Appia, was never seen by the Emperor himself, who had left for the East in 114 and died en route in 117. Here is the inscription found on both faces of the Arch of Trajan (see picture in the student's book, page 112):

> **Im(perātōrī) Caesarī dīvī Nervae fīliō, Nervae Trāiānō Optimō Aug(ustō) Germānicō Dācicō, Pontif(icī) Max(imō), Trib(ūniciā) Potest(āte) XVIII, Im(perātōrī) VII, Cō(n)s(ulī) VI, P(atrī) P(atriae), fortissimō prīncipī, Senātus P(opulus) q(ue) R(ōmānus)**

The Senate and People of Rome (dedicate this arch) to the Emperor and son of the deified Nerva, Caesar Nerva Traianus Optimus Augustus Germanicus Dacicus, Pontifex Maximus, holder of the power of tribune 18 times, victorious general 7 times, consul 6 times, Father of his Country, and bravest **prīnceps**.

3. *An Imperial Building Program:* The following is said of the Emperor Constantius II (A.D.

351–361) upon seeing Trajan's Forum for the first time:

> But when he (Constantius) came to the Forum of Trajan, a construction unique in any view under the whole canopy of heaven, admired even by the unanimous verdict of the gods, the vast complex around him which is far beyond any description, and not again to be rivaled by mortal man, all hope of attempting anything like it was put aside, and he simply said that Trajan's horse, which stands in the middle of the court and carries the emperor (i.e., an equestrian statue), was something that he could and would imitate. Then the Persian prince Hormisdas remarked with his native wit, "Sire, first you must order a stable if you can; the horse you propose must be as free to exercise as this which we see."
>
> —Ammianus Marcellinus XVI.13–18

Trajan's Forum (see the plan on page 110 of the student's book), which measured 384 feet (118 meters) by 289 feet (89 meters), included a temple dedicated by Hadrian to Trajan, a basilica known as the Basilica Ulpia, Greek and Latin libraries, and the triumphal column pictured on page 113. Trajan's column was erected in the courtyard of the Greek and Latin libraries in A.D. 113 in celebration of the Emperor's victories over the Dacians in A.D. 102 and 106. The spoils from this conquest enabled Trajan to pay each Roman 500 **dēnāriī**, and the five million pounds of gold and double that of silver helped to finance his building projects (for Augustus' building program, see 62D and background note 4f for Chapter 62). The inscription at the base of the column records the fact that the column was built to a height "which shows how much of the (Quirinal) Hill had to be removed" for the construction. Trajan's column has survived in its fine state of preservation owing to a decree of the Roman Senate in A.D. 1162, which provided the death penalty for anyone tampering with the monument. The hollow interior of the column has now been re-opened to the public. For coins illustrating Trajanic monuments, see plates 4 and 64 of *Rome: Its People, Life and Customs*. A reconstruction of the interior of the Basilica Ulpia appears on p. 17 of *Roman Towns*. For handsome photographs of the relief sculpture and column base inscription, see *Pictorial Dictionary of Ancient Rome*, Vol. I, pp. 283–286 and 452; for Trajan's Forum, see Vol. I, pp. 450–456; for Trajan's markets, see Vol. II, pp. 49–58. See also "Trajan's Markets," *The Architecture of the Roman Empire*, pp. 00, and "Trajan: Port, Forum, Market and Column," *The Mute Stones Speak*, pp. 251–272.

4. Teaching the Text

a. In connection with question 1 for Reading A, and as extended background for this chapter, reports on each emperor could be shared with the class and supplemented with a "Who's Who?" bulletin board display of surviving portrait busts of the emperors (see above, background notes 3c1 and the illustrated timecharts of imperial Rome available from the American Classical League Teaching Materials and Resource Center). The teacher may also design a game of "Imperial Charades" to draw students into the lives of the various emperors and into the role of Emperor. Activities promoting library research are also appropriate at this time.

b. Reading A (Pliny) consists of 8 lines and may be taught in one class period. In connection with this letter and with discussion of public life in imperial times, the teacher should introduce the passage from Pliny's *Panegyricus* provided in background note 3c1 above, to assist students in understanding the extent to which successful careers depended upon the patronage of the emperor. The inscription summarizing Pliny's political career found in the supplementary readings at the end of this handbook may also be used at this time. With regard to Reading A, the following questions should be addressed in discussion:
   1. What does Pliny's closing salutation imply about his purpose in writing the letter?
   2. How do you think those in public life hoped to advance themselves during the imperial period?

c. The appearance of the globe on Trajan's coin and the notion of Trajan as protector of the world (A:5–7 and the quotation from Pliny's *Panegyricus* above) reinforce statements by Eutropius that Trajan was interested in territorial expansion of the Empire, as Augustus had been (62C:4–6 and 63B:3–5). With regard to the fact that the Roman Empire reached its greatest extent under Trajan, see the activity entitled "Geography Ancient and Modern" in the supplementary materials at the end of this handbook (page 110). The following **sententia** from Vergil may also be presented to assist in student appreciation of the Roman Empire as a world-community:

> **Tū regere imperiō populōs, Rōmāne, mementō, (hae tibi erunt artēs) pācīque impōnere mōrem, parcere subiectīs et dēbellāre superbōs.**
>
> You, Roman, remember to rule the nations with power (these will be your special skills), and to add civilization to peace, to spare the defeated and to conquer the proud.
>
> —*Aeneid* VI.851–853

Discussion of the use of imperial propaganda begun in the previous chapter should be continued. Students should be asked how the emperors, through inscriptions, coins, statues, and buildings, communicated to their subjects the virtues of Roman imperial rule. In this regard, the subject of modern imperialism may be discussed.

d. As students complete the readings in Chapter 63, the lives and accomplishments of Augustus and Trajan should be compared. Here are some points of comparison, to which the teacher may add others:

1. Both were soldier-emperors and increased the territory of the Empire.
2. Both enjoyed long reigns.
3. Both were considered divine after their deaths.
4. Both used building programs to celebrate and define their reigns.
5. Both were known for their strength of personal character and for their fair treatment of others.
6. Both were honored with special **agnōmina** ("Augustus" and "Optimus").
7. Both were memorialized by funerary monuments in Rome.
8. Both treated Rome's subjects with clemency.
9. Both were fiscally responsible.
10. Both ruled with the good will of the Senate.
11. The success of future emperors was measured against both Trajan and Augustus.

In summation of Chapter 63, the teacher should point out that Eutropius' account bears out the fact that Pliny's hopes for Trajan's reign had been realized. Eutropius depicts Trajan as a fair and just ruler, who had concern for his subjects and enjoyed resulting popularity. (Trajan is praised by Dante in his *Divine Comedy*, and there is a legend that Pope Gregory the Great obtained the Emperor's release from Purgatory by his prayers.) Pliny, Eutropius, and Trajan himself all considered that the Emperor enjoyed the good will of the gods. These observations will be further explored in the next chapter.

e. New syntax introduced in this chapter: genitive of description: **inūsitātae cīvīlitātis et fortitūdinis** (B:2–3)

Opportunities for review: comparative and superlative adverbs and adjectives (A:2, 3, and 7; B:4, 14, and 22); present participle (B:7, 8, 9, 10, 11, 12 and 13); gerundive (B:7 and 11); subjunctive clauses (indirect command: A:2–3 and 5–7; result: B:1–2 and 20–22; and **cum** circumstantial: B:8–9).

5. Reading Notes

A.

a. **IMPERATORI** (1): Students should take note of the formal appellation of the Emperor (cf. 2 and 7), for which, see 59C:1 and notes. By Trajan's time, words such as **sānctissimus** had become almost conventional when referring to the emperor. When used of a private individual, **sānctus** refers to moral qualities.

b. **pietās** (2): This word, together with **sānctus, dī immortālēs** (3), and **precor** (5), implies that Trajan rules by divine sanction.

c. **ut . . . succēderēs patrī** (2–3): In the early Empire, few imperial sons succeeded their fathers. Four of the first five emperors were adopted out of necessity, and it was a weakness of the Roman principate that no permanent provision for succession was ever made. Emperors could be proclaimed by the army or the imperial bodyguard, appointed by the Senate, recognized by right of adoption, and even, as in the case of Claudius, raised to the purple by chance!

d. **festīnāvērunt** (3–4): Nerva's reign lasted little more than a year, from 18 September 96 to 23 January 98.

e. **gubernācula** (4): The plural refers to the large double steering oars, one on either side of the stern; the meaning here is transferred, i.e., "the course." Students met the word **gubernāre** in Chapter 57. For the "ship of state" image, see Horace, *Odes* I.14.

f. **Fortem tē et hilarem . . . optō** (7–8): This is equivalent to the modern catch-phrase, "I wish you health and happiness."

B.

a. **Marcus Ulpius Trāiānus** (1): This was Trajan's given name. Son of M. Ulpius Traianus and a Spanish mother, Trajan was born in Italica, in the province of Baetica (Spain) in A.D. 53. The Basilica Ulpia in Trajan's forum was named after the Emperor's **gēns**.

b. **inūsitātae cīvīlitātis et fortitūdinis** (2–3): genitives of description. With regard to **cīvīlitās**, cf. Eutropius' use of **cīvīlissimē** (56A:12) in regard to Augustus.

c. **Rōmānī imperiī . . . fīnēs . . . diffūdit** (3–5): Students should be cautioned not to assume that, because of its position, **Rōmānī imperiī** is the subject of the sentence.

d. **amīcōs salūtandī causā** (7–8): The Romans preferred to avoid the awkward and heavy sounds of the gentive plural with **causā** (i.e., **amīcōrum salutandōrum causā**).

e. **aedificāns multa** (12): Trajan built the most of any emperor. See *An Imperial Building Program* on page 113 of the student's book.

f. **immūnitātēs cīvitātibus tribuēns** (12–13): In the time of Trajan, **cīvitās** was a technical term referring to provincial communities that enjoyed the lowest status of patronage from Rome, i.e., possessing some local autonomy but remaining under the jurisdiction of the Roman provincial government and owing taxes or tribute to Rome. These local **cīvitātēs** might be given Roman municipal status (**mūnicipium**; cf. 57A:2), including Roman citizen rights and exemption from certain fiscal responsibilities, when sufficiently Romanized.

g. **sōlusque omnium intrā urbem sepultus est** (17–18): The mausoleum of Augustus was located in the Campus Martius and thus outside the **pomerium** (sacred boundary) of the city.

h. **ad nostram aetātem** (21): Trajan died in A.D. 117; Eutropius' history was published in 380.

6. *VERBS: Impersonal Verbs*: For the introduction and previous discussion of impersonal verbs, see the fourth teacher's handbook, Chapter 49, Student's Book, note 4. Students have seen **licet** since Chapter 19 and **taedet, oportet**, and **decet** in Chapter 49 (for a review exercise of these verbs, see Activity 49e in the fourth language activity book). For passive verbs used impersonally, see Chapter 61 of the fifth student's book, page 92.

a. The following sentences may be used for additional practice or evaluation of students' knowledge of impersonal verbs:
1. I am weary of life. (**Mē taedet vītae.**)
2. We will all be sorry we did this. (**Nōs paenitēbit hoc fēcisse.**)
3. Pliny takes pity on his slaves. (**Plīnium miseret suōrum servōrum.**)
4. It is proper for a senator to praise the emperor. (**Decet senātōrem laudāre prīncipem.**)
5. Trajan must leave Rome at once. (**Trāiānum/Trāiānō necesse est statim Rōmā exīre** *or* **Necesse est statim Trāiānus Rōmā exeat.**)

7. Exercise 63a: suggested translations:
1. The Senate was happy to send envoys to the Dacians.
2. Since Nerva had died (was dead), it was necessary for Trajan to become emperor.
3. It is proper for a senator to go to the Forum for the sake of greeting the emperor.
4. You ought to write a letter to congratulate the emperor.
5. I am ashamed of my foolishness.
6. Since he has written many letters, Pliny will be allowed to enjoy the holidays.
7. The emperor tires of always hearing the same things.
8. Trajan gave his ailing friends aid because he pitied them.

9. The Romans were allowed to bury Trajan's remains inside the city.
10. Pliny does not regret having praised Trajan.
11. The soldiers were ashamed of having run away in battle.
12. The gathering at the Forum is for the sake of listening to the emperor.
13. The best emperors do not do what they like, but what is appropriate.
14. I am not ashamed to admit that I do not know what I do not know.
15. Trajan is well spoken of (i.e., enjoys a good reputation).

With regard to the mention of the Dacians in this exercise, it might be of interest to remind students that a Romance language might not be spoken in modern Rumania today were it not for Trajan's conquests in this area.

8. Supplementary Activities

a. *Geography Ancient and Modern* (page 110): Since the text stresses the fact that the Roman Empire reached its greatest extent under Trajan, it is desirable for students to have a sense of how great that extent was. This activity will help develop such an understanding; it will also reinforce geography and skills in map reading, in which many students are weak. Answers:
1. territories added: Britain, Dacia (Rumania), Armenia, Assyria, and Mesopotamia (parts of Turkey, Syria, Iraq, and the U.S.S.R.); in addition, Arabia Petraea (Jordan and part of Arabia), Thrace, and Cappadocia, which had been client kingdoms under Augustus, had been taken over as provinces by Trajan's time.
2. modern countries: Albania, Algeria, Austria, Belgium, Britain, Bulgaria, Cyprus, Egypt, France, Germany, Greece, Hungary, Iraq, Israel, Italy (including Corsica, Sardinia, and Sicily), Jordan, Lebanon, Libya, Luxembourg, Malta, Morocco, the Netherlands, Portugal, Rumania, Spain, Switzerland, Syria, Tunisia, Turkey, the U.S.S.R., and Yugoslavia.
3. cities: Ancyra = Ankara, Turkey; Burdigala = Bordeaux, France; Carthago Nova = Cartagena, Spain; Colonia Agrippinensis = Cologne, Germany; Neapolis = Naples, Italy; Gades = Cadiz, Spain; Hierosolyma = Jerusalem, Israel; Mediolanum = Milan, Italy; Londinium = London, England; and Vindobona = Vienna, Austria.

The less obvious connections between the ancient and modern names, e.g., Vienna from Vindobona, may be determined by the process of elimination. The activity is designed to extend the map exercise above and to reinforce the fact that it was partly by means of urbanization that the Empire was Romanized. If a world map is available in the classroom, the teacher may wish to ask students to point out the location of the various cities and countries in this activity. Roman colonies (e.g., Colonia Agrippinensis, founded in A.D. 50 by the Emperor Claudius in honor of his wife Agrippina) were often created to settle legionary troops after their retirement, not only to reward soldiers for their loyalty but also to establish a formal Roman presence at strategic locations along the imperial frontiers. Trajan built the city of Thamugadi (modern Timgad) in Numidia (modern Algeria) in A.D. 100 to settle soldiers of the Third Legion. This excavated site contains the most complete Roman remains in Africa and illustrates how Rome served as a model of town planning and construction for cities of the Empire. For an excellent aerial photograph, see *The Ancient Romans*, pp. 136–137, and *Atlas of the Roman World,* p. 123.

b. *Two Inscriptions from Britain* (page 111) also illustrates the extent of the Empire and provides an excellent opportunity to discuss the process of Romanization, which is so clearly revealed in this inscription, as well as the nature of ancient religion. Translation of the first inscription:

> A temple to Neptune and Minerva, for the health of the imperial family, by the authority of Tiberius Claudius Cogidubnus, king, imperial legate in Britain, the guild of metalworkers and its members gave [the temple], with Clemens, son of Pudentinus, donating the site.

This inscription not only reveals the fact that Roman religion had penetrated to the furthest frontiers of the Empire but also illustrates the way in which Roman emperors extended their political patronage into the provinces to control native populations. This inscription is from a first century A.D. temple at Noviomagus (modern Chichester), **cīvitās** or capital of the Regnenses tribe; it reveals the extent of Romanization among barbaric tribes of southern Britain. During the conquest of Britain by the Emperor Claudius in A.D. 43, King Cogidubnus had gone over to the Romans, thus retaining his kingdom and ultimately acquiring the title **lēgātus Augustī** (cf. Pliny's title as imperial legate, page 95 of the student's book). He ruled as a client king

from about A.D. 45 to 80. A magnificent palace recently excavated at Fishbourne may have belonged to him. For this, see *Atlas of the Roman World*, p. 139, and, for the king, see "Cogidubnus," *The Oxford Classical Dictionary*, p. 258.

This inscription may be assigned for oral or written translation or for discussion, using the comprehension questions provided. The content may prompt student reports on the emperor Claudius and the conquest of Britain.

Suggested answers to the comprehension questions:

1. The temple was dedicated to Neptune and Minerva, revealing the fact that Roman gods had penetrated the northernmost frontiers of the Empire.
2. **Prō salūte domūs dīvīnae**, "for the health of the divine house (of the emperor)," is an indication of the devotion of the donors toward the emperor and his family.
3. Dedication was made by authority of Tiberius Claudius Cogidubnus, king and imperial legate in Britain. Cogidubnus' adoption of the **praenōmen** and **cognōmen** of the emperor and his recognition by the emperor with the title **lēgātus Augustī** reveal that he has placed his **cīvitās** under the power of Rome and the patronage of the emperor. Cogidubnus' titles combine the roles of native chief and Roman official.
4. The temple was funded by the **collēgium fabrōrum**, the guild of metalworkers of Noviomagus. The existence and financial stability of this guild imply that this area of Britain enjoyed the prosperity provided by Roman imperial rule.
5. The land for the temple precinct was donated by Clemens, son of Pudentinus.

Translation of the second inscription:

> Quintus Sittius Caecilianus, prefect of the first Aquitanian cohort, has paid his vow to the god Mars Braciaca.

Students may need help with the concept of "paying" a vow. **Brācae** have been encountered previously in the supplementary activity *Political Jokes about Caesar* (page 92), which also contains an illustration of an archer wearing them.

CHAPTER 64: RELIGION AND THE STATE

1. The aims of this chapter are:

    a. to provide a perspective on how the Romans governed their Empire, with specific reference to policies affecting religion
    b. to present the earliest literary evidence for the treatment of Christians by the Romans
    c. to complete the character study of the Emperor Trajan
    d. to summarize the nature of Roman imperial rule
    e. to present the relative clause of characteristic and the opportunity for review of all subjunctive clauses.

2. Translations

    A. Pliny to the Emperor Trajan

    In the meantime, with respect to those who were brought to me accused of being Christians, I observed the following procedure. I asked them personally whether or not they were Christians. When they confessed, I asked them a second and a third time, threatening punishment; if they persevered [in claiming to be Christian], I ordered them to be led [to execution]. For I did not doubt that, whatever it was that they were admitting, stubbornness and unyielding obstinacy ought certainly to be punished. There were others of a similar fanaticism whom, since they were Roman citizens, I ruled had to be sent back to Rome.

    Soon, because of the investigation itself, as so often happens, accusations spread and more cases came to light. An anonymous notice has been published containing the names of many [accused of being Christian]. Those who denied that they were or ever had been Christians, when, at my prompting, they invoked the gods and made offerings of wine and incense to your statue, which, together with the images of the gods, I had ordered to be brought [into court] for this reason, and furthermore cursed [the name of] Christ, none of which those who are truly Christians are said to be able to be compelled [to do], I thought must be set free.

    Others, named by an informer, said that they were Christians and soon denied [it]; [they said] that they had indeed been [Christians] but had ceased [to be so], some more than three years ago, some more years ago [than that], and others even more than twenty years ago. All these also worshiped your statue and the effigies of the gods and cursed [the name of] Christ. They also declared that the following was the sum total of their guilt or [if you prefer] their error: that they had been accustomed to meeting before dawn on a fixed day and to chanting verses back and forth among themselves in honor of Christ, as if to a god, and also to binding themselves by oath, not for any crime, but not to commit any fraud, rob-

bery, or adultery, not to breach any trust, and not to deny [possession of] any deposit when called upon to return it. After these things were done, [they said that] it had been their custom to disperse and then come back together again for the purpose of taking food—of an ordinary and harmless kind, however; [saying that] they had ceased to do the latter following my edict in which I had outlawed political societies according to your orders. Because of this, I believed it more necessary to seek the truth, even by torture, from two slave-women, who were called deaconesses. I found nothing but a depraved and excessive superstition.

    B. Trajan to Pliny

    You have followed the procedure that you ought [to have followed], my Secundus, in examining the cases of those who had been brought to you [on the charge of being] Christians. For, in general, nothing can be legislated which might provide, as it were, a fixed rule. These people must not be hunted down; if they are indicted and convicted they must be punished, with this stipulation [literally, in such a way, however], that whoever denies that he is a Christian and makes this explicitly clear, that is, by offering prayers to our gods, although under suspicion for his past, he is to receive pardon for his repentance. Notices published anonymously ought to have no place in any accusation. For [that] is [characteristic] of the worst example [i.e., sets a very bad precedent] and is not [characteristic] of our era.

3. Background

    a. The two letters of Pliny presented in this chapter are organized into three passages of a total of 45 lines, which bring Part IV to a close. These passages were selected because of their intrinsic interest as documents for the early history of Christianity and because they reflect the nature of Roman imperial government under Trajan. Students will have the opportunity to decide for themselves, after discovering how Trajan handles Pliny's inquiries about treatment of the Christians, whether or not the accounts of Trajan presented in the previous chapter are valid. It is hoped that, in general, the materials presented in Part IV will allow students to discover for themselves the value of comparative analysis of historical sources in forming accurate impressions about the nature of life in Roman times. Part IV will be concluded with a suggested exercise (presented below) that asks students to summarize what they have learned about the nature of the Roman Empire in the previous three chapters.

    b. During the several years of Pliny's tenure as imperial legate for the province of Bithynia-Pontus, he wrote over sixty letters to the Emperor, seeking advice on a wide range of administrative matters. Published as the tenth book of Pliny's *Epistulae*, these letters, and the Emperor's replies, serve as valuable documents of Roman provincial administration during the early Empire.

c. The lifeblood of Rome was its provinces, which, at the beginning of the second century A.D., consisted of more than fifty cultural and geographical areas, governed either by the Senate or by the emperor himself. The unprecedented size of the Empire under Trajan and the growing dependency of Rome upon the resources of her conquered or annexed territories led to an increasing centralization of provincial government in the hands of the emperor in Rome. This fact is illustrated by the passing of Bithynia-Pontus from senatorial to imperial jurisdiction during Trajan's reign and by Pliny's subsequent nomination as imperial legate to address problems in that province (see page 95 of the student's book). Pliny's discussion of the status of Christians in a Roman province whose language and culture were Greek reveals the complicated nature of Roman jurisdiction in a conquered or annexed territory. Did the provincial charter, the provincial governor, the emperor, Roman custom elsewhere, or the local community itself establish law? The fair and just resolution of these questions in many instances reveals the particular genius of the Romans in governing a world community. The following **sententia** may be of interest as the teacher attempts to communicate this point:

> **Difficilius est prōvinciās obtinēre quam facere; vīribus parantur, iūre retinentur.**
> It is harder to hold onto provinces than to acquire them; they are obtained by might but retained by justice.
> —Florus, *Epitome*, II.2.30

Trajan's reply to Pliny's letter about the Christians illustrates the Roman tendency toward accommodating local laws and customs as much as possible, within the framework of the provincial administrative structure, a fact consistent with the fair-mindedness attributed to Trajan by Eutropius (63B:6–7 and 12–13). The following resources are useful for further information about Roman provincial administration:

1. For excellent discussions, see "Trajan and the Provinces" and "Bithynia and its Moral," *Five Roman Emperors*, pp. 200–207 and 207–211. See also "A Short Account of Roman Provincial Administration in the Age of Augustus."

2. For a beautifully-illustrated pictorial survey of the provinces of the Empire, see "Life in the Provinces," *Rome and Her Empire*, pp. 210–265.

3. "Provinces of the Empire," *Atlas of the Roman World*, pp. 113–166, provides excellent topographical maps of the various provinces (including Bithynia-Pontus), as well as a map illustrating their historical acquisition, pp. 106–107.

4. "Everyday Life in a Roman Province" is a 12-minute sound film which dramatically recreates the life of a young woman in a north African city of the early Empire (available from the University of Illinois film bureau).

d. For previous appearances of Roman religion in ECCE ROMANI, see the rituals associated with coming of age (50:15–24), marriage (52:10–11), and death (53), along with the background essay "Augury," found on pages 88–90 of the fourth student's book. See also 62C and D in this book.

e. The subject of the history of early Christianity and its place in the Roman Empire has brought about a vast and growing body of scholarship. Pliny's letter is a prime source for knowledge about the spread of Christianity in Asia Minor and about the official Roman policy toward the Christians in the two centuries between Nero and Decius, in whose reign (A.D. 249–251) the organized imperial persecution of Christians was begun. After several decades of such persecution, the emperor Constantine was converted to Christianity and, in A.D. 313, proclaimed that Christianity was a legally permitted faith. It was not until A.D. 395 that it was made the official religion of the Roman Empire. During the period leading up to Trajan's reign, Christians were treated by Romans with an animosity based on political, rather than religious, considerations. Lewis and Reinhold, in *Roman Civilization Sourcebook II*, p. 582, write:

> Christians were constantly exposed to prosecution for such overt acts as obstinate disobedience of imperial officials, violation of the statutes on illegal associations, disloyalty and treason (evidenced in their refusal to participate in the state religion and the imperial cult), and other specific offenses involving suspicion and misunderstanding of the liturgy and ritual associated with the Eucharist. In addition, there was persistent popular agitation against Christians locally, so that provincial governors often employed their police powers for summary repression of the growing religion in the interest of maintaining civil order.
>
> The refusal of Christians to recognize other forms of worship troubled the Romans, whose polytheistic religion was tolerant of foreign gods. The Christian insistence on conversion, however, may have closed minds usually receptive to religious diversity.

Through misunderstanding of the rites associated with the Eucharist and with the idea of Christian brotherhood, the Romans attributed to Christians such practices as cannibalism, promiscuity, and incest, crimes (**flagitia**) associated with foreign cults that had been banned by the state as subversive of public morality. Political fear and suspicion of the Christians as a secret society led to "Christian-baiting" and their use as ready scapegoats. The historian Tacitus, writing roughly at the same time as Pliny, gives the impression that he felt Christians deserved the tortures inflicted upon them by Nero after Rome had burned in A.D. 64:

> Accordingly, an arrest was first made of all who pleaded guilty; then, upon their information, an immense multitude was convicted, not so much of the crime of firing the city, as of hatred against mankind. Mockery of every sort was added to their deaths. Covered with the skins of beasts, they were torn by dogs and perished, or were nailed to crosses, or were doomed to the flames and burnt, to serve as a nightly illumination, when daylight had expired.
>
> —*Annales* XV.44
> tr. Chester A. Starr

For further information on early Christianity, see the following:

1. "Christianity," *The Oxford Classical Dictionary,* pp. 231–234.
2. "The Conflict of Religions and the Triumph of Christianity," *Roman Civilization Sourcebook II*, pp. 552–610, a collection of source readings on the Roman state religion, the imperial cult, oriental cults, and Christianity up to Constantine.
3. "The Expansion of Christianity," *The Ancient Romans*, pp. 185–194, especially the interesting graffito on p. 190, and "The Development of Christianity," (source readings), pp. 235–238.
4. "The Rise of Christianity," *Roman Religion*, pp. 43–48. This pamphlet also contains much information on the evolution of Roman religion, family religion and public worship, and the Roman pantheon.
5. For specific background on Pliny's letter, see "Trajan and the Christians," *Five Roman Emperors*, pp. 53–58, and "The Letters from Bithynia," *The Letters of Pliny: A Historical and Social Commentary*, pp. 691–710 (X.96) and pp. 710–712 (X.97).

For films (available on videotape) on Roman, Christian, and Jew, see:

1. *Quo Vadis* (1951), a story of the winning over to Christianity of a young Roman officer during the time of Nero's persecutions. After the novel by Hendryk Sienkiewicz (1896). 171 minutes.
2. *The Robe* (1953), a story about the effects of Christ's robe, after his crucifixion, on the Roman officer charged with carrying out the sentence. After the novel by Lloyd C. Douglas (1942). 135 minutes.
3. *Ben Hur* (1959), a story (somewhat propagandistic toward Christianity) of Roman and Jew in Judaea at the time of Christ. After the novel by Lew Wallace (1880). 217 minutes.
4. *Masada* (1981), a story of the "Siege of the Rock" by Roman legions during the time of Vespasian, ending in the mass suicide of Jewish defenders. 131 minutes.

f. The translation of the Christian epitaph found on page 118 of the student's book is as follows:

> Here lies in (Christian) peace Agricius, who lived three years, three months, and three days. (His) mother Syrica and sister Euonyma put up this epitaph out of love.

Students may be asked to translate this simple epitaph or to ask or answer questions about it. Attention should be paid to the Christian context of the phrase **in pāce** and the symbols of the dove of peace and the "chi-rho" (X = the Greek letter *chi*, the first letter of Christ's name; P = the Greek letter *rho*, the second letter of Christ's name). The teacher might introduce in this regard the emblem of a fish used by Christians during the ages of persecution to identify one another. The secret lay in the meaning of the initial letters of the Greek word for fish, *ichthys*: i = *Iesous*, ch = *Christos*, th = *theou*, y (u) = *uios*, s = *soter*: Jesus Christ, son of God, savior. For additional Christian graffiti, see *Roman Religion*, pp. 44, 46, and 48, and for additional Christian epitaphs, see *Introduction to Latin Epigraphy*, pp. 183–185, numbers 98–100 (plate 64), including the epitaph of a "handmaiden of Christ" (cf. 64A:31–33).

g. The coin pictured on page 119 of the student's book shows a frontal view of the Temple of Trajan, surrounded by porticos, built for the Emperor and his wife Plotina by Trajan's successor Hadrian. See the plan on page 110 of the student's book. The legend on the coin reads: **SPQR Optimō Prīncipī**. For additional coins depicting Trajanic structures, see *Roman Coins* #356 (#377 provides a portrait of Plotina), *Pictorial Dictionary of Ancient Rome*, Vol. I, p. 450, and *Rome: Its People, Life and Customs*, plate 64.

4. Teaching the Text

a. The subject of Christianity during the early Principate has always been a fascinating one and should be of natural interest to students. The treatment of Christians during the Empire and the subject of religious toleration by the Romans, in general, may be introduced by establishing the historical context of Christianity during the first century A.D. through reading and discussion of the *Acts of the Apostles* in the New Testament of the Bible, especially Acts 22:22–25:12 where Paul, under indictment by the Jews as a Christian, appeals to Nero as a Roman citizen in A.D. 60. Students may also show interest in the Neronian persecutions following the great fire of A.D. 64, for which, see Tacitus, *Annales* XV.44, and the cultural background readings in the third teacher's handbook, pages 39–40. While teaching this chapter, teachers should remember that religion can be a very sensitive subject and should procede from an awareness of what is appropriate with their own students and in their local community.

b. At the beginning of his letter to Trajan, Pliny confesses: "I am not at all sure whether a pardon ought to be granted to anyone retracting his beliefs, or if he has once professed Christianity he shall gain nothing by renouncing it; and whether it is the mere name of Christian which is punishable, even if innocent of crime, or rather the crimes associated with the name." The teacher may wish to present this translation as a preface to the Latin text, as it goes to the very heart of the ambiguity felt by the Romans about the Christians. Pliny's reference to punishment for the name "Christian" refers to what later Christian apologists called **accūsātiō nōminis**, or membership in or association with a cult or sect banned by the Roman state. Cults such as that of Bacchus were banned because the Romans wished to discourage elements of these sects that they considered to be criminal.

c. The text of the excerpts provided in the letter from Pliny to Trajan may be divided into three parts, providing information about (1) admitted Christians (lines 2–8), (2) those who are falsely accused (11–16), and (3) former Christians who are no longer practicing the faith (17–31). As students read the Latin, they should be asked to identify these topics and to observe the ways in which each topic is similarly presented, e.g., **Cōnfitentēs . . .** (3), **Quī negābant . . .** (11), and **esse sē Chrīstiānōs dīxērunt et mox negāvērunt** (17–18). This organization may lead to assignment of each topic to a small group for exploration. Each group may be asked to design comprehension questions to be shared with the rest of the class or to respond to those questions provided in the student's book. After students work through the text, the teacher may wish to ask them to read the entire letter in translation to summarize the content for discussion. The complete translation of this letter (X.96) is provided in Volume II of the Loeb edition of Pliny and in *Roman Civilization Sourcebook II*, pp. 582–583.

d. After the meaning of the text has been established, ensuing discussion may center on any or all of the following themes:

1. The teacher may wish to relate, in a general way, what students already know about Christian liturgy and ritual to the uninformed account of Pliny, who uses the testimony of witnesses who no longer practice their faith. References to the Mass, the Sacraments (especially Baptism and the Eucharist), the Ten Commandments, and the *Agape*, or fellowship meal, have been seen in lines 22–29.

2. In addition to information about the ritual and liturgy of early Christianity, something of the attitudes and character of Pliny emerges from this letter. Pliny certainly over-reacts in his response to a situation about which he admits he has very little information. His discretionary execution of Christians for their refusal to deny their faith is tyrannical and certainly at odds with **hūmānitās**.

3. Discussion of the subject of religious tolerance by the Romans may include comments on the recent popularity of religious cults, particularly those from the Far East, and their reception by and impact on modern society.

e. At some point, perhaps with regard to the reference to the Roman gods in lines 12–14, the teacher may wish to summarize the nature of Roman religion for students. For source readings, illustrations, and project ideas on the subject, see *Roman Religion*.

f. Grammar and syntax for review: present participle (A:3, 4, 9, and 11), past participle (A:4 and 27, B:8 and 10), ablative absolute (A:9, 12, 23 and 27), gerund (A:28), gerundive (A:8, 16, and 28–29, B:5 and 6), indirect statement (A:8, 11–12, 15, 16, 17–18, 21–31 and B:7), subjunctive clauses (circumstantial A:12–15, indirect command A:25–27, indirect question A:5 and 33, and result, B:6–9).

The following constructions and usages should also be noted:

double indirect question: **an essent** (A:2–3)

verb of doubt + infinitive: **dubitābam . . . dēbēre** (A:5–6)

iubeō + infinitive: A:4 and 13–14

quod clause + subjunctive: **quod essent** (A:23)

future less vivid condition: **sī dēferantur** (B:5–6)

predicate gentive of characteristic: **pessimī exemplī** and **nostrī saeculī** (B:11)

5. Reading Notes

A. Pliny to Trajan

   a. dēferēbantur (1–2): Dēlātiō was a legally recognized process of private accusation by a third party who genuinely believed that a law had been broken. The formal charge (the Roman state had no police force or state attorney) would then lead to trial before the provincial governor. The dēlātōrēs were sometimes Jews, who objected to the perversion of Jewish religious beliefs by the Christians and who resented the Roman attitude of "guilt by association."

   b. supplicium minātus (4): This means that Pliny gave confessed Christians an opportunity to recant by warning them that punishment was inevitable should they refuse. Confession was proof of guilt.

   c. dūcī (4): Capital crimes such as murder, treason, magic, or "impious rites" could lead to execution by beasts, fire, crucifixion, or decapitation by the sword. Pliny's authority as provincial governor gave him the right of life and death over provincial subjects, but he could have pronounced a lesser sentence or ignored the charges altogether.

   d. pertināciam . . . pūnīrī (5–6): Pliny chose to punish Christians for failing to yield to his authority, rather than for any specific crimes they might have committed. It was Pliny's opinion that the Christians were openly defying a magistrate's order to abandon an undesirable cult. His imperial mission to restore peace and security in the restive province of Bithynia-Pontus may have made him overly zealous in the pursuit of his duty.

   e. quōs, quia cīvēs Rōmānī erant (7): The most famous example of this is the case of St. Paul, indicted on Jewish charges that he was an agitator and profaner of the Temple (auctor sēditiōnis sectae Nazarēnōrum, *Acts* 24:5).

   f. adnotāvī in urbem remittendōs (esse) (8): Adnotāre was a technical term referring to a magistrate's notation of an official decision in his records. This is an example of Pliny's use of ellipsis, for which, see also dīmittendōs (esse) (16).

   g. ipsō trāctātū . . . plūrēs speciēs incidērunt (9–10): It was only natural that, as more Christians received judicial attention, more accusations would be made on less valid grounds, such as personal grudges.

   h. libellus (10): This word, a diminutive of liber, is a technical term, referring to an anonymous (sine auctōre, 10–11) written accusation.

   i. Quī negābant . . . dīmittendōs (esse) (11–16): The test which Pliny describes here was only applied to those who had been accused of being Christians and denied the charge, as opposed to the confessed Christians referred to in the first paragraph. The test required invocation of the Roman gods and the emperor and the execration of the name of Christ.

   j. deōs (12) and simulācrīs nūminum (13–14): The Capitoline triad: Jupiter, Juno, and Minerva.

   k. imāginī tuae . . . tūre ac vīnō supplicārent (13–14): Pliny speaks elsewhere of the statue of Trajan placed in the Temple of Jupiter Optimus Maximus (*Panegyricus* 52). Worship of the emperor was not compulsory and usually involved the upper classes in the provinces. Failure to worship the emperor was not yet a treasonable offense. Pliny does not charge Christians with impiety on this ground but characterizes them with the terms obstinātiō (6), āmentia (7), and superstitiō prāva (34). For emperor worship, see page 94 of the student's book.

   l. Aliī ab indice nōminātī (17): This probably refers to the anonymous charges, often filed by pagan slaves of Christians, mentioned in the previous paragraph (10–11). The previous sentence referred to those who had been falsely accused as Christians; the present sentence refers to those who at one time had belonged to the sect but no longer did. It is implied by affirmābant that Pliny was holding these former Christians pending decision by Trajan.

   m. statō diē (23): This was the diēs sōlis or diēs dominica. The week as a unit of time was unknown to the Romans (see Word Study XV, page 113 in the Appendix to this handbook). For a complete discussion of the contribution of this letter to an understanding of early Christian liturgy, see "The Christian Liturgy," *The Letters of Pliny: A Historical and Social Commentary*, pp. 702–708.

   n. quod essent solitī (23): causal clause with the subjunctive, because Pliny is citing the testimony of witnesses, rather than speaking from his own knowledge.

   o. sacrāmentō (25): Scholars have seized upon this word as an early reference to the Christian sacraments, or perhaps the Ten Commandments, an observation perhaps reinforced by the "Thou shalt not" elements of the oath forbidding theft, robbery, adultery, breaking a promise, or withholding a loan (25–27). To a Roman, the word sacrāmentum meant "military oath" sworn upon induction (cf. coniūrātiō). Such a word used in the context of a foreign cult certainly would carry with it connotations of secret, and perhaps military, activity, which would place Christian activity under the ban against hetaeriae (but see below, 29–31). Pliny is apparently using the word the Christians themselves used or his word for it, if they spoke Greek. Others believe that the word sacrāmentum refers to the Eucharist or to the baptismal vow, which was a promise to "renounce all that was worldly."

p. **discēdendī . . . coeundī ad capiendum cibum** (28–29): This is an excellent opportunity for students to compare the gerund with the gerundive and to contrast both with the previous appearances of the gerundive of obligation (8 and 16).

q. **ad capiendum cibum, prōmiscuum tamen et innoxium** (28–29): **Ad capiendum cibum** refers to the *agapē* (ah-gah-pay), a Greek word meaning "love feast," held later in the day in association with the Eucharist, or it may refer to the Eucharist itself. Before Pliny's edict banning **hetaeriae**, when these clubs were officially legal, such fellowship meals were common. The words **prōmiscuus** and **innoxius** address the terrible suspicions of non-Christians about the Eucharist. It was claimed that Christians were ritual murderers, cannibals, and drinkers of blood (by consuming the "body" and "blood" of Christ). Early references to the Eucharist included the charge of its being a "Thyestean banquet." Thyestes was the brother of the Greek king Atreus, who had served up to Thyestes Thyestes' own children cooked in a stew, after Thyestes had seduced his wife.

r. **quod ipsum facere . . . hetaeriās esse vetueram** (29–31): In accordance with his imperial mandate (**mandāta tua**, 31) to guarantee the security of the troublesome province of Bithynia-Pontus, Pliny had issued an edict suppressing **hetaeriae** in the province. Elsewhere, Trajan refuses Pliny's request for a fire department in Nicomedia because of the imperial fear of such associations as sources of political unrest. Pliny seems to believe that no charges could be brought against Christians for violation of his ban on **hetaeriae**, since the love feasts had ceased after his edict.

s. **Quō magis necessārium . . . per tormenta quaerere** (31–33): However barbarous, it was perfectly legal for slaves to be tortured to extract the truth, and, indeed, evidence was not admissible unless gained under torture. Pliny tortures the **ministrae** to confirm his impression from the accounts of witnesses that Christianity was nothing more than a **superstitiō prāva et immodica** (33–34).

B. Trajan to Pliny

a. **dēlātī fuerant** (3): The double pluperfect, instead of **dēlātī erant**, reflects Trajan's recognition of the fact that the Christians had already been dealt with at the time Pliny wrote his letter.

b. **Neque enim in ūniversum aliquid . . . cōnstituī potest** (4–5): Trajan fails to give Pliny specific guidelines for punishing Christians, but forestalls mass persecution by forbidding inquisition (5).

c. **id est supplicandō dīs nostrīs** (8): Trajan clarifies what he means by **rē ipsā manifestum**

(7), using the phrase **id est**, which has become the conventional *i.e.* in English. Trajan does not insist on **maledīcere Chrīstō** (cf. A:15 and 21).

d. **veniam ex paenitentiā impetret** (9): This phrase answers Pliny's uncertainty regarding whether or not a Christian retracting his beliefs could be pardoned (see 4b under Teaching the Text).

6. *VERBS: Relative Clauses of Characteristic:* The use of the relative pronoun in clauses with verbs in the indicative mood was introduced in Chapter 27 and should be reviewed before its use with subjunctive clauses is presented. Students have seen the relative clause of characteristic several times in previous readings: see 56B:16, 61C:4–5, 7, and 9–10, among others.

7. Exercises 64a and b: suggested translations:
64a
1. There are those who think that Bithynia is the most troublesome of all provinces.
2. Trajan was the type of person who would pardon wrong-doing.
3. What is there that does not annoy Pliny in this province?
4. Surely you are not the type of person who would condemn Christians?
5. There is no emperor who has recognized every senator.
6. Who is there to whom the possession of liberty is not dear?
7. There are those who say that Christians do not worship many gods.
8. Let those who obey the emperor live in peace and happiness.
9. Trajan was the type of person who wished to be a good emperor.

64b
1. (a) I saw nothing of which I was [truly] afraid.
   (b) I saw nothing of the type that would frighten me.
2. (a) There is no one who saw what had happened.
   (b) There is no one who has (really) seen what had happened.
3. (a) Pliny is the type of man whom Trajan would often praise.
   (b) Pliny is a man whom (in fact) Trajan often praises.

8. Exercise 64c: This is a review of the uses of the subjunctive. Suggested translations:

1. Pliny was asking Trajan what plans had to be made concerning the Christians. (indirect question)
2. Is there any emperor who considers himself to be the worst of all? (relative clause of characteristic)

3. Because he had more soldiers, Pompey hoped that the battle would be brief. (**cum** causal)

4. Roman citizens who were Christians were permitted to be sent back to Rome. (subjunctive with impersonal verb)

5. Trajan manages the state in such a way that he seems to be very close to a god. (result)

6. The Senate ordered Octavian to see to it that no harm should come to the Republic. (indirect command)

7. Was Pliny afraid that all Christians would not be loyal to the Emperor? (indirect question)

8. Was Octavian making ready an army to free the state from Antony's tyranny? (purpose)

9. When Pompey had observed our men inside the rampart, he obtained a horse and hurled himself out of the camp. (**cum** circumstantial)

10. Pliny, as Trajan had ordered, sailed at once for Bithynia. (**ut** + indicative)

9. *Part IV: Emperor and Empire* may be summarized with the following exercise:

Imagine that Rome is on trial in an international court of law and is being asked to defend her place in world history. Read the following quotations and then, from the point of view of either the prosecuting or defense attorney, write a brief essay discussing which of these best represents an accurate assessment of Roman imperial rule. Be sure to support your observations by referring to the materials in Chapters 62, 63, and 64.

1. O Rome, the world is yours and you its queen. Far distant tribes became one fatherland beneath your power, which brought to conquered men the rule of law; and through this common right, you made a city out of all the world.
   —Rutilius Namatianus, *On His Return*, I.62–66
   (translated by R. Nichols and K. McLeish)

2. Plunderers of the world, now that there are no more lands for their all-devastating hands, they search even the sea. If the enemy is rich, they are rapacious, if poor they lust for dominion. Not East, not West has satisfied them; alone of all mankind they covet riches and power with equal passion. They rob, butcher, plunder, and call it *empire*; and where they make a desolation, they call it *peace*.
   —Tacitus, *Life of Agricola*, 30
   (translated by N. Lewis and M. Reinhold)

This activity, which can be done either orally or in writing, asks students to summarize what they have learned about the nature of the Roman Empire in the previous three chapters and is designed to provoke thought and discussion of the impressions left by the coins, inscriptions, monuments, and literary evi-

dence. Themes which can be used in support of Namatianus include the rule of law, urbanization, a common language, economic prosperity, religious tolerance (toward most religions, although not toward Christianity), and security provided by a strong central government. Arguments in support of Tacitus include loss of cultural identity, "rape of the provinces" through taxation and loss of political autonomy, and use of military might to "impose peace." For interesting discussions on Rome's place in history, see *The Idea of Rome from Antiquity to the Renaissance*, a collection of source readings including the complete texts of the quotations from Namatianus (pp. 126–130) and Tacitus (pp. 85–87).

10. Supplementary Materials

a. *Epitaph of a Young Christian Boy* (page 112):
   1. Suggested translation: An innocent boy named Siddus lived here for four months [and] 24 days, [and was] taken in peace three days before the Ides of April during the consulship of Anicius Auchenius Bassus.
   2. Background: This epitaph is included to give an additional illustration of the spread of Christianity. It may be compared to the one printed on page 118 of the student's book; notice the same symbols, and the similar language. This epitaph also clearly shows the linguistic changes that led to the modern Romance languages; the evolution of Latin into Romance will be picked up by the last two Word Studies (XVI and XVII) in Part V. The teacher may wish to discuss with the class how and why language changes (e.g., the change from the English of Shakespeare and the King James Bible to that of the twentieth century).
   3. Answers to questions
      1. He was four months, 24 days old.
      2. He died 11 April A.D. 408.
      3. It probably means that Siddus was taken to heaven.
      4. Alpha and omega represent the beginning and the end, symbolizing the all-encompassing power of God. The crossed *chi* and *rho* symbolize Christ, while the birds may be doves, symbols of the Holy Spirit.
      5. **Bīxit** for **vīxit** and **bīgintī** for **vīgintī**; **mēsēs** for **mēnsēs**.
      6. The spellings **innocus** and **quator**; this implies that they were relatively poor.

b. *Word Study XV* (page 113):
   1. The origins and development of the planetary week are somewhat obscure. Although the system seems to have been in general use in the Empire by A.D. 200, a writer of that period implies that schoolchildren still had to

memorize the names and order of the week-days as part of their elementary education. Nevertheless, as the Pompeian inscription (*CIL* IV.8863) given here shows, some Romans were using the seven-day week as early as A.D. 79. Translation of inscription:

> To the deified spirits of Saturnina, born on Saturn's day, died on Saturn's day; she lived three years, five months, twenty days.

2. The month, on the other hand, was a familiar and highly organized concept among the Romans from early times (see *Home and School*, pp. 59–60). The illustration on the student's sheet shows one side of a four-sided calendar stone (**kalendārium**) that gives basic information about each month; the number of days it contains, the date of its Nones, the approximate number of hours of daylight and darkness per day, the zodiacal sign in which the sun is located, the month's patron divinity, agricultural activities appropriate to it, and festivals. Students might enjoy deciphering part of this inscription, e.g., in January, **Sōl Capricornō** ("Sun in Capricorn"), **Tūtēlā Iūnōnis** ("under the protection of Juno"), and in February, **segetēs sāriuntur, vīneārum superfic(iēs) colit(ur), harundinēs incendunt(ur)** (*crops are hoed, the surface of vineyards is cultivated, weeds are burned*).

3. Answers to questions:
    1. Friday
    2. Venus, Freya
    3. From the name of the god Woden
    4. Sunday, the Lord's Day
    5. Saturday, the Sabbath Day
    6. Pompeii, Saturday; Rome, Friday; Nola, Tuesday
    7. Saturday
    8. luna
    9. none
    10. Tiw is equivalent to Mars, and Freya to Venus.

PART V
Three Individuals of the Early Empire

CHAPTER 65: THE MILLIONAIRE

1. The aims of this chapter are:
   a. to return students to some of the themes of everyday life they studied in Books 1–4 of ECCE ROMANI
   b. to introduce one of the great comic masterpieces of ancient literature
   c. to teach the jussive and hortatory subjunctives formally
   d. to review all types of commands.

2. Translations

A. Trimalchio said, "My friends, slaves, too, are human and have drunk one milk equally [with us], even if a bad fate has overwhelmed them. But as long as I'm alive, quickly they will taste the water of freedom. In short, I free them all in my will. And I make it all public for this reason, so that my household will love me right now just as [when I'm] dead."

They all began to give thanks for their master's indulgence, when he, getting down to business, ordered a copy of his will to be brought and read the whole thing aloud from beginning to end while the staff groaned. Then looking back at Habinnas, he said, "What do you say, my very dear friend? Are you building my tomb, as I have ordered you? I ask you very much to portray a puppy near the feet of my statue and garlands and perfumes and all the fights of Petraites, so that it may befall me through your kindness to live on after death; moreover, [I ask] that there be a hundred feet in frontage and two hundred feet in depth. I want there to be every kind of fruit tree around my ashes, and plenty of grape vines. For it is completely wrong for a man to have an elegant house while he's alive, [and] not to care about the one where we must live for a longer time. And for this reason, above all I want [these words] to be added: 'This monument is not to pass to my heir.'

B. "I ask you to make [some] ships on my tomb, too, going along under full sail, and me sitting up on the tribunal in a bordered toga with five gold rings and pouring coins from a sack for the public; because you know that I gave a feast, two denarii per person. Let a dining room be made also, if it seems good to you. Also make the whole population enjoying themselves. At my right hand put a statue of my Fortunata holding a dove, and let her be leading a puppy tied with a leash, and my little pet [slave], and wine jars sealed with gypsum so they don't spill the wine out. And

you may carve a broken urn, and above it a boy weeping. [Let there be] a sundial in the middle, so that whoever looks at the time may read my name whether he wishes to or not.

"Also, consider carefully whether this inscription seems suitable enough to you: 'Here rests Gaius Pompeius Trimalchio Maecenatianus. A sevirate was decreed for him in his absence. Although he could have been on every board in Rome, he didn't wish to. Loyal, brave, faithful, he grew from small [beginnings], left thirty million sesterces, and never listened to a philosopher. Farewell. 'And [the same] to you.'" After he had said all this, Trimalchio began to weep copiously. Fortunata wept too, Habinnas wept, and finally the whole household, as if [they'd been] invited to a funeral, filled the dining room with lamentation.

C. "But, as I began to say, my frugality brought me to this [good] fortune. I came from Asia as tall as this lampstand is. In short, every day I used to measure myself at it, and in order to have a beard on my chin more quickly, I smeared my lips [with oil] from the lamp. Moreover, as the gods want, I became master in the house, and look, I caught my master's fancy [literally, I captured his brain]. To make a long story short, he made me co-heir with the emperor, and I received a fortune fit for a senator. But no one is ever satisfied [literally, nothing is enough for no one]. I got an urge to go into business. Not to bore you with a long story [many words], I built five ships, I loaded wine—and it was worth its weight in gold then—and I sent [them] to Rome. You would think I had ordered this; all the ships were wrecked, fact, not fiction. In one day Neptune devoured 30,000,000 sesterces. Do you think that I gave up? No, by Hercules; this loss was hardly noticeable, as if nothing had happened. I built other [ships], bigger and better and luckier, so that no one could say that I'm not a brave man. You know, a big ship has lots of strength. I loaded wine again, lard, beans, perfume, slaves. At this point Fortunata did a dutiful thing; for she sold all her gold [jewelry], all her clothes, and she put a hundred gold pieces in my hand. This was the leavening of my nest egg. What the gods want happens quickly. In one voyage I made approximately 10,000,000 sesterces. Immediately I bought back all the farms that had been my patron's. I build a house, buy slaves [and] draft animals; whatever I touched grew like a honeycomb.

D. "After I began to own more than my entire homeland has, [I took my] hand off the tablet; I took myself out of business and began to finance freedmen. And indeed an astrologer encouraged me when I didn't want to do any business, who had come by chance to our town, a little Greek named Serapa, an adviser to the gods. This man told me even things that I'd forgotten; he showed me everything from thread and needle; he knew my guts; the only thing he hadn't told me was what I'd had for dinner the day before. You would have thought he'd always lived with me.

"Meanwhile, while Mercury watched [over me], I built this house. As you know, it was a little hut; now it's a temple. It has four dining rooms, twenty bedrooms, two marble porticos, a dining room above, the room in which I myself sleep, a sitting room for this viper, a very good room for the doorkeeper; the lodgings captivate [capture] the guests. In short, when Scaurus came here, he preferred to be lodged nowhere [else], and he has a family place by the shore. And there are many other things, which I'll show you right away. Trust me; if you have a penny, a penny is what you're worth; you are judged by what you have. So your friend, who was a frog, is now a prince."

3. Background

The *Satyricon (Book of Satyric Matters)* seems to have been, in its original form, an unusually long work by ancient standards, perhaps as much as 400,000 words (about two-thirds of the length of *War and Peace*). An amalgam of novel, satire, and comic epic larded with occasional lyric poems, the book has defied scholarly attempts to assign it definitely to any of these genres. It certainly has much in common with the picaresque novel in its loose, episodic structure and the amoral character of its two young protagonists, Encolpius and Giton. The adventures of this disreputable pair in various parts of Italy and southern France involve murder, theft, sexual escapades, shipwreck, and cannibalism. Given the fragmentary state of the *Satyricon* as it exists today, it is impossible to be certain how much unity the plot originally had, but the thread that tied it loosely together may have been the theme of the Wrath of Priapus, in parody of the Wrath of Poseidon in the *Odyssey*.

In the course of their wanderings, the protagonists encounter a down-at-the-heel professor of rhetoric named Agamemnon, who cadges a dinner invitation for all three of them at the house of an acquaintance of his, the parvenu millionaire Trimalchio. Petronius' account of this dinner, which has been preserved virtually complete and is referred to as the *Cena Trimalchionis*, is deservedly the best known of the surviving fragments, not only because of its greater length and coherence but also because of the sheer brilliance of its comic portrait.

For more extensive excerpts from the *Cena*, the teacher is referred to the cultural background readings in the third teacher's handbook. Or, the teacher might read the entire *Cena* in translation (about 45 pages in William Arrowsmith's version) and perhaps have students read at least part of it also. Sections 28–30 would be particularly good for students to read, since they contain references to many things that appear in the Latin texts of this chapter: Trimalchio's pet slave; Mercury as Trimalchio's patron god; wall-paintings that combine scenes from Homer with the gladiatorial fights that Trimalchio wants on his tomb; and references to Trimalchio's sevirate. For a more detailed introduction to Petronius' work, see *The 'Satyricon' of Petronius: A Literary Study*.

Immediately prior to the passage printed as Reading A, Trimalchio invited his slaves to share the dining couches with his guests, and he took the opportunity to show off his "philosophical" sophistication, which consists of ill-digested and ill-assorted Stoic ideas. Trimalchio's gesture has been seen by some as a satire on a passage in Seneca (*Epistulae morales*, 47, a version of which appears in *The Romans Speak for Themselves* Book I, Chapter 6, pp. 40–46), but it is probably better to regard it in more general terms as an uncultured person's vulgarized version of ideas concerning the brotherhood of man that were in the air when both Seneca and Petronius were writing.

The other aspect of this passage that should be emphasized is the way in which Trimalchio paints his own portrait with his own words. His longing to be regarded as a knowledgeable and cultivated person is as apparent in this speech as in several others where he shows off his (non-existent) familiarity with literature, history, and mythology; equally obvious is his total lack of understanding of any of these subjects. Trimalchio is also concerned with respectability, with making sure that his life is in every detail exactly like that of the wealthy, leisured, and cultured class with which he identifies. The humor arises from his inability to discriminate and select; any dish that has ever appeared on any aristocratic table must appear on Trimalchio's, preferably in an even more elaborate form; every funeral convention that has ever appeared on any aristocratic tombstone must likewise appear on Trimalchio's—considerations of taste, compatibility, or even space be damned. Hence the jumble of funerary motifs on his monument.

Another aspect of Trimalchio's character that is apparent from these passages is the pride he takes in his career, in his spectacular rise from "frog" to "prince" (D:43). Also important, and perhaps less obvious, are his concern and affection for his family and friends. It is easy to lose sight of these in the midst of his noisy self-advertising, but the fact remains that Trimalchio has given his friends a lavish dinner, his former constituents free food and money, his slaves generous bequests in his will, and most of his huge estate to his wife.

4. Teaching the Text

a. The readings in Part V have been chosen as a contrast to those in Parts I–IV, which focus on historical and political developments. The readings in this Part bring the student back to the lives of individuals, where the ECCE ROMANI program began, and at the same time offer students a chance to examine some aspects of life under the Principate. Students certainly should be encouraged to laugh at Trimalchio; his comic behavior provides a welcome change of pace at this point in the course.

b. Introductory discussion of the issues raised in this reading could focus on self-made men in our own society. Some students may have a parent who has moved a long way up the socio-economic scale, but the class would probably feel more comfortable discussing someone's grandparent, someone in the news, or a character from fiction or the movies. In the latter context, it could be pointed out that F. Scott Fitzgerald consciously intended his novel *The Great Gatsby* as a contemporary version of the *Cena Trimalchionis* (see "The Great Gatsby and Trimalchio"). Some students may have seen the movie version of this novel (1974), with Robert Redford as the Trimalchio figure, Jay Gatsby.

c. The marble relief illustrated on page 123 could also be analyzed and discussed as an introduction to reading Trimalchio's description of his own tomb. Though different in detail from the monument described by Trimalchio, Haterius' notion of the ideal tomb is quite close to Trimalchio's in spirit; they share an exuberant determination to include every funerary convention they have ever heard of; an unabashed pride in the "vulgar" sources of their wealth (symbolized by Haterius' crane and Trimalchio's ships); and a predilection for sentimental references to family life (Haterius' children and nurse; Trimalchio's wife with dove and puppy). In class discussion, students might be encouraged to work out these parallels for themselves. The Haterius relief is thus described by B. Andreae in *The Art of Rome*:

> A building crane is shown being operated by slaves on a treadwheel alongside a tomb in the form of a temple. Since the crane is decorated with palm fronds and laurel—utilized in the cult of the dead to signify the triumphant completion of existence on earth and as evergreen symbol of the transmutation of the mortal defunct into the divine hero—this suggests that it was not meant to be depicted in action but only to indicate the profession of the owner of the tomb. . . .
>
> The funerary temple in the shape of a *heroon*, a memorial chapel for a mortal or deified person, sits on a high podium of the sort used as a burial chamber and scarcely a millimeter of it is not covered with some sort of sculpture. But the most remarkable peculiarity is that, in the upper right, above the roof of the temple, one has a visionary view of the interior of the tomb itself, where the heroized dead reposes on a *klinē* [couch]. At the left the fragrance of a burnt offering rises from an incense burner, at the right the tiny figure of the dead man's nurse brings a sacrifice to the altar. The three children of the deceased . . . play on the ground in front of the *klinē*. To the right of the reclining dead man there is a statue of Venus in her shrine, which also serves as a kind of house altar for the ancestors' masks set out on top of it. The juxtaposition of realistic and virtually dreamlike elements, something characteristic of Flavian wall paintings as well, occurs here within the same densely filled pictorial field. . . . Large and small figures are placed directly next to one another, their size is commensurate only with their importance to the subject, and the spatial cohesion of the scene is sacrificed to the interests of the narrative. . . . The relief has more to do with folk art than with the aristocratic character of the official reliefs on public monuments.

What Andreae calls the relief's "fantastic toying with reality" may be familiar to students from modern painting and sculpture; they could also be reminded that similarly non-realistic treatments of spatial relationships, proportion, and probability (e.g., the crane spouting palm fronds) are widely used in the videos they watch on MTV. For a modern drawing of a Roman crane in use, based on the Haterius relief, see *The Roman Engineers*, p. 36. Students may also enjoy drawing what they think Trimalchio's tomb would look like.

d. Since part of the humor of this passage lies in Trimalchio's exaggerations and distortions of actual Roman customs and conventions concerning death and burial, another valuable introductory activity would be to review, or preview, other materials on these topics that appear in the ECCE ROMANI program. They include:

1. Book 2: Chapter 21, page 47, three women's epitaphs; Chapter 26, page 91, a charioteer's epitaph.

2. Book 4: Chapter 46, page 57, epitaph of a **rētiārius**; Chapter 53, pages 108–109, various epitaphs; also the material in English on funerals, pages 103, 107, and 109–110.

3. Book 5: Chapter 56A, pages 41 and 46, Augustus' tomb, and Chapter 62, its inscription, the *Res gestae*, pages 97 ff.; Chapter 57C, page 53, the "funeral pyre" of Clodius; teacher's handbook, page 106, tombstone of a centurion; student's book, Chapter 63B, page 109, the unusual honor extended to Trajan, who was allowed to be buried within the city limits; student's book, page 118, a Christian tombstone; teacher's handbook, page 109, two honorary inscriptions; teacher's handbook, page 112, tomb of young Christian boy;

student's book, page 129, tomb inscription; teacher's handbook, page 115, epitaph from children's tomb; and teacher's handbook, page 115, epitaph of Faustus. Teachers who want additional epitaphs should consult *Roman Voices* and *Themes in Greek and Roman Epitaphs*. Wills are another aspect of this topic that could be treated; students might enjoy reading the *Testamentum Porcelli*, a very funny "will" dating from the later Roman Empire, written by a little pig who was about to be slaughtered. It is printed in *Claimed by Vesuvius*, pp. 143–146; like Trimalchio, the little pig includes in his will the inscription he wants on his tomb. Perhaps students would also like to try their hand at writing their own wills in Latin. On the importance of wills and epitaphs in Roman society in general, see "Wills," pp. 29–31, and "The Publicity of the Tomb," pp. 169–171, *A History of Private Life, Vol. I*. Some Roman wills and epitaphs in translation can be found in *Roman Civilization Sourcebook II*, pp. 277–286.

e. Students may need help with the colloquial and sometimes elliptical style that Trimalchio uses, particularly in passages A and B. It is also helpful for students to realize that the Romans did not always express themselves in the rather formal style of a Pliny, Cicero, or Caesar!

f. New grammar and syntax found in this chapter:

> independent subjunctive: **sequātur** (A:20), **faciātur** and **faciās** (A:25), **pōnās** (A:A:26), and **dūcat** (A:28)
>
> dative of possession: **vīvō ... domūs cultās esse** (A:17–18)

g. The following items are available for review: passages A and B are very rich in subordinate subjunctives: purpose (5–6, 29, and 31–32), result (14), indirect command (12–14, 15–16, and 21–22), after an impersonal verb (30), and **cum**-concessive (35–36). **Cum**-concessive clauses are not frequent in ECCE ROMANI; examples have occurred at 59D:2 and 62C:15. Also, passive periphrastic (18–19); ablative absolute (3 and 9); present participle (22, 24, 26, 27, and 30); and past participles (28, 29, and 30).

5. Reading Notes

A.

a. **lactem** (2): This and Trimalchio's other grammatical mistakes have not been regularized. The teacher should help students understand that Trimalchio's imperfect Latin contributes to his characterization as a *nouveau riche*; it may also suggest his Greek background (he came from Asia Minor, but most likely grew up speaking Greek, the *lingua franca* of the East).

The phrase **ūnum lactem bibērunt** expresses the common humanity of all members of society, since all received nourishment in the same way as babies. In fact, since rich matrons often employed slave women as wet-nurses, slave and free would literally have drunk the same milk.

b. **corōnās et unguenta** (13): These items suggest a **commissātiō** (cf. *Home and School*, page 43). Notice how Trimalchio wants his favorite things in life on his tomb: his dog, banquets, and gladiatorial fights.

c. **nōn sequātur** (20): Another example of Trimalchio's shaky Latin; it should read **nē**. Students will probably need help with this, the first occurrence of the jussive subjunctive in this chapter. The teacher might also remind students that Roman tombs were placed on the roads leading out of town, e.g., the Street of Tombs in Pompeii, the various tombs on the Via Appia as it left Rome (cf. *Rome at Last*, pages 41 and 47), and Titus' burial on the Via Flaminia (*Pastimes and Ceremonies*, Chapter 53:25). These tombs have provided us with many interesting and informative inscriptions.

B.

a. **mē in tribūnālī sedentem. . . .** (22): The office of **sēvir Augustālis**, one of the six priests in charge of the imperial cult, was normally filled by freedmen and was one of the few civic distinctions open to them. The topic of emperor worship has already been touched upon in Chapters 63 and 64 .

b. **bīnōs dēnāriōs** (24): It was customary for rich citizens to give free meals to their fellow-townsmen, as Pliny did posthumously (*Credit Where Credit Is Due*, page 109 in this handbook). **Bīnōs dēnāriōs** may refer to the cost of the dinner or to a cash handout in addition to the dinner (cf. Trimalchio's desire to be portrayed handing out coins, in lines 23–24).

c. **Faciātur** (25): Again, students may need help with the jussive subjunctive.

d. **Faciās, pōnās** (25–26): These subjunctives may be understood either as a continuation of the indirect command after **rogō** (21) or as jussives parallel to **Faciātur** (more likely the latter).

e. **nec umquam philosophum audīvit** (38): Compare Trimalchio's declaration that he has "never listened to a philosopher" with his display of current philosophical ideas about human brotherhood (A:1–4). He wants to be thought of as cultured, like the upper class he emulates, but at the same time as a strictly practical Roman.

C.

a. **Putārēs** (11): This is a potential subjunctive, related to contrary-to-fact conditions, which will be introduced in Chapter 66: "You would think (if you thought about it)." This need not be formally discussed.

b. **nihil factī** (14): **Factī** is a partitive genitive.

D.

a. lībertōs (27): The story of Trimalchio provides a good opportunity to discuss the role of freedmen in the Empire. Some of them became wealthy but still suffered from social stigma (cf. *Credit Where Credit Is Due*, page 109 in this handbook, where Numerius Popidius Ampliatus was ineligible for election as a **decuriō**); many also served in the imperial bureaucracy (as Trimalchio claims he could have done, B:35–36) and as such attained great influence (cf. *Home and School*, Chapter 27:18–21 and 29–31, where Cornelia and her mother see one of the imperial freedmen being carried in a litter). The class of freedmen was an important economic force in the Empire, much more so than during the Republic, and it also provided a source of new talent for society outside of the traditional ruling class. See "The Household and its Freed Slaves," *A History of Private Life*, Vol., I, pp. 79–91, for a good discussion of freedmen and the difficulties they faced.

b. mathēmaticus (28): Most Romans believed in astrology, magic, and related ideas; cf. the love charm printed in Exercise 65b, page 129 of the student's book. Students may also remember the curse against chariot drivers (*Rome at Last*, page 91) and the werewolf story from Petronius (*Pastimes and Ceremonies*, pages 115–116). For additional Latin texts dealing with the occult, see *Roman Voices*; for a large variety of texts in translation, with discussion, see *Arcana Mundi*. See also "Magic," *The Oxford Classical Dictionary*, pp. 637–638; and "Superstition, Magic, and Spells," *Rome: Its People, Life, and Customs*, pp. 279–291.

c. hanc domum (34): This passage provides a good chance to review what students know about Roman villas from Book 1 (pages 35–38, with many references for further reading in the first teacher's handbook, pages 25–26, and the passage from Columella on pages 42–44) and, if desired, to develop the topic further. Students might be encouraged to study the floor plans of some imperial villas and then come up with their own version of how Trimalchio's **templum** might have been arranged.

6. EPITAPH FOR A SON (page 129): This text (*CIL* XII.4938) illustrates the Roman custom of specifying burial-plot dimensions in epitaphs, as Trimalchio does in his instructions to Habinnas (A:15–16). Often, as here, this results in what may strike us as an incongruous juxtaposition of the practical and the sentimental.

7. *VERBS: Jussive and Hortatory Subjunctives*: These uses of the subjunctive will call for a slight change in students' thinking, since up to now they have experienced the subjunctive in the context of various types of subordinate clause. (A review of the uses of the subjunctive already learned was provided on page 121 [Chapter 64] of the student's book; additional review could be done after the presentation of conditional sentences in Chapter 66.) Also, the jussive subjunctive is often translated by "let . . . ," a construction which is no longer part of the speech of most students and may seem unnatural to them. Occasionally, the jussive subjunctive appears in the second person, e.g., **Faciās** (25) and **pōnās** (26), "You should . . . . " This usage expresses a polite request, as opposed to the more peremptory imperative.

8. Exercise 65a: Suggested translations:
   1. Trimalchio said, "Let my will be brought in."
   2. Let us all taste the water of freedom!
   3. Let the masters free all their slaves.
   4. Let a statue of Fortunata be placed on the tomb.
   5. Let us not listen to philosophers!
   6. Let us all thank our very dear friends!
   7. Let this tomb come to [literally, receive] no harm.
   8. Let Trimalchio's name and deeds be read by all.
   9. May I have a suitable inscription on my tomb.
   10. May C. Pompeius Trimalchio Maecenatianus rest in peace.

9. Exercise 65b: Suggested translation:
   May Vettia whom Optata bore do whatever I desire, for the sake of love for me, may she not sleep or be able to take food. Let her love me, Felix whom Fructa bore; may she forget her father and mother and her relatives and all her friends and other men. Let her have me alone in [her] mind, [whether] sleeping [or] waking may Vettia burn, freeze, be on fire for the sake of love and desire for me.

   Jussive subjunctives: **faciat, dormiat, possit, amet, oblīvīscātur, habeat, ūrātur, frīgeat,** and **ardeat.**

10. Exercise 65d: Answers and suggested translations:
    1. (**afferrent**) Trimalchio ordered the slaves to bring in a copy of his will.
    2. (**affer**) "My friend," he said, "Bring in my will!"
    3. (**Afferant**) Trimalchio said, "Let the slaves bring in my will."
    4. (**sequiminī**) Friends, follow me, all of you!
    5. (**Adiciātur**) "Let this monument not pass to the heir" should be added to my tomb.
    6. (**Nōlī**) "Don't cry, Fortunata!" said Trimalchio.
    7. (**flēret**) However, he did not persuade Fortunata not to cry.
    8. (**audīrent**) He advised the guests not to listen to philosophers.
    9. (**audiāmus**) He said, "Let us not listen to philosophers."

10. (aedificēs) Finally he said to Habinnas, "My friend, you should build me a very beautiful monument."

Note: in the gloss at the bottom of page 135 we have given the expression as **nē sequātur**, rather than the ungrammatical **nōn sequātur** that Trimalchio himself used (A:20).

11. Supplementary Materials

a. *Roman Names* (page 115): These exercises expand upon a topic with which students are already somewhat familiar (cf. *Meeting the Family*, page 8, and *Pastimes and Ceremonies*, page 94), with special reference to freedmen such as Trimalchio.

1. Answers for Exercise A: 1. **Cn. Pompeius Hilarus**. 2. **Tychē Iūlia**. 3. **C. Iūlius Fortūnātus Cicerōniānus**. 4. **C. Pompeius**: the **praenōmen** and **nōmen** of the man who freed him; **Trimalchiō**: his name as a slave; **Maecēnātiānus**: the adjectival form of **Maecēnās** (genitive **Maecēnātis**), Trimalchio's first owner. Note: students will need help in forming the adjectival form of the name **Cicerō**.

2. If students have read the supplementary reading from Caelius' tombstone (page 106), they should be shown the tombstone again after completing Exercise A and be invited to comment on the names, before and after manumission, of the freedmen who are shown on either side of Caelius (**M. Caelius M[arcī] l[ībertus] Prīvātus** and **M. Caelius M[arcī] l[ībertus] Thiaminus**). Their names before manumission were Privatus and Thiaminus; and, as is usual in formal inscriptions, they identify themselves as freedmen of their **patrōnus**, whereas a freeborn citizen identifies his father, as Caelius himself does (**T[itī] F[īlius]**).

   Students should become aware that the name changes that followed manumission were similar to those that followed adoption. They may remember from Part I that when Gaius Octavius was adopted under Julius Caesar's will, he became Gaius Julius Caesar Octavianus; his **agnōmen** is similar to that used by Trimalchio (**Maecēnātiānus**). Students who will read Cicero's *Somnium Scipionis* (one of the Longman Latin Readers) later in their Latin course will encounter this phenomenon again in the case of Scipio the Younger, who was born the son of L. Aemilius Paulus and became after adoption P. Cornelius Scipio Aemilianus.

3. Exercise B involves names also, and, in addition, it provides another funeral inscription that may be compared with Trimalchio's. Here is a translation:

   To the deified spirits [and] eternal memory of Valeria Leucadia, a very sweet child who lived six years, thirty days, and of Vireius Vitalis, a youth of incomparable talent in the art of ironwork, brother of the same Leucadia, whose deaths were separated by only thirty days; he lived nineteen years, ten months, nine days; his wisdom was the wonder of all his friends and relations. Val[erius] Maximus his stepfather, who had adopted him as his son and trained him in the craft, in whom he had placed the hope of his old age, and Julia Secundina his most unhappy mother, who [both] had hoped that this would be done for them by them [the children], and Vireius Marinianus and [Vireius] Secundianus and Valerius Secundinus their brothers had [this monument] set up.

   Answers to questions: 1. Five. 2. Vireius Vitalis, Vireius Marinianus, Vireius Secundianus; their father's **nōmen** was Vireius. 3. Valeria Leucadia and Valerius Secundinus; Valerius Maximus. 4. Vireius Secundianus and Valerius Secundinus. 5. Valeria Leucadia and Valerius Secundinus.

   Answers to family tree: under (1), Vireius; his children are Vireius Vitalis, Vireius Marinianus, and Vireius Secundianus; under (2), Valerius Maximus; his children are Valerius Secundinus and Valeria Leucadia.

   If students need additional help in working out the relationships referred to in this epitaph, the following questions could be asked:

   1. Who has died? (Valeria Leucadia, age 6, and her brother Vireius Vitalis, age 19.)
   2. Who set up their monument? (Their mother, Julia Secundina, and Vitalis' stepfather, Valerius Maximus; also the children's brothers Vireius Marinianus, Vireius Secundianus, and Valerius Secundinus.)
   3. Who is Julia's present husband? (Valerius Maximus—who is not the father of Vitalis.) Who are her children by him? (Valerius Secundinus and Valeria Leucadia—deduced from the **nōmen**, **Valerius** (feminine **Valeria**.)
   4. What do you notice about the names of the other three children? (All are Vireius.)
   5. So who was their father, Julia's former husband? (Vireius—we cannot deduce his **cognōmen**.)

   It is likely that some students will not have been exposed to genealogical charts before, and so conventions such as the equal sign for marriage will need to be explained.

4. Reproduced on the same page as the preceding exercise is another epitaph, which may be compared to the funeral monuments of Trimalchio and Haterius. As Trimalchio portrays the ships, and Haterius the construction-crane, which sum-

bolize the sources of their wealth, so Faustus carves on his tombstone the tools of his trade, land-surveying: the **groma**, consisting of two horizontal cross-bars at right angles to each other, supported on a vertical post, and two of the four triangular plumb-weights that were suspended from the ends of the crosspieces to determine verticality. (For a picture of a **groma** in use, see *City*, p. 17.) Also like Trimalchio, Faustus commemorates his sevirate, symbolized by the honorary seat (**bisellium**) and **fascēs** displayed just above the **groma**. The inscription above reads:

> **(L.) Aebutius L(ūcī) l(ībertus) (F)austus mēnsor VI vir sibi et Arriae Q(uīntī) l(ībertae) Auctāī [= Auctae] uxōrī et suīs et Zep(h)yrē [= Zephyrae] lībert(ae) v(īvus) f(ēcit).**
> *Lucius Aebutius Faustus, freedman of Lucius (Aebutius), surveyor and sēvir, made (this monument) during his lifetime for himself and his wife Arria Aucta, freedwoman of Quintus (Arrius) and his (household) and Zephyra his freedwoman.*

The common formula **vīvus fēcit (hoc monumentum)** indicates that Faustus, like Trimalchio, planned and executed his own tombstone during his lifetime.

b. *Word Study XVI* (page 117): The various mistakes that Trimalchio makes in his Latin may be used as the starting point for this exercise. It is clear from inscriptions and other sources that Trimalchio was not the only Roman who made grammatical mistakes. You may wish to have students find all of Trimalchio's errors (identified in the notes). For more graffiti and inscriptions, often with grammatical mistakes, see *Pompeian Graffiti, Roman Voices*, and *Claimed by Vesuvius*.

CHAPTER 66: A NOBLE WOMAN

1. The aims of this chapter are:

   a. to show how the political system under the Principate could affect the life of an individual
   b. to provide an opportunity for additional discussion of the Principate, especially its "darker side"
   c. to review future more vivid conditions and to present future less vivid and contrary to fact conditions.

2. Translation

   A. Pliny sends greetings to his friend Priscus.
   Fannia's illness has me worried. She contracted it while she was nursing Junia the [Vestal] Virgin, first of her own free will (for she is a relative), then also by the authority of the priests. For the [Vestal] Virgins, when they are compelled to leave the **ātrium Vestae** by the force of an illness, are entrusted to the care and custody of married women. Fannia was conscientiously performing that duty, [when] she was caught up in this crisis. The fevers are settling in, the cough increases; she is very thin and weak. Only her mind and spirit are strong, very worthy of her husband Helvidius [and] her father Thrasea; her other faculties are failing, and they wear me out not only with fear, [but] also in fact with grief. For I grieve that a great woman is being snatched from the eyes of the state, which may not see her like [again]. What loyalty she has, what holiness, what seriousness, what steadfastness! Twice she followed her husband into exile, the third time she herself was banished because of her husband.
   For when Senecio was on trial on the grounds that he had written a biography about the life of Helvidus, and he had said in his defense that he had been asked by Fannia, with Mettius Carus threateningly questioning [her] whether she had asked [for this], she replied: "I did"; whether she had given [Helvidius'] diaries to the author, [she replied]: "I did"; whether [she had done this] with her mother's knowledge: "Without her knowledge"; in the end she uttered no word that yielded to the danger. Why even those books themselves, although [ordered] destroyed (from necessity and from the fears of the times) by decree of the Senate, after her possessions were confiscated she saved [and] kept [them], and took [them] into exile, the cause of her exile.

   B. This same [woman], how pleasant [she was], how friendly, finally not less deserving of love than of respect ([a thing] which is given to few)! Will there be [anyone] whom hereafter we will be able to show to our wives? Will there be [anyone] from whom we men also can take examples of courage, whom we will wonder at, when we see and listen to [her], like those who are read about? But to me her very house seems to totter, and having been torn from its foundations seems about to collapse on itself, although it may still have descendants. With what merits [and] with what deeds will they [her descendants] [have to] follow, so that she won't have perished, the last [of her line]. Indeed, that also crushes and torments me, [the fact] that I seem to be losing her mother a second time, that mother of such a great woman (I can say nothing more complimentary), [her mother] whom she, just as she brings back and restores to us, will likewise take away with her, and will affect me all over again [literally, equally] with a newly-opened wound.

I cultivated and loved them both; which one more I don't know, nor would they want a choice to be made. They had my help in good times, they had it in bad times. I was their comforter in exile, I was their champion upon their return; even so, I did not pay my debts and all the more I want her to be saved [from her illness], so that there will be time left for me to repay [my debts]. I was in these difficulties when I wrote to you; if some god turns them into joy, I will not complain about my fears. Goodbye.

3. Background

a. The nature of the "Augustan compromise" has already been explored in Part IV; Augustus established one-man rule while preserving the outward forms of Republican government. However, the powers of the emperor and the Senate were not precisely defined by Augustus or his successors. The Senate still governed a number of provinces and exercised judicial functions. It was uncertain how much independent action the Senate could take in making policy; this fluctuated depending on the tolerance of the emperor and the will of the senators. The senatorial class remembered the days when they had ruled the world and frequently chafed under the necessity of pleasing the emperor. The emperor in turn did not trust the senatorial class completely, since (aside from any tendency on the Senate's part to act independently of the **prīnceps**) it was from this class that any potential usurper would come (one of the fundamental weaknesses of the principate was the lack of any reliable mechanism for securing the succession). At the same time, the emperor could not rule entirely without the senators, since most high-ranking officials came from this class (although the bureaucracy that ran the Empire was largely staffed by imperial freedmen, and freedmen and equestrians held offices under the Empire that would have been unthinkable during the Republic). While Augustus lived, he skillfully kept the Senate happy, and Trajan also respected the Senate and received its goodwill in return. The potential tension between the Senate and the emperor never died out until the Empire was openly transformed into a military autocracy in the third and fourth centuries, by which time it was clear that the Senate was something of a superfluous relic.

b. In the absence of an Augustus or a Trajan, this underlying tension between Senate and emperor could cause serious difficulties. In the case of Nero, Rome had a young emperor who was more interested in indulging his own interests than in running the Empire. During the first years of Nero's reign, Afranius Burrus, the commander of the Praetorian Guard (the Emperor's bodyguard) and L. Annaeus Seneca, the philosopher who had been appointed Nero's tutor, effectively ran the government. After the death of Burrus (A.D. 62), Seneca was forced to retire and Nero was in control. Almost immediately a series of treason trials began, occasioned partly by Nero's suspicions about plots against him and partly by his desire to confiscate the wealth of convicted senators (Nero was a spendthrift, and his treasury needed all the money it could get). The senators began to feel that they could not be safe under Nero, and in 65 an actual conspiracy was formed under the leadership of C. Calpurnius Piso. Discovery of this conspiracy only fueled Nero's fears, and from then on no member of the upper class was safe. Nero employed spies and informers (**dēlātōrēs**—cf. the use of the verb **deferō** in readings 64A:1 and B:3) to root out any opposition. Among Nero's prominent victims were a group of senators who followed the Stoic philosophy, including the ex-consul Thrasea Paetus and Barea Soranus; in addition, Thrasea's son-in-law, Helvidius Priscus (husband of the Fannia in our letter), was exiled. Although these men seem not to have actually plotted against Nero, they made no secret of their disapproval of his conduct, and they held the old Republican ideals of government. (C. Petronius, author of the *Satyricon*, was also one of Nero's victims in the aftermath of Piso's conspiracy.)

c. After his accession in A.D. 69, Vespasian made it clear that, while he would accord the Senate a certain respect, it would play no active role in the government. The majority resigned themselves to this situation, but a group of Stoic philosophers led by Helvidius Priscus, now returned from exile, continued vocally to espouse Republican ideals. Priscus carried on a cult of Brutus and Cato the Younger (two of Julius Caesar's most prominent opponents) and went so far as to revile the Emperor in public. For this he was banished (after A.D. 70) and later executed, perhaps about A.D. 75.

d. Domitian ascended the throne upon the death of Titus in 81. Like his father and elder brother, he was an efficient administrator who cared for the well-being of the Empire. Like Nero, however, he made no bones about considering himself sole ruler, and his reign in some ways parallels that of Nero. His autocratic behavior alienated the upper class; after an abortive rebellion in Upper Germany in 88–89, Domitian hunted down all those whom he suspected of complicity, and from then on he was only too ready to listen to the false accusations of the **dēlātōrēs** against the nobility (informers received a portion of the convicted person's property, which explains their continued activities). Toward the end of his reign he seemed to do little but try suspected conspirators. A group of senators finally did conspire against him, to preserve themselves; with the aid of Domitian's wife and two praetorian prefects, they assassinated him in 96.

e. Fannia herself was the daughter of Thrasea Fannius Paetus and the younger Arria (and thus grand-daughter of Arria the elder, whom students may remember from *Pastimes and Ceremonies*, pages 101–102). She was married by A.D. 66 to Helvidius as his second wife, which means she was probably born no later than 53. Her trial and subsequent exile took place after August of 93; Pliny's letter was probably written no later than 107 (we do not know the exact date of Fannia's death).

f. For the ancient sources dealing with the topics discussed in this background section, see Tacitus, *Annales* XIV.12 and 48–49 (Thrasea's defiance of Nero); XV.48–74 (Piso's conspiracy and aftermath, including the death of Seneca); XVI.18–19 (death of Petronius); 16.21–34 (deaths of Thrasea and Barea); *Historiae* IV.4–8 (early career of Helvidius Priscus). See also *The Oxford Classical Dictionary*, "Arria (2) Minor," p. 122; "Helvidius Priscus", p. 496; and "Thrasea Paetus," p. 1066

g. For a good modern summary of the events discussed above, usable by students, see *Roman Society: A Social, Economic and Cultural History*, pp. 194–199.

h. On the **ātrium Vestae**, mentioned in A:5 and illustrated on page 138 of the student's book, and the temple of Vesta associated with it, see *Forum Romanum*, pp. 26–28.

4. Teaching the Text

a. One can introduce this chapter by contrasting emperors such as Augustus and Trajan, whom students have already met, with less attractive emperors such as Nero and Domitian. This can lead to a discussion of those aspects of the Principate that were less than satisfactory (lack of a good mechanism for choosing an emperor, leading to over-reliance on the military; no restraints on the power of an emperor to punish those whom he disliked or distrusted; etc.).

b. Before taking up the actual text, it would be wise to give at least a brief introduction to the characters involved and their relationships to each other.

c. This letter provides a natural springboard for exploring the role of women in Roman society. Students encountered Aurelia as organizer of the home in the first four student books, and Cornelia's marriage was featured in Chapters 49 and 52, along with the supplementary reading "A Noble Wife" (*Pastimes and Ceremonies*, pages 101–102). Certainly Roman men thought that the ideal woman was one who managed the house well and remained steadfastly loyal to her husband, however confining this may seem to con-

temporary women. Octavia, wife of Mark Antony (pictured on page 32 of the student's book and discussed on page 17, note 7 in this handbook) was one historical figure who exhibited this familial loyalty, and it is for this very virtue of loyalty that Pliny praises Fannia so highly. Additional materials for the study of Roman women include "Women in the Roman Family," *Rome: Its People, Life, and Customs*, pp. 113–119; "Marriage," *A History of Private Life, Vol. I*, pp. 33–50; *Women in Greece and Rome* (good for students); *Roman Women: Their History and Habits*; and *Goddesses, Whores, Wives, and Slaves: Women in Classical Antiquity*.

d. Students may become interested in the Stoic philosophy, which motivated Thrasea and Helvidius to oppose imperial despotism. See "Stoa (1)," *The Oxford Classical Dictionary*, pp. 1015–1016; *From the Gracchi to Nero*, pp. 10–12, 204–205, and 357–359; and "Philosophical Sects," *A History of Private Life, Vol. I*, pp. 223–229. A basic outline of Stoic principles, suitable for use with students, appears in *The Romans Speak for Themselves*, Book I, pages. 40–41.

e. The following grammatical items are available for review:
   1. relative clauses of characteristic (a good follow-up to Chapter 64): lines 27 and 28–29
   2. participles (12, 21, 23, 29, 30, 31, and 37) and ablative absolutes (18, 20, and 23)
   3. **fungitur** + abl. (6–7).

5. Reading Notes

a. Words to be deduced: **custōdiae** (6), **composuisset** (17), **exempla** (28), **adversīs** (40)

b. **PRISCO SUO** (1): Pliny had several acquaintances with the **cognōmen** Priscus, so we do not know for certain to whom this letter is addressed.

c. **S.** (1): This would be a good time to review Roman epistolary conventions, first presented in Chapters 34 and 38 and reviewed in Chapter 59. The letters in Chapter 64 between Trajan and Pliny, that students have recently read, use the most abbreviated form of salutation: the names of author (nominative) and recipient (dative), with the formulaic **salūtem dīcit** to be supplied.

d. **ex auctōritāte pontificum** (4): The College of Pontifs, a group of sixteen priests led by the Pontifex Maximus, had jurisdiction over the Vestal Virgins, with authority to punish them if they neglected their duties.

e. **ātriō Vestae** (5): For more on this building, and its associated temple, see *Forum Romanum*, p. , and *The Mute Stones Speak*, p. . The Vestal Virgins were introduced in 62C:11.

f. **febrēs, tussis** (7): Fannia apparently suffered from tuberculosis.

g. **castitās, sānctitās, gravitās, cōnstantia** (13–14): Devotion to her family and especially faithfulness to her husband were traditional virtues for a Roman woman. Compare the figure of Lucretia in Book I of Livy, in many ways the paradigm of Roman womanhood. Lucretia stayed at home and tended to the management of her household while her husband was away fighting (unlike some other wives). After being raped by the wicked Sextus Tarquinius, she told her husband and father to avenge her and then killed herself rather than live with her family dishonored. Lucretia is perhaps one of those whom Pliny has in mind when he mentions those women **quae leguntur** (29–30). **Gravitās** (especially as contrasted with the "frivolity" attributed by Romans to the Greeks) is another traditional Roman virtue, more often encountered in reference to men but clearly applicable to women as well.

h. **illī** (13): If the verb **est** is supplied, this can be considered a dative of possession ("What chastity . . . she has"); or it could be taken as a dative of reference ("What chastity . . . is in her").

i. **Bis . . . relēgāta** (14–15): Fannia went into exile with Helvidius first during Nero's reign (A.D. 66), then during Vespasian's (probably before 75), and the third time after her condemnation under Domitian (date uncertain).

   Exile was a punishment reserved for the upper classes (cf. the exile of Cicero, discussed on page 21, note c in this handbook, and of Milo, mentioned in reading 57E), and during the Empire it had various grades. The mildest form was **relēgātiō** (cf. **relēgāta [est]**, 15), which was what Fannia suffered; this was either exclusion from certain places (e.g., Italy) or confinement in a particular place. A more severe form was **dēportātiō**, which involved transportation to an island, confiscation of property, and loss of Roman citizenship. **Exsilium** (14) is used as a generic term for all types of exile.

j. **Mettiō Cārō** (18): Mettius Carus was one of Domitian's henchmen, who brought charges against many senators.

k. **an sciente mātre: "Nesciente"** (20): Arria was banished with Fannia, despite her daughter's denial of any involvement on her mother's part. They both returned from exile in 97.

l. **quamquam** (22): Strictly speaking, **quamquam** is not necessary, since a perfect participle by itself can express the idea of concession. Pliny uses it to make sure that the participle is not taken in a causal or temporal sense.

m. **senātūs cōnsultō** (23): The Senate often served as a court, where charges were brought against its members (often at the behest of the Emperor). It was doubly difficult for the Roman nobility during the reigns of Nero and Domitian; they not only had to watch as these men sought out any

opposition, real or imagined, but also had to serve as jury for many of those who were charged. Occasionally they would find someone innocent, but usually, when it was known that the Emperor wanted someone convicted, a conviction was obtained. The Senate was also involved in carrying out the Emperor's wishes by such actions as the book-burning mentioned here. Cf. Tacitus, *Agricola* 45, who comments that Agricola was fortunate in not living to see the horrible events that took place toward the end of Domitian's reign:

> Agricola did not see the Senate House beseiged and surrounded with weapons, and the destruction of so many ex-consuls with the same blow, and the exile and flight of so many very noble women. Carus Mettius was still credited with [only] one victory, . . . soon our [i.e., Senatorial] hands took Helvidius to jail, . . . Senecio spattered us with his innocent blood.

Tacitus also discusses this book-burning (*Agricola* 2):

> We have read that, when Thrasea Paetus had been praised by Arulenus Rusticus, and Herennius Senecio by Helvidius Priscus, it was declared a capital [offense], and that [the Emperor's] rage was directed not only at the authors themselves, but also at their books, and the assignment was given to the **trēsvirī capitālēs** [commissioners in charge of carrying out executions] to burn in the Comitium and the Forum the monuments of very great genius.

The first three chapters of Tacitus' *Agricola* give a good sense of what the senatorial class felt during the reigns of Domitian, Nerva, and Trajan.

n. **quam** (25, 26, 27): Students may need help here since we have in these three lines the three meanings of **quam**: "how" (followed by an adjective or adverb), line 25; "than" (in a comparison), line 26; and "whom" (fem. sing. relative pronoun), line 27. This is an excellent review (the various meanings of **quam** were first brought together in *Home and School*, page 67).

6. *Conditional Sentences*: Students have met many simple conditions throughout ECCE ROMANI and have met future more vivid conditions since Chapter 22, although the technical term has not been employed in the student's books. Therefore, future more vivid conditions make an excellent starting point for this lesson; after reviewing these and introducing the technical terms such as protasis and apodosis, one can proceed to a discussion of future less vivid and contrary to fact conditions. (There is a future more vivid condition in lines 43–44 of this reading, which would make an excellent starting point.) Mixed conditions (protasis and apodosis in different tenses) are

not discussed in the student's book, but one such sentence, along with a brief note on mixed conditions, occurs in Exercise 1 of the supplementary activity *Practice with Conditionals* (page 118).

This might also be a good time to discuss the nature of the three moods, indicative, subjunctive, and imperative. Each of these shows that the speaker is looking at the action in a different way: as a factual statement or question, as a non-fact, or as a command. (The infinitive, which is sometimes said to be a fourth mood, is in fact a sort of verbal noun and not a true mood.) In ECCE ROMANI, the subjunctive has been presented simply as a form that must be used in certain grammatical situations. However, students may now be ready for the notion that the subjunctive often shows that the speaker regards an action as uncertain, doubtful, or impossible. This aspect of the subjunctive is clearly seen in structures such as purpose clauses, indirect commands and questions, and hortatory and jussive usages; it is less obvious in result and **cum** clauses. Once the idea of the subjunctive expressing a non-factual idea is established, then students should have no trouble seeing why it is used in contrary to fact and future less vivid conditions.

A review of all subjunctive forms and constructions would be appropriate either now or in conjunction with Chapter 67, which will present no new grammar.

4. Exercise 66a: Answers and suggested translations:
   1. If Pliny had visited Fannia, she would have been very happy. (past contrary to fact)
   2. If Pliny should visit Fannia, she would be very happy. (future less vivid)
   3. If Fannia's parents were alive, they would help their daughter. (present contrary to fact)
   4. If Fannia goes into exile, she will take with her the books about her husband Helvidius. (future more vivid)
   5. If a Vestal Virgin leaves the house of the Vestals, she is entrusted to the care of a married woman. (simple)
   6. If Fannia had not been nursing Junia the Vestal Virgin, she would not have contracted this disease. (past contrary to fact)
   7. Pliny would be glad, if Fannia should get well. (future less vivid)
   8. Unless Pliny were very upset, he would not be writing this letter to his [friend] Priscus. (present contrary to fact)
   9. If Trimalchio gives a dinner, everyone wants to be there. (simple)
   10. If Trimalchio should build a plain tomb, everyone would be stunned. (future less vivid)
   11. If Fortunata had not sold her jewelry, Trimalchio would not have been able to buy other ships. (past contrary to fact)
   12. If we are invited to dinner by Trimalchio, certainly we will be present. (future more vivid)
   13. If Trimalchio were a modest man, he would not be showing the guests all his riches. (present contrary to fact)
   14. If they had not drunk so much wine, they would not have fallen down in the street. (past contrary to fact)
   15. If Trimalchio should talk about his life, we would listen carefully. (future less vivid)

Notes:
   1. The translation of future less vivid conditions with the auxiliaries "should" and "would" is now rather archaic. You may prefer to allow students to translate sentences such as number 7 above using the normal English contruction, "Pliny would be happy if Fannia got well."
   2. You may wish to point out that if the subject of both protasis and apodosis is the same, Latin prefers to put the subject first and then the subordinate clause (e.g., number 4 above, "Fannia, if she goes. . . . "), while in English we normally put the subordinate clause first, with the main subject ("If Fannia goes . . . ."). This observation applies not only to conditions but to many types of subordinate clauses.

7. The Pliny manuscript shown on page 143 is now in the Pierpont Morgan Library, New York City (MS 462) and was written in an uncial hand about A.D. 500. We have no manuscripts that have come down to us from the classical period of Latin literature; the earliest ones (some Vergil manuscripts and a copy of Terence) date from the fourth century, although we do have papyri from earlier dates. The uncial hand, developed during the fourth century, is distinguished from the earlier capital scripts primarily in the shapes of the letters *a, d, e,* and *m* (notice especially the *d*'s in this photo). The Romans also had a cursive script that was used for letters, contracts, graffiti, etc., but not for good-quality books; for examples of cursive, see *Claimed by Vesuvius* and *Pompeian Graffiti*.

The photograph shows the beginning of *Epistulae* III.3, a well-known letter in which Pliny recommends Junius Genitor as a tutor for Corellia's son. The portion printed on page 142 has been enlarged so that students can actually read the script. Transcription: **C. Plinius Corelliae salutem. Cum patrem tuum gravissimum et sanctissimum virum suspexerim magis an amaverim dubitem, teque et in memoriam eius et in honorem tuum unice diligam, cupiam necesse est atque etiam quantum in me fuerit enitar, ut filius.**

This photograph provides an opportunity to discuss with students how ancient books have come down to us. Since all books had to be copied by hand, time and effort were spent in copying only those volumes for which there was a real need. Because most classical authors were not in demand during the early Middle Ages, few copies were made; as the older manuscripts were gradually destroyed, many authors were lost forever. Others survived only by the most slender threads until ancient learning became more fashionable toward the close of the Middle Ages, and additional copies were made. For example, the poems of Catullus depend on a single manuscript; this is also true for parts of Tacitus, whose *Annales* and *Historiae* both survive in an incomplete state. Since copyists were likely to make mistakes (especially when they came to a word they did not know or an unusual proper name), the various manuscripts contain many errors. Scholars since the Renaissance have attempted to correct these errors and restore the true readings, which has given rise to the science of textual criticism. For a fascinating and readable discussion of all these matters, see *Scribes and Scholars: A Guide to the Transmission of Classical Literature*.

8. Supplementary Materials

a. *Practice with Conditionals* (page 118): Three exercises to consolidate students' understanding of conditional sentences. Answers and suggested translations:

Exercise 1
1. (simple) I am unhappy if I don't see you.
2. (simple) I was unhappy if I didn't see you.
3. (future less vivid) I would be unhappy if I didn't see you. (More traditional translation: I would be unhappy if I should not see you.)
4. (past contrary to fact) I would have been unhappy, if I hadn't seen you.
5. (simple) I was unhappy if I didn't see you.
6. (future more vivid) I will be unhappy if I don't see you.
7. (future more vivid) I will be unhappy if I don't see you.
8. (present contrary to fact) I would be unhappy if I weren't seeing you.
9. (mixed contrary to fact) I would be unhappy if I hadn't seen you.

Exercise 2
1. (dīcerēs, crēderet) Even if you were telling the truth, no one would believe you.
2. (dīcās, crēdat) Even if you told the truth, no one would believe you. (More traditional translation: Even if you should tell the truth, no one would believe you.)
3. (dīxissēs, crēdidisset) Even if you had told the truth, no one would have believed you.
4. (dīcis, crēdit) Even if you tell the truth, no one believes you.
5. (dīcēs or dīxeris, crēdet) Even if you tell the truth, no one will believe you.

6. (dīxissēs, crēderet) Even if you had told the truth, no one would believe you.

Exercise 3
1. If you wish to be loved, love! (simple)
2. The gods don't care what the human race does. For if they cared, it would be good for good people, and bad for bad ones. A situation which doesn't exist now. (future less vivid)
3. If he were alive, you would be hearing his words. (present contrary to fact)
4. You will say "Alas" if you see yourself in the mirror. (future more vivid)

CHAPTER 67: THE DEATH OF PLINY THE ELDER

1. The aims of this chapter are:

   a. to end *From Republic to Empire* with a dramatic and compelling narrative
   b. to provide opportunity to study the eruption of Mt. Vesuvius and the towns of Pompeii and Herculaneum.

2. Translation

A. He was at Misenum and in charge of the fleet, personally in command. On the ninth day before the Kalends of September [24 August] at about the seventh hour [12:00–1:15 P.M.], my mother points out to him that a cloud of unusual size and shape is appearing. He climbs up to a place from which that strange sight could best be seen. The cloud was rising—[it was] unclear to those gazing from a distance from which mountain (later it was learned to have been Vesuvius)—[a cloud] whose likeness and form no other tree than the pine conveyed more. To him, as a very learned man, it seemed a great thing and one that had to be observed at closer range. He orders a light galley fitted out; he gives me the chance, if I want to come along; I answered that I preferred to study, and by chance I was writing what he himself had given [me]. He was on his way out of the house; he receives a message from Rectina, [wife] of Tascius, who was terrified by the threatening danger (for her villa lay at the foot [of Mt. Vesuvius], nor was there any escape except by ship); she begged that he rescue her from such a danger.

He changed his plans and what he had begun with a scholar's mind he completes with a hero's. He launches quadriremes, [and] goes on board intending to bring help not only to Rectina but to many (for the pleasant shore was thickly populated). He hastens to that place from where others were fleeing, and he holds a straight course and a straight helm [right] into the danger, so free from fear that he dictates and notes down all the movements [and] all the forms of that disaster as he caught them with his eyes.

B. Now the ash was falling on the ships, the hotter and thicker the closer they approached; now also pumice stones and black rocks burned up and broken by fire [were falling]; now suddenly [there was] shallow water and the shore rising up because of the destruction of the mountain. After hesitating a little whether he should turn back, he said to the helmsman who was advising that he do so, "Fortune helps the brave; head for Pomponianus." At Stabiae he was cut off by the middle of the bay; there, although the danger was not yet coming close, it was nevertheless visible and very close as it increased, he had put his luggage on ships, determined to escape if the contrary wind died down. Then my uncle, brought in by the favorable wind, embraces the panic-stricken man, consoles him, encourages him, and in order to lighten his fear through his own [Pliny's] lack of concern, orders [himself] carried into the bath; after he bathes he sits down [and] dines, either cheerful or (a thing equally great) apparently cheerful.

C. Meanwhile from Mt. Vesuvius in many places very wide flames and high fires were glowing, whose brilliance and brightness was accented by the shadows of the night. He kept on saying, as a remedy for their fear, that fires left through the terror of peasants and deserted villas were burning in the countryside. Then he lay down to rest and rested in fact with a very real sleep; for the motions of his breathing [i.e., snoring], which in his case were rather heavy and loud because of the size of his body, were heard by those who attended outside his door.

But the [level of the] courtyard from which the living room had its entrance had now risen so much, filled with ash and mixed pumice stones, that if there was any longer delay in the bedroom, exit would be denied. After being woken up he comes forth, and rejoined Pomponianus and the others who had stayed awake all night. They consult together, [whether] they should stay indoors or wander in the open. For the house was shaking with frequent, heavy tremors, and as if moved from its foundations, now here now there, it seemed to move away and [then] be brought back. Again, although under the open sky the falling of light and porous pumice stones was feared, [a thing] which a comparison of the dangers chose [i.e., they considered the dangers in the open less threatening than those in the house]; and in his case [Pliny's] one reason overcame the other, in the case of the others one fear overcame the other. They place pillows on their heads and tie them with pieces of cloth; this was a protection against things falling.

D. Now [it was] day elsewhere, there [it was] a night blacker and thicker than all nights; which, however,

many torches and different lamps lessened. It was decided to go out onto the shore and to look from up close [whether] the sea would now allow any [escape]; it still remained vast and forbidding. There, lying on a cloth thrown [on the ground] once and again he demanded and drank cold water. Then the flames and the odor of sulphur, the herald of flames, turn the others to flight, [and] rouse him. Leaning on two little slaves he stood up and immediately fell down, as I infer, with his breathing blocked by the rather thick fumes, and with his windpipe (which in his case was naturally unhealthy and narrow and frequently inflamed) closed. When daylight returned (this was the third from that which he had last seen), his body was found intact and unharmed and covered as he had been dressed; the appearance of the body was more like a person asleep than a dead person.

3. Background

a. The story of the eruption of Mt. Vesuvius in A.D. 79 is well known and needs no introduction. There is only one surviving eyewitness account, that of Pliny the Younger, in the two letters he wrote in response to the historian Tacitus' request for material to incorporate into his *Historiae*; by this point in the course, Pliny needs no introduction either. After students have read the account of Pliny the Elder's death in this chapter, they might like to read what happened to Pliny the Younger and his mother, who stayed behind; see Pliny, *Epistulae* VI.20 (use the Penguin or Loeb versions).

b. The exact date when the letter was written cannot be determined, but it seems to have been about A.D. 106–107.

c. Mt. Vesuvius has erupted several times since 79, most recently in 1944; the cone created by this eruption is considerably smaller than that of 79. Sensors along the rim continue to monitor the seismic activity. It is possible at the present time for tourists to climb Mt. Vesuvius. The excavations around Vesuvius are still continuing; for coverage of recent, important discoveries in Herculaneum, see the following articles in *National Geographic*: "A Buried Roman Town Gives Up its Dead," December 1982, pp. 687–693; and "The Dead Do Tell Tales at Vesuvius," May 1984, pp. 589–613.

d. There are many books and articles available on Pompeii and Herculaneum. The following are among the more recent and are listed in the Bibliography: "Pompeii 2000 Years Ago"; the catalogue of the "Pompeii, A.D. 79" exhibition; *Pompeii*; "Victims of Vesuvius"; *Cities of Vesuvius*; *Herculaneum: Italy's Buried Treasure*; and *Southern Italy: An Archaeological Guide* (for visitors to the site).

e. For audio-visual materials, see the film "Pompeii: Once There Was a City"; the *National Geographic* video "Cities of Vesuvius;" and the computer game "Escape from Pompeii."

4. Teaching the Text

a. This letter is a fine example of the storyteller's art, fast-moving, full of drama and danger. The teacher should emphasize these dramatic qualities, doing nothing to take away from or slow down the action. The goal of the entire ECCE ROMANI series has been to teach the student to read Latin; the student's final reading experience in the series should be a memorable one.

b. The Latin is not easy. In order to create as dramatic an atmosphere as possible, Pliny has used a number of rhetorical and literary devices such as asyndeton, the historical present (preserved in the translation given above), omission of words (especially forms of **esse**), and a generally compressed style. The teacher should give plenty of help, as required, so that students can move quickly through the text and develop the picture as Pliny lays it out. After finishing the first reading, the teacher may go back and pick out things to look at in more detail; mature and able students may be asked to appreciate some of the literary devices that Pliny uses in his narrative, some of which are identified in the notes below; some of them were also used in the letter students read in Chapter 66 (e.g., asyndeton, 66A:23 and B:38, and omission of **esse**, 66A:8 and 13–14). But if students have enjoyed this account, it would not be bad to omit detailed analysis this time; let their final experience of the book be an enjoyable one.

c. An interesting parallel to the eruption of Vesuvius is the destruction of St. Pierre, Martinique, by an eruption of the volcano Mt. Pélée in 1908. *Claimed by Vesuvius* has an appendix, "An American Pompeii," which presents newspaper and other accounts of this disaster, which are quite comparable to Pliny's accounts of Mt. Vesuvius. After completing the readings and studying some background material on the eruption, students might be asked to write a first-person "you are there" account describing their own escape from the city or from a nearby villa.

d. The picture of page 151 of the student's book is "The Eruption of Mt. Vesuvius" by Jean-Baptiste Genillon (1750–1829), now in the Musée des Beaux-Arts, Lille, France.

e. Students may already have learned something about Pompeii and Herculaneum, two of the towns destroyed in the eruption of Mt. Vesuvius; if not, this would be an excellent opportunity to spend some time studying them. They are extremely important because so much of what we know about everyday life in Roman towns during the first century A.D. is based on materials found there. *Claimed by Vesuvius* presents a number of interesting materials for students to read, such as copies of tablets, inscriptions, etc.

f. The following are available for grammar development and review:

> historical present (3, and *passim*)
> ablative of description (3–4)
> gerundive (8–9)
> mixed conditions: **sī venīre ūnā vellem, facit cōpiam** (10), **certus fugae [erat] sī ventus resēdisset** (31–32);
> contrary-to-fact condition: 47–48 (**esset** understood in protasis)
> ablative of separation (14, 21, and 52)
> present participles used as substantives (5 and 58)

5. Reading notes

a. **Nōnum** (2): Short for **Ante diem nōnum**.

b. **nōn alia magis arbor quam pīnus** (7–8): This is the same shape as the "mushroom cloud" familiar to us from nuclear explosions. The umbrella pine is still found throughout Italy.

c. **nōscendum** (8–9): The gerundive is in fact the future passive participle. It is more often found in its various idiomatic uses (e.g., with **ad** to express purpose) than in its simple function as future passive participle, as it is here ("a thing to be observed").

d. **ipse . . . dederat** (11): Pliny the Elder was helping his nephew with his education in rhetoric, presumably and had given him a composition assignment.

e. **gubernacula** (20: Students met this word in a metaphorical sense at 63A:4.

f. **ruīnā** (25): Ablative of cause, "because of the destruction."

g. **Pompōniānum** (28): No clear reason is given for Pliny the Elder's decision to head for Pomponianus' villa rather than Rectina's. Perhaps the ship could not reach her villa because of the rise in the sea floor (lines 25–26). Sherwin-White suggests (*The Letters of Pliny*, p. 373) that Tascius and Pomponianus were the same man, whose original **cognōmen** was Pomponius, and that after adoption by Tascius was called Tascius Pomponianus.

h. **complectitur . . . hortātur** (33): Another instance of asyndeton. Previous examples have occurred at 66A:9 and 23 (with note in facing vocabulary), B:32, and 67A:21–22; an additional example will occur at B:35.

i. **dictitābat** (41): A frequentative verb. The concept of frequentatives was first introduced in Word Study XI (*Pastimes and Ceremonies*, pages 29–30).

j. sē quiētī dedit (42): This idiom was first introduced in Chapter 22.

k. quasi ēmōta . . . vidēbantur (52–53): Notice that Pliny's description of the real house shaken by an earthquake is very similar to his comparison of Fannia's family to a "house" struck by an earthquake and tottering on the brink of destruction (66B:30–31).

l. Iam diēs alibi (59): The morning of 25 August, the second day of the eruption.

m. spiritū obstructō (68): Pliny the Elder may have suffered from asthma. This would account for his death, while others in his party survived, just as in modern cities asthmatics often have to remain indoors when air pollution reaches levels that are still tolerable for others. The problem then would have been really in his lungs, not his windpipe (**stomachō**).

n. Ubi diēs redditus (70): The morning of 26 August.

o. integrum inlaesum opertumque (71–72): From a literary point of view, it is somehow appropriate that the body of Pliny the Elder, who did not fear the eruption, remained undamaged after his death. These words also make it clear that he died a natural death and was not killed either by his slaves or by looters after Pomponianus and his friends ran away.

6. Supplementary Materials

a. *Summary of Case Usages* (pages 120–121): This activity is designed to help the student review and assimilate the various usages of the genitive, dative, and ablative cases. (The nominative, accusative, and vocative cases are not treated here because they have a relatively small number of uses, all of which have been familiar to students for some time. If the teacher wishes to review them also, fine.) Students should be very comfortable with some of the uses described here, such as the genitive of possession (Chapter 12), dative of indirect object (Chapter 21), and ablative of means (Chapter 9). Others, such as the ablative of manner, have also occurred frequently in the readings but have not been formally discussed. A few have occurred only rarely (e.g., the ablative of price). It should be kept in mind when doing this activity that the names for some of these constructions have not been presented in the body of the student's books, although they are used in the Syntax section at the end of the student's book.

Some teachers feel that the ability to identify case usages using the traditional terminology presented here has no direct relationship to the student's ability to comprehend Latin (and it is usually true that the students must understand the sentence before they can apply the correct la-

bel); others feel that such practice is quite valuable. We have provided this activity for those who wish to use it.

Suggested translations and answers:

1. Clodius' wife had no fear of death. (dative of possession; possessive genitive; objective genitive)
2. He will be ashamed of his crimes. (genitive with impersonal verbs of feeling)
3. Let her not forget her friends. (genitive with special verbs)
4. Art for art's sake. (genitive with **grātiā**)
5. This book is not suitable for students. (dative with special adjectives)
6. Milo did not trust Pompey. (dative with special verbs)
7. The state was a great concern to Cicero. (dative of reference, dative of purpose = double dative)
8. You must not touch the gold. (dative of agent)
9. Clodius and Milo were equal in crime. (ablative of respect)
10. The poet accepted the gift with great pleasure. (ablative of manner)
11. Martial was a much better poet than Cicero. (ablative of degree of difference, ablative of comparison)
12. Cicero made use of Greek literature. (ablative with special verbs)
13. The poet bought the book for ten sesterces. (ablative of price)
14. C. Julius Caesar, a man of outstanding knowledge of military science, fought many battles. (ablative of description, objective genitive)
15. The soldiers fled from the field of Pharsalus because of their fear. (ablative of cause)

b. *Word Study XVII* (pages 122–123): This activity continues the focus on the development of Latin into the Romance languages that was begun in Word Study XIV (found on page 100 of this handbook). The first half is also a useful review of several important Latin suffixes, while the second half serves as a culmination of the various Word Study sections in this book. It provides an excellent opportunity for teachers to explore with students how Latin words changed as they came into Romance. If students in the class are studying French, Spanish, or Italian, they can pronounce the words and the **sententiae** correctly for the group. Otherwise, teachers should check with their colleagues in modern languages to make sure they are using correct pronunciation.

Answers:

Exercise 1

cīvitās, city ("state" or "citizenship" in classical Latin)

glōriōsus, glorious

lībertās, freedom

imperātor, emperor

sevērā mente, with a severe mind (Latin), severely (Romance)

ambitiōsus, ambitious

senātor, senator

pestilentia, plague

līberā mente, with a free mind (Latin), freely (Romance)

positiō, placement, position

locātiō, locātiōnis, leasing, rental (the Latin word is connected with **locus** and **locō** (1), and literally means "placement," but even among the Romans it soon acquired the meaning of "lease," and this is its meaning in Romance)

ignōrantia, ignorance

Exercise 2

1. **Ō Lībertās, Ō Lībertās, quot crīmina committuntur (or commissa sunt) in tuō nōmine!** (For the Romans, the sense of **crīmen** was more properly a charge or accusation, rather than "crime," which was rendered by a word such as **scelus** or **facinus**.)

2. **Nōn omnis flōs facit bonum odōrem.**

3. **Rēx novus, lēx nova.**

Bibliography

Note that the references have usually been restricted to books that are currently in print. Many other resources can be found in libraries. Asterisks in the list below mark books regarded as highly recommended for the school library. Double asterisks mark books that should be available as basic resources in the Latin classroom. The lists below contain those books and articles referred to in this handbook.

I. RESOURCES AVAILABLE FROM THE AMERICAN CLASSICAL LEAGUE TEACHING MATERIALS AND RESOURCE CENTER

"A Debate for the Cicero Class" (Mimeo packet 1, #101).

"A List of Consuls from 77 B.C. to 43 B.C. and Some Important Events in Each Consulship" (Mimeo packet 6, #657).

"A Meeting of the Senate" (Mimeo packet 6, #109).

"Ancient Elections and Politics" (Item B316).

"A Short Account of Roman Provincial Administration in the Age of Augustus" (Mimeo packet 6, #414).

"A Simple Account of Legal Procedure in a Roman Court" (Mimeo packet 6, #82).

Asterix in Latin (7 different stories) (Item B709).

"Caesar in the Curriculum—Some New Approaches" (Item B12).

"Cicero vs. Catiline" (Cassette tape T2202).

"Classics of Latin Poetry and Prose" (Cassette tape T2).

"Directions for Making a Costume of a Roman Legionary" (Mimeo packets 4 and 6, #434).

"Escape from Pompeii" by Paul Tatarsky (Item W301). A computer game; demo disk available.

"Exitium Caesaris" (Mimeo packets 1 and 4, #231).

"Fifteen Anecdotes about Caesar" (Mimeo packet 1, #229).

"Government in Rome in the Time of Cicero: A Summary" (Mimeo packets 1 and 6, #1).

How We Know about Antiquity, by William J. King (Item B403).

"Oro Vos Faciatis . . . : An 'Election Unit' " (Item B11).

"Parallel Chronological Tables for the Lives of Caesar, Cicero, and Pompey" (Mimeo packets 1 and 6, #652).

"Pompeian Graffiti" by Philip R. Kirkpatrick (Item B717). New England Classical Newsletter Publications, 1980. 16 pp., paper.

Pompeii 2000 Years Ago by A. C. Carpiceci (Item B426). A book imported from Italy; many color photos, plans, reconstructions, etc.

"Roman Coins for the Latin Class" (Mimeo packets 3, 6, and 7, #744).

"Stories about Caesar: Translations from Classical Authors" (Mimeo packet 1, #5).

Timecharts of Roman History (Item P30)

Victims of Vesuvius by Elizabeth Heimbach (Item B427). A book with emphasis on daily life in the towns; makes use of Latin terminology and provides inscriptions, graffiti, etc. in Latin and in English. An accompanying videotape is available.

II. BOOKS AND ARTICLES REFERRED TO IN THE TEACHER'S HANDBOOK

A History of Private Life, Vol. I: From Pagan Rome to Byzantium, edited by Paul Veyne. Harvard University Press, Cambridge, Massachusetts, 1987. 670 pp., illustrated. Although sometimes given to overly broad generalizations, this new book contains much useful material about Roman life that is not readily available elsewhere.

*A History of Rome to A.D. 565, by William G. Sinnigen and Arthur E. R. Boak. Macmillan, New York, 1977 (6th ed.). xviii + 557 pp., maps, illustrations. One of the standard narrative histories of Rome, for teachers or mature students.

Arcana Mundi: Magic and the Occult in the Greek and Roman Words, by Georg Luck. Johns Hopkins University Press, Baltimore, MD, 1985. 395 pp., paperback. Ancient texts (in translation) on all aspects of magic, with introductions and notes. Best general introduction to the subject.

"A Selected Bibliography of Recent Work on C. Julius Caesar," by J. C. Douglas Marshall, New England Classical Newsletter, Volume XVI, Number 3, February (1989), pp. 11–14. An annotated discussion of recent scholarship on Caesar (general works, Caesar and Gaul, and Caesar the Author) suitable for secondary school students.

**"And Never Say No—Politics as Usual in Ancient Rome," by Lionel Casson, Smithsonian magazine, Volume 15, Number 7, October (1984), pp. 130–138. An anecdotal and amusing piece comparing ancient and modern politics, for student and teacher.

*Atlas of the Roman World, by Tim Cornell and John Matthews. Facts on File Publications, New York, 1986. 240 pp., illustrated. The best available topographical and geographical atlas of the Roman world, organized chronologically. Includes a gazeteer.

Art and the Romans, by Stephen Bertman. Coronado Press, Lawrence, Kansas, 1975. 83 pp., illustrated. An excellent general appreciation of the relationship of art to the character of imperial Rome. Includes Ara Pacis, Trajan's Column, Colosseum, Baths of Caracalla, and the Arches of Titus and Constantine.

As the Romans Did: A Source Book in Roman Social History, by Jo-Ann Shelton. Oxford University Press, New York, 1988. xx + 492 pp., cloth or paper. A new collection of sources for Roman social life, relatively little on politics and government.

New translations, wide coverage, aimed at contemporary students. Highly recommended.

Catapult Design, Construction, and Competition, by Bernard F. Barcio. Pompeiana, Inc., Indianapolis, IN, 1978. 111 pp., illustrated. Construction blueprints and photographs of the finished models in action.

Cities of Vesuvius by Michael Grant. Penguin Books, 1971. 240 pp., paper, many black-and-white illustrations.

**City: A Story of Roman Planning and Construction*, by David Macaulay. Houghton Mifflin Company, Boston, MA, 1974. 112 pp., many superb line drawings, cloth or paper. The layout and building of an imaginary town in northern Italy. Captivating illustrations, for all ages.

Claimed by Vesuvius, by Walter H. Marx. Longman, Inc., White Plains, NY, 1975; available also from the American Classical League, Miami University, Oxford, OH, 1979 (2nd ed.). 228 pp., illustrated, paperback. Graffiti from Pompeii, with notes and vocabulary; supplement on the "American Pompeii" on Martinique.

Five Roman Emperors, by Bernard W. Henderson. Barnes and Nobles, Inc., New York, 1969. Readable biographical studies of the Emperors Vespasian, Titus, Domitian, Nerva, and Trajan.

**Forum Romanum, by William M. Seaman and Carolyn Matzke. American Classical League, Miami University, Oxford, OH. 36 pp., illustrated, paperback. A concise, well-illustrated guide, containing descriptions of each of the principal structures in the Forum.

**From the Gracchi to Nero: A History of Rome, 188 B.C.–A.D. 68,* by H. H. Scullard. Barnes and Noble, Inc., New York, 1983 (5th ed.). 460 pp., paperback. The best general history of the period, with excellent notes. For the teacher and mature students.

Goddesses, Whores, Wives, and Slaves: Women in Classical Antiquity, by Sarah B. Pomeroy. Schocken, New York, 1976. 280 pp., illustrated, paperback. A widely-used book by a well-known scholar of women in antiquity, for teachers or mature students.

Greece and Rome: Builders of Our World. National Geographic Society, 1971. 448 pp., lavishly illustrated. An excellent general survey, with emphasis on Hannibal and Caesar.

**Greek and Roman Voting and Elections*, by E. S. Staveley. Cornell University Press, Ithaca, NY, 1972. 271 pp., illustrated. An excellent reference book for student and teacher, including a survey of the development of Roman political processes.

Herculaneum: Italy's Buried Treasure, by J. J. Deiss. Harper and Row, New York, 1985. 244 pp., paper.

**Illustrated Introduction to Latin Epigraphy,* by Arthur E. Gordon. University of California Press, Berkeley, 1983. xxv + 264 pp. and 100 plates, paperback. A beautifully organized survey of 100 representative examples of Roman inscriptions, including translations. Useful for student projects and as background for the teacher.

*Imperial Rome, by Moses Hadas. Time-Life Books, New York, 1972. Great Ages of Man series. 190 pp., illustrated, maps, charts, and quotations in translation. An excellent general introduction to Roman life and culture from its beginnings through early Christianity.

Life and Leisure in Ancient Rome, by J. P. V. D. Balsdon. Bodley Head, London, 1969. 463 pp. Good general introduction to daily life.

**Pictorial Dictionary of Ancient Rome,* by Ernest Nash. Hacker Art Books, New York, 1981 (2nd ed., reissued). Volume I, 544 pp., Volume II, 535 pp., both lavishly illustrated in black and white. An authoritative pictorial survey of the monuments and ruins of ancient Rome, arranged alphabetically. Extremely useful.

Pompeii by Ian Andrews. Cambridge Introduction to the History of Mankind series. Cambridge University Press, New York, 1978. 48 pp., paper, illustrated. Also available from ACL Materials Center (Item B408).

**Pompey and Caesar*, by Martin Forrest, et al. Cambridge University Press, New York, 1986. 72 pp., illustrated, paperback. A chronological account of Caesar and Pompey using Plutarch, Suetonius, and other sources in translation. Book III of the Cambridge School Classics Project.

**Roman Civilization*, by Napthali Lewis and Meyer Reinhold. "Harper Torchbooks" edition. Harper and Row, New York, 1966. *Sourcebook I: The Republic,* ix + 544 pp.; *Sourcebook II: The Empire,* viii + 625 pp., paperback. Passages from ancient authors and documents in English translation. An excellent reference work for the teacher and a useful book for student's reports and projects.

*Roman Coins, by C. H. V. Sutherland. G. P. Putnam's Sons, New York, 1974. 311 pp., illustrated. A brief history of Roman coinage, with many closeup photographs. Useful as background for the teacher.

Roman History from Coins, by Michael Grant. Cambridge University Press, New York, 1968. 96 pp., 32 plates, paperback. A study of the uses of imperial Roman coinage as historical evidence.

"Roman Politics in the 1st Century B.C.: A Basic Bibliography," by Mark Morford. *The Classical Outlook,* Volume 62, Number 4, May-June (1985), pp. 126–128. An annotated bibliography, including all standard works, as well as recent contributions, on the Roman Republic.

*Roman Religion, by Michael Massey. "Aspects of Roman Life" series. Longman, Inc., White Plains, NY, 1980. 48 pp., illustrated, paperback. A student's textbook for the subject, containing discussion of various topics, quotations from ancient sources, illustrations, study questions, and suggestions for projects. Suitable for junior high and high school.

Roman Society: A Social, Economic, and Cultural History, by Henry C. Boren. D. C. Heath and Company, 1977. 320 pp., paper. A text that emphases aspects other than political history, although much of the latter is necessarily included. Sound but less detailed and scholarly than *A History of Rome* or *From the Gracchi to Nero*; could be used by students.

Roman Towns by Peter Hodge. "Aspects of Roman Life" series. Longman, Inc., White Plains, NY, 1977. 48 pp., illustrated, paperback. Also available from ACL Materials Center (Item B417).

Roman Women: Their History and Habits, by J. P. V. D. Balsdon. Harper and Row, New York, 1983 (reprint of 1962 edition). 354 pp., paper. One of the standard books on the topic, although now slightly dated.

*Rome and Environs, by Alta Macadam. Rand McNally and Company, Chicago, 1979. The Blue Guide series. 402 pp., maps and plans, paperback. Detailed historical background on the ancient, medieval, and Renaissance monuments of Rome, including some guidebook information. Very useful for the teacher planning a trip to Rome.

*Rome and Her Empire, by Barry Cunliffe. McGraw Hill Book Company, New York, 1978. 322 pp., gorgeously illustrated. A thematic study of the development of Rome, with charts, maps, plans, and many unusual photographs, for student and teacher.

**Rome: Its People, Life, and Customs, by Ugo Enrico Paoli, translated by R. D. Macnaghten. Longman, Inc., White Plains, NY., 1983. xii + 336 pp., illustrated, paperback. Excellent, detailed, well-documented accounts of most major aspects of Roman culture. A basic background book for students and teachers for use in conjunction with ECCE ROMANI.

Scribes and Scholars: A Guide to the Transmission of Greek and Latin Literature, by L. D. Reynolds and N. G. Wilson. Oxford University Press, 1974 (second edition). 275 pp., illustrated, paperback. An excellent introduction for teachers who are interested in knowing more about how ancient works have come down to us. Includes information on book publishing in antiquity.

Selections from Cicero Read in Classical Latin, by Robert P. Sonkowsky. "The Living Voice of Greek and Latin Literature" series. Guilford, CT: Jeffrey Norton Publishers, 1984. Two cassettes + booklet with texts in Latin and English. Includes a wide variety of selections, both well-known (*In Catilinam I, Pro Archia*) and lesser-known (oratorical works, fragments of Cicero's poetry); note particularly the inclusion of the end of section 9, and sections 10 and 11, of the *Pro Milone* (section 10 appears in Chapter 58). Sonkowsky has carefully

studied the issues involved in reconstructing ancient pronunciation and has also had much practical experience in giving recitations. Very highly recommended!

Social Conflicts in the Roman Republic, by Peter A. Brunt. W. W. Norton, New York, 1971. 164 pp. Useful background for Catiline, Clodius, etc.

Southern Italy: An Archaeological Guide by Margaret Guido. Noyes Publishing, Park Ridge, New Jersey, 1973. Illustrated. Designed for those who will be visiting the sites, but useful in other situations as well; a standard work.

**The Ancient Romans, by Chester G. Starr. Oxford University Press, New York, 1972. 256 pp., generous photographs, maps, charts, and source readings. The best comprehensive treatment of the high points of Roman history and culture for the student.

The Architecture of the Roman Empire: An Introductory Study, by William L. MacDonald. Yale University Press, New Haven, CT, 1982. 225 pp., illustrated. Discussions of the palaces of Nero and Domitian, Trajan's markets, the Pantheon, and architects, materials, and styles.

The Art of Greece and Rome, by Susan Woodford. "Cambridge Introduction to the History of Art" series. Cambridge University Press, 1982. 122 pp., paperback, well illustrated. An excellent book for the teacher who does not have an extensive background in art history but wants to approach the subject.

**The Classical Companion, by Charles F. Baker and Rosalie Baker. Cobblestone Publishing, Inc., Peterborough, NH, 1988. 160 pp., copiously illustrated, puzzle keys, paperback. Excellent anthology of background essays, sources in translation, and project ideas on ancient Greece and Rome.

"The Great Gatsby and Trimalchio," by Paul L. MacKendrick. *The Classical Journal*, Volume 45, Number 7, April (1950), pp. 307–314. A study of the many parallels (some of them deliberate) between F. Scott Fitzgerald's novel and the *Cena Trimalchionis*.

The Idea of Rome from Antiquity to the Renaissance, ed. by David Thompson. University of New Mexico Press, Albuquerque, NM, 1971. xviii + 211 pp., paperback. A collection of thirty–eight source readings, from Polybius to Machiavelli, describing what Rome has meant to the history of the world.

The Letters of Pliny: A Historical and Social Commentary, by A. N. Sherwin-White. Oxford University Press, New York, 1966. 824 pp. The definitive scholarly commentary on Pliny's letters.

Themes in Greek and Roman Epitaphs, by Richmond Lattimore. University of Illinois Press, Urbana, IL, 1962. 354 pp., paperback. Epitaphs, grouped by theme and discussed; translations of the Greek (but not the Latin) texts are provided.

The Military Institutions of the Romans, a translation of Flavius Renatus Vegetius, by John Clark, edited by Thomas Phillips. Greenwood Publishers, 1985. viii + 114 pp. A translation of the fourth century A.D. treatise on Roman military science, containing much anecdotal information. For student and teacher.

*The Mute Stones Speak: The Story of Archaeology in Italy, by Paul MacKendrick, St. Martin's Press, New York, 1960. 369 pp., illustrated, paperback available. A history of Roman archaeology, covering the prehistoric period through the Christian era, with excellent chapters on the imperial structures. The classic in the field and suitable for the general reader.

**The Oxford Classical Dictionary, ed. by N. G. L. Hammond and H. H. Scullard. Oxford University Press, New York, 1970 (2nd ed.). xxii + 1176 pp. Detailed, scholarly background material for the teacher; an excellent place to find quick information on a vast variety of topics.

*The Oxford History of the Classical World, by John Boardman, et al. Oxford University Press, New York, 1987. 882 pp., illustrated, maps, plans. A collection of thirty–one essays on various aspects of Greece and Rome, with each chapter containing annotated suggestions for further reading that reflects current scholarship.

The Power of Images in the Age of Augustus, by Paul Zanker. University of Michigan Press, 1988. Clothbound. A new book for teachers who want to look more closely at Augustus and how he created the image of himself that he wanted; Zanker uses art, buildings, rituals, ceremonies, and passages from poetry as evidence.

*The Roman Army, by Peter Hodge. "Aspects of Roman Life" series. Longman, Inc., White Plains, NY, 1984. 32 pp., illustrated with artist's conceptions. An appreciation of the subject for younger students, following the text of Vegetius.

The Roman Emperors: A Biographical Guide to the Rulers of Imperial Rome, 31 B.C.–476 A.D., by Michael Grant. Scribner, New York, 1985. 367 pp., illustrated. Biographies of all the emperors with examples of their coin portraits.

The Roman Engineers by L. A. and J. A. Hamey. Cambridge University Press, New York, 1981. 48 pp., illustrated, paperback. Also available from ACL Materials Center (item B411).

*The Romans and Their Empire, by Trevor Cairns. Cambridge University Press, Lerner Publications Company, Minneapolis, MN, 1974. 99 pp., illustrated with maps and drawings. Excellent introduction to Roman history for younger students. Also available from ACL Materials Center (item B410).

*The Romans and Their Gods in the Age of Augustus, by Roger M. Ogilvie. W. W. Norton & Co., New York, 1970. 135 pp., maps, illustrations. A topical study of Roman religion, from 80 B.C. to A.D. 69, including the gods, sacrifice, worship, and ritual.

The 'Satyricon' of Petronius: A Literary Study, by J. P. Sullivan. Indiana University Press, Bloomington, IN, 1968. Best general introduction to the *Satyricon* as a whole.

Trials in the Late Republic, 149 B.C.–50 B.C., by Michael C. Alexander. University of Toronto Press, Toronto, 1989. Clothbound, 224 pp. Synopses of and interesting information about 391 civil and criminal trials of the last century of the Republic. Useful for the teacher and for research by more able students.

Vox Latina by W. Sidney Allen. Cambridge University Press, New York, 1978 (2nd ed.). xiv + 132 pp., cloth or paper. The standard scholarly work on pronunciation of classical Latin.

Women in Greece and Rome, by Michael Massey. Cambridge Introduction to World History Series. Cambridge University Press, New York, 1986. Accessible to students; includes primary sources in translation. Also available from the ACL Teaching Materials Center (Item B431).

*Warfare in the Classical World, by John Warry. St. Martin's Press, New York, 1980. 224 pp., richly illustrated, including maps and battle plans. A presentation of the historical development of all aspects of Greek and Roman military science, for student and teacher.

III. ANCIENT AND MODERN PRIMARY SOURCES

Caesar, The Civil War, translated with an introduction by Jane F. Mitchell, Penguin Books, Baltimore, MD, 1967. 360 pp., paperback.

Fall of the Roman Republic: Six Lives of Plutarch (Marius, Sulla, Crassus, Pompey, Caesar, and Cicero), translated by Rex Warner. Penguin Books, Baltimore, MD, 1964. 320 pp., paperback.

Lives of the Later Caesars, by Anthony Birley. Penguin Books, New York, 1976. 336 pp., chronological tables, maps, family trees, paperback. A translation of the *Historia Augusta*, with lives of Nerva and Trajan newly compiled from ancient sources.

Petronius: The Satyricon and the Fragments, translated by J. P. Sullivan. Penguin Books, Baltimore, MD, 1965. 204 pp., paperback.

Res Gestae Divi Augusti: The Achievements of the Divine Augustus, by P. A. Brunt and J. M. Moore. Oxford University Press, New York, 1973. 90 pp., paperback. The best text edition, with translation, notes, and commentary.

Roman Voices: Everyday Latin in Ancient Rome, by Carol Clemeau Esler. Available from *NECN* Publications, 71 Sand Hill Rd., Amherst, MA 01002. 1982,

161 pp., paperback. *Teacher's Guide to Roman Voices*, by Carol Clemeau Esler. Available as above. 1984, 62 pp., paperback. A translation key for the book above; also contains additional non-literary and literary Latin texts.

Selected Political Speeches of Cicero, by Michael Grant. Penguin Books, New York, 1979. xxxii + 335 pp., paperback. Translations of seven important political speeches of Cicero, including the *Pro Milone* and the Catilinarians.

Suetonius, The Twelve Caesars, translated by Robert Graves. Penguin Books, New York, 1978. 315 pp., includes coin portraits, paperback.

The Letters of Pliny the Younger, translated with an introduction by Betty Radice. Penguin Books, Baltimore, MD, 1963. 319 pp., paperback.

The Satyricon of Petronius, translated by William Arrowsmith. Mentor, New American Library, New York, 1959. 192 pp., paperback.

Ancient authors quoted in the teacher's handbook (except for the Tacitus passages on page 70) come from the translations of the Loeb Classical Library series, sometimes with adaptations. These translations are published with permission of Harvard University Press (all rights reserved). The following list of authors and works in the Loeb Classical Library series is provided for reference (each volume contains the Latin text and facing translation, plus introduction and notes). The list is alphabetical by name of author.

Caesar, *Civil Wars*, tr. A. G. Peskett
Cicero, *Letters to Atticus*, tr. E. O. Winstedt
Cicero, *Letters to His Friends*, tr. W. Glynn Williams, et al.
Cicero, *Pro Milone*, et al., tr. N. H. Watts
Horace, *Odes and Epodes*, tr. C. E. Bennett
Lucan, *De bello civili (Pharsalia)*, tr. J. D. Duff
Petronius, *The Satyricon*, tr. Michael Heseltine
Pliny, *Letters and Panegyricus*, tr. Betty Radice
Plutarch, *The Parallel Lives* (Greek), tr. B. Perrin
Scriptores Historiae Augustae, tr. D. Magie
Suetonius, *Lives of the Twelve Caesars*, tr. J. D. Rolfe
Tacitus, *Agricola, Germania, Dialogus*, tr. M. Hutton, R. M. Ogilvie, E. H. Warmington, Sir W. Peterson, and M. Winterbottom
Tacitus, *Histories and Annals*, tr. C. H. Moore and J. Jackson
Velleius Paterculus and *Res gestae divi Augusti*, tr. F. W. Shipley

For general books on ancient Rome and its culture and civilization, on word study and on the Latin language, see the bibliographies in the teacher's handbooks for Books 1 through 4 in the series. Information will also be found there on audiovisual resources, national Latin examinations, and classical associations.

Latin Vocabularies
(Including Principal Parts of Verbs)

Only those words with asterisks or bullets are given; it is assumed students are being held responsible for these words, and that the teacher will therefore want to make particular use of them in constructing drills or tests. For the significance of asterisks and bullets, see page 5 of this handbook. There is no separate list of principal parts (as in the second, third, and fourth teacher's handbooks) because the principal parts of all the verbs listed below are given in the facing vocabulary list when the verb is first introduced.

Part I, Chapters 54 to 56

NOUNS

54C	aciēs
54C	aetās
54A	carcer
54C	castra
55A	cīvitās
54D	cōnsuētūdō
54A	cōnsul
54C	cōnsulāris
54B	cōnsulātus
54C	cōpia
54C	cornū
54B	dux
54C	eques
54B	exercitus
55B	famēs
54B	fortūna
54A	genus
54D	honor
55B	imperium
54A	ingenium
56A	initium
54B	iniūria
55B	iūdex
54A	legiō
54D	lībertās
56B	mūnus
54D	nepōs
54A	obses
54C	orbis
54C	Oriēns
54A	patria
54C	pedes
54D	praecipuus
56A	prīncipātus
54A	proelium
54D	rēs pūblica
56B	rīpa
54B	senātus
56B	signum
54A	socius

54D	testāmentum
55B	triumphus

ADJECTIVES

54A	clārus
54A	immānis
55B	iūstus
54A	nōnus
56A	ūllus
54B	ūniversus
54B	vacuus
55B	venēnum
54D	voluntās

VERBS

55A	āmittō
55B	admittō
56A	aequō
54A	aggredior
54A	appellō
56B	caedō
55A	commoveō
54D	compōnō
54A	condō
54A	dēcernō
54B	dēferō
54B	dīmicō
54C	dīripiō
55A	dīvidō
54B	ēvādō
56A	flōreō
54A	imperō
54A	interficiō
54C	intueor
54D	iūdicō
54B	mūtō
56A	obtineō
54D	potior
54D	praestō
54A	prōcēdō
55B	regnō
54B	succēdō
55A	suscipiō
54A	vincō

55A	vindicō

PREPOSITIONS

54B	apud
54B	contrā
54B	praeter

MISCELLANEOUS

54C	adhūc
54D	amplius
55A	bellum gerere
54A	bellum īnferre
54D	ergō
54A	ferē
54B	hinc
56A	penitus
54b	quia
54C	quīngentī
54C	quondam
56B	scīlicet
56B	sīcut
54B	tribus (from trēs)
54A	usque ad

Part II, Chapters 57 to 58

NOUNS

57A	agmen
58E	bona
58B	caedēs
57A	comes
58B	comitātus
58D	crīmen
57A	eques
58E	exsilium
58A	facinus
57A	familiāris
58A	fundus
58A	furor
57C	invidia
58E	iūdex
57A	mōs
57A	mūnicipium

57A	plēbs
57B	pugna
58C	tēlum
57B	tumultus
57C	vulgus

ADJECTIVES

58C	adversus
57C	īdem
57A	posterus
58D	praesēns
58D	quisque
58C	ūndecimus

VERBS

58C	adorior
57C	augeō
58C	caedō
57B	cōnficiō
58A	collocō
57B	dēferō
58A	dēsīderō
58C	dēsiliō
57C	flagrō
58E	ignōrō
58D	imperō
58C	incipiō
58C	interficiō
57C	iungō
57B	lateō
58B	mūtō
58A	obeō
57B	orior
57C	ostendō
57C	perferō
58D	prohibeō
57B	revertor
57C	studeō
57B	tollō
57A	vehō

MISCELLANEOUS

57B	graviter
57C	item

58B	paulīsper
58A	prīdiē
58B	quoad

Part III, Chapters 59 to 61

NOUNS

60B	aciēs
61B	aestus
59A	anima
61C	argentum
61A	caedēs
61C	comitātus
60A	cornū
60B	cursus
59D	dignitās
60B	eques
60B	equitātus
59A	famēs
61C	fīdūcia
59D	grātia
61C	īnsigne
60A	imperātor
61B	imperium
60B	impetus
61A	initium
60B	lātus
61B	merīdiēs
59C	ops
60B	ōrdō
59B	potestās
60C	praesidium
59C	salūs
60B	spatium
61A	statiō
59C	studium
61B	vāllum
59C	virtūs
61C	voluptās

ADJECTIVES

59A	āmēns
59C	commūnis
60A	dexter
60C	inermis
60B	īnfestus
61A	integer
61C	nōnnūllī
61B	plērīque
59C	pristinus
61A	recēns
61A	reliquus
60B	sinister
60A	superior

VERBS

60C	adorior
59C	afflīgo
60B	cēdō
59C	cēnseō
61A	circumeō
59D	cōnfīdō
61A	cōnfirmō
60B	cōnsistō
60A	cohortor
61A	collocō
60B	concurrō
61C	conquīrō
61C	contendō
60B	dēsum
59D	dubitō
60B	excipiō
61B	exīstimō
60B	explicō
61A	fallō
59B	hortor
59D	ignōscō
60B	imperō
60C	īnstituō
60B	īnstō
59D	mereor
61C	nancīscor
61B	oppugnō
61A	orior
61B	pareō
61A	pellō
59B	persequor
61B	pertineō
60B	praecipiō
60A	praedicō
59D	praemittō
60A	prīvō
61C	prōdō
61A	prōnūntiō
59D	properō
59A	prōsum
61C	queror
60A	recuperō
61B	relinquō
60B	renovō
60B	stringō
61A	succēdō
60C	summoveō
60A	supersum
61A	sustineō
61A	tueor
59D	ūtor
59A	valeō
61C	versor

PREPOSITIONS

| 59C | prō |

MISCELLANEOUS

60A	circiter
59B	equidem
59D	etsī
59D	grātiās agere
59B	iste
61B	magis
59C	magnopere
60B	paulātim
60C	prōtinus
61A	quīn
59A	sīn
60B	sponte

Part IV, Chapters 62 to 64

NOUNS

62C	āra
62B	aedēs
63B	aetās
62B	auctōritās
64A	carmen
64B	causa
62B	collēga
62B	cōnsultum
64A	crīmen
62A	facinus
62A	factiō
62C	fīnēs
64A	fūrtum
62C	gēns
62D	hērēs
62A	imperium (= "right to command")
63B	imperium (= "empire")
64A	index
64A	latrōcinium
62B	magistrātus
64A	nūmen
62D	opus
62A	ōrdō
63A	pietās
62B	potestās
62A	propraetor
62C	reditus
62C	sacerdōs
62A	sententia
64A	supplicium
64B	venia

ADJECTIVES

62C	externus
62C	fīnitimus
62D	grandis
63A	hilaris
64B	manifestus
63A	sānctus
62A	uterque

VERBS

62D	ampliō
62B	appellō
62C	augeō
62C	cēnseō
62A	comparō
64B	conquīrō
62D	cōnsūmō
62A	creō
63B	dēferō
64A	dēsinō
63B	diffundō
62A	expellō
62B	exstinguō
64A	fallō
64A	fateor
62B	fīgō
62C	ignōscō
62D	immittō
64B	impetrō
63B	laedō
63B	obeō
63A	optō
62C	parcō
62C	pariō
62B	potior
62B	praestō
62D	reficiō
63A	succēdō
63A	suscipiō
62B	testor
62A	ulcīscor

PREPOSITIONS

| 62D | praeter |

MISCELLANEOUS

62C	bellum gerere
62A	bellum īnferre
63B	meritō
63B	nōn aliter
62C	omnīnō
62C	orbis terrārum
64B	quamvīs
62A	sponte suā
62C	tūtō
63B	usque ad

Part V, Chapters 65 to 67

NOUNS

67C	anima
67C	cāsus
67A	classis
66A	cōnsultum
67A	cursus
67A	discrīmen
66A	febris
67B	fuga
66B	gaudium
67B	lapis
67B	lītus
67D	lūmen
66A	metus
67A	mōtus
66A	mūnus
66B	officium
67A	speciēs
67C	tēctum
67C	tenebrae
67B	vādum
66A	valētūdō

ADJECTIVES

67C	agrestis
66B	aliquis
67B	ambustus
67D	angustus
67C	crēber
66A	dignus
67A	ērudītus
67A	frequēns
66B	illūstris
67C	lātus
67A	nōnus
67A	rēctus
67A	septimus
67B	trepidāns
67A	ūllus
65A	vīvus

VERBS

66B	āmittō
67B	accēdō
67D	adspiciō
66B	afflīgō
67A	appāreō
66B	cernō
66B	colō
67B	complector
67D	concidō
67B	crēscō
66B	dīligō
67A	ēripiō
65D	expōnō
67A	exprimō
67B	flectō
67D	hauriō
67B	iuvō
67B	lavō
67C	negō
65D	nōscō
65A	oblīvīscor
67A	orior
67A	properō
66B	queror
67A	regō
67D	solvō
66B	supersum
67C	surgō
67C	vagor
66B	vertō

PREPOSITIONS

65B	super

MISCELLANEOUS

67A	adeō
67B	aequē
66A	an
66B	dēnique
65A	diūtius
65D	interim
65D	negōtium agere
67A	procul
67A	ūnā

Appendix:
Supplementary Materials

The materials in this Appendix may be reproduced for classroom use by teachers who have adopted *From Republic to Empire*. For general discussion of these materials and suggestions for their use, see "Supplementary Materials," page 6; teaching suggestions specific to individual readings or exercises, as well as translations/answer keys, will be found under the heading "Supplementary Materials" at the end of the corresponding chapter section of this handbook (e.g., for information about the reading *A Casualty of War*, see the notes for Chapter 61, pages 42–43).

List of Materials

Exercises for the Introduction (Ch. 54) 91

Political Jokes about Caesar (Ch. 54) 92

Synopsis Blank (Ch. 54/55) 93

Irregular Third Principal Parts (Ch. 55) 94

Practice with Subjunctive Clauses (Ch. 56) 95

Practice with Gerunds (Ch. 57) 96

Politics in the Late Republic (Ch. 57) 97

Practice with Gerunds and Gerundives (Ch. 58) 98

Oratory in Republican Politics (Ch. 58) 99

Word Study XIV (Ch. 59) 100

Genitive and Dative with Special Verbs (60 or 61) 101

Practice with Fear Clauses and Impersonals (Ch. 61) 104

The Deaths of Caesar and Cicero (Ch. 61) 105

A Casualty of War (Ch. 61 or 62) 106

Comparison of Sculptures (Ch. 62) 107

Credit Where Credit is Due (Ch. 62 or 63) 109

Geography Ancient and Modern (Ch. 63) 110

Two Inscriptions from Britain (Ch. 63) 111

Epitaph of a Young Christian Boy (Ch. 64) 112

Word Study XV (Ch. 64) 113

Roman Names (Ch. 65) 115

Word Study XVI (Ch. 65) 117

Practice with Conditionals (Ch. 66) 118

Summary of Case Usages (65 or 66) 120

Word Study XVII (Ch. 68) 122

Exercises for the Introduction

(With Chapter 54)

Exercise 1

On a separate sheet of paper, answer the following questions based on the introduction to Part I:

1. What was the sequence of offices that made up the **cursus honōrum**? How long was each term of office? What were the duties of each office?
2. List as many events as you can (in chronological order) that show that the Roman government was not stable during the first century B.C.
3. Why was the government unstable during this period? Can you think of any similar situations in our own time?
4. How did Augustus try to solve this instability?
5. Historians often identify three periods of Roman history—the Monarchy, the Republic, and the Empire. Give dates for each and briefly describe the form of government in each period.

Exercise 2

By referring to the time line on page 6, answer the following questions:

1. How old was Vergil when Caesar crossed the Rubicon?_____

2. How many years did the emperor Augustus live?_____

3. Who was older, Cicero or Pompey?_____

4. How old was Octavian when Caesar was assassinated?_____

5. How old was Pliny when Vesuvius erupted and destroyed Pompeii?_____

6. What emperor was born in Cicero's consulship?_____

7. By how many years did Cicero outlive Caesar?_____

8. What famous poet was born the year Cicero died?_____

9. When was Petronius born?_____

10. Who was older, Pliny or Martial? By how many years?_____

11. How old was Ovid at the time of the battle of Actium?_____

12. How old was Cicero at the time of Catiline's conspiracy?_____

Political Jokes about Caesar

(With Chapter 54)

The Romans, like many other people, frequently made fun of their politicians, either because they resented things the politicians had done or because politicians were generally easy targets for jokes. The Roman historian Suetonius, who wrote biographies of the first twelve Caesars (Julius Caesar to Domitian) preserved the following political jokes. Translate them.

1. During his consulship in 59 B.C., Caesar became notorious for his high-handed disregard of his colleague Bibulus (and Bibulus later opposed Caesar's attempts to become sole ruler of Rome; cf. Reading 54B). Remember that the standard way of designating a year was by the names of its consuls; 59 should have been **C. Iūliō Caesare et M. Calpurniō Bibulō cōnsulibus** (ablative absolute), but contemporaries jokingly referred to it as "the consulship of Julius and Caesar." An anonymous humorist expressed the idea thus:

   > Nōn Bibulō quiddam nūper sed Caesare factum est:
   > nam Bibulō fierī cōnsule nīl meminī.

   Nōn . . . quiddam: "not a thing"
   Bibulō . . . Caesare: supply **cōnsule** with each name
   meminī, I remember

2. Caesar's policy of admitting large numbers of provincials to the Roman Senate was unpopular:

   > Gallōs Caesar in triumphum dūcit — īdem in Cūriam;
   > Gallī brācās dēposuērunt, lātum clāvum sūmpsērunt.

   īdem, also, likewise
   brācae, -ārum (*f pl*), trousers (regarded by Romans as outlandish and effeminate)
   lātum clāvum, the "broad (purple) stripe" of the senatorial toga

3. A mock public "announcement" on the same subject:

   > Bonum factum: nē quis senātōrī novō Cūriam mōnstrāre velit!

   factum, -ī (*n*), deed, action
       Bonum factum: a phrase used at the beginning of official decrees
   Nē quis . . . mōnstrāre velit: "Let no one point out . . . !"

4. The following is directed against Caesar's arrogant behavior during his dictatorship:

   > Brūtus, quia rēgēs ēiēcit, cōnsul prīmus factus est;
   > Hic, quia cōnsulēs ēiēcit, rēx postrēmō factus est.

   Brūtus: the legendary first consul of Rome, who drove out the
   Etruscan kings
   ēiēcit: from ē + iacere
   Hic: = Caesar

Synopsis Blank

Principal parts: _____, _____, _____, _____.

	ACTIVE	PASSIVE
Indicative		
Present	_____	_____
Imperfect	_____	_____
Future	_____	_____
Perfect	_____	_____
Pluperfect	_____	_____
Future Perf.	_____	_____
Subjunctive		
Present	_____	_____
Imperfect	_____	_____
Perfect	_____	_____
Pluperfect	_____	_____
Participles		
Present	_____	
Perfect		_____
Future	_____	_____
Infinitives		
Present	_____	_____
Perfect	_____	_____
Future	_____	

Irregular Third Principal Parts

(With Chapter 54 or 55)

The third principal part of many Latin verbs, especially those in the 3rd conjugation (occasionally in the 2nd and 4th), looks quite different from the first principal part. There is more logic behind these irregular forms, however, than there may appear to be. Most of them can be accounted for in one of three ways:

1. *Lengthening* of the present-stem vowel (sometimes with a change in the vowel itself), e.g.: **fugiō/fūgī, capiō/cēpī**

2. *Reduplication* of the present-stem vowel and the preceding consonant (sometimes with present-stem *a* changing to *e* or *i* in the perfect), e.g.: **currō/cucurrī, cadō/cecidī**

3. *Sigmatic* formations (so called from *sigma*, the name of the Greek letter *s*); this kind of perfect is formed by adding *s* to the present stem, sometimes with assimilation of the final consonant of the present stem, e.g.: **gerō/(gersī) gessī, lūdō/(ludsī) lūsī**; sometimes with respelling of the consonant clusters *-cs-* and *-gs-* as *-x-*, e.g.: **dīcō/(dīcsī) dīxī, augeō/(augsī) auxī**

Give the third principal part of each of the following verbs, and indicate whether it is lengthened, reduplicative, or sigmatic:

1. poscō: _____

2. dūcō: _____

3. faciō: _____

4. discēdō: _____

5. claudō: _____

6. dō: _____

7. legō: _____

8. scrībō: _____

9. veniō: _____

10. iungō: _____

11. sedeō: _____

12. stringō: _____

13. parcō: _____

14. adiuvō: _____

15. praestō: _____

Practice with Subjunctive Clauses

(With Chapter 56)

Circle the correct form to complete each sentence, following the rules for sequence of tenses (cf. pages 38–39 of the student's book). Then translate and tell what use of the subjunctive is found in each sentence (a list of subjunctive uses is found on page 44 of the student's book).

1. Eutropius haec scrīpsit ut Augustum (laudāret, laudāre, laudet).

   _____

2. Cum Octāviānus Aegyptō potītūrus (esset, sit, est, erat), Cleopatra sē interfēcit.

   _____

3. Proeliō ad Actium factō, Antōnius intellēxit cūr Octāviānus sē (vīcerat, vīcerit, vīcisset).

   _____

4. Nāvēs Antōniī Cleopatraeque tam magnae erant ut nōn facile gubernārī (possent, possint, poterant, possunt).

   _____

5. Antōnius ad Actium victus ōrat mīlitēs nē sē (dēsererent, dēserant, dēserent).

   _____

6. Antōnius et Octāviānus inter sē pugnāvērunt ut cōnstituerent quis orbem terrārum rēgnātūrus (sit, esset).

   _____

7. Cum Aegyptus imperiō Rōmānō (adiecta esset, adiecta sit, adiecta erat), Octāviānus Rōmam rediit.

   _____

8. Augustus erat prīnceps tantae virtūtis ut Eutropius eum maximē (laudāret, laudet, laudāvit, laudābat).

   _____

9. Multī senātōrēs Octāviānum Antōniumque monent nē bellum cīvīle (commovēre, commovent, commoveant).

   _____

10. Omnēs discipulī sciēbant ubi Antōnius et Octāviānus inter se (pugnāvissent, pugnāverant, pugnāverint).

    _____

    gubernō (1), to steer, maneuver   **dēserō, dēserere** (3), to desert

Practice with Gerunds

(With Chapter 57)

Exercise 1

Form gerunds (accusative case) from the following verbs:

cōnspicere _____

monēre _____

collocāre _____

venīre _____

vehere _____

redīre _____

arripere _____

orīrī _____

cōnārī _____

pellere _____

Exercise 2

Read aloud and translate:

1. Milō Rōmā profectus est Lānuvium eundī causā.

   _____

2. Cicerō spērābat sē posse Milōnem adiuvāre dīcendō in Forō.

   _____

3. Cicerō ad Forum īvit ad loquendum.

   _____

4. Impetū in Milōnem factō, complūrēs servī adiuvandī grātiā ad raedam cucurrērunt.

   _____

5. Magister omnia explicandō discipulōs adiūvit.

   _____

6. Octāviānus erat cupidus imperandī.

   _____

7. Octāviānus et Antōnius in Graeciam ad pugnandum īvērunt.

   _____

Politics in the Late Republic

(With Chapter 57)

A candidate for political office, when canvassing for votes in the Forum, an activity called **ambitiō**, wore a toga of bright white rubbed with chalk (**toga candida**) as a symbol of his purity and fitness for office. The candidate was accompanied by a slave (**nōmenclātor**), who reminded him of voters' names, and by a crowd of partisans (**sectātōrēs**), mostly freedmen clients, whose task it was to secure votes through promises and even bribery.

In 64 B.C., Cicero's brother Quintus wrote a campaign handbook titled *On Being a Candidate for the Consulship*, to assist his elder brother's election bid for the consulship of 63. This political pamphlet lists some things for a candidate to consider during a campaign:

Take care to have followers at your heels daily, of every kind, class, and age; because from their number people can figure out how much power and support you are going to have at the polls.

You particularly need to use flattery. No matter how vicious and vile it is on the other days of a man's life, when he runs for office it is indispensable.

Getting votes among the rank and file requires calling everyone by his name. Make it clear you know people's names; practice, get better at it day to day. Nothing seems to me better for popularity and gaining favor.

If you make a promise, the matter is not fixed. It's for a future day, and it affects only a few people. But if you say no, you are sure to alienate people right away, and a lot of them.

But, of all the forces at work in determining the outcome of an election, it was usually the character of the candidate himself that was the most influential factor.

When Scipio Nasica was seeking the office of curule aedile and, in the custom of a campaigner, had firmly grasped the hand of a certain man worn leathery with farm work, to get a laugh he asked the man whether or not he usually walked on his hands. This comment, when heard by bystanders and passed around, was the source of Scipio's downfall; for all the country voters thought he was laughing at poverty.

—Valerius Maximus, VII.5.2

Virtūs, probitās, integritās in candidātō, nōn linguae volūbilitās, nōn ars, nōn scientia requīrī solet. *Moral courage, honesty, and integrity are usually sought in candidates, not a glib tongue, skill, or knowledge.* (Cicero, *Pro Plancio*, 62)

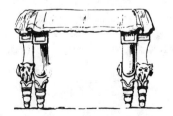

Practice with Gerunds and Gerundives

(With Chapter 58)

Select (if required), read aloud, and translate:

1. Lānuvium (ā Milōne, Milōnī, Milō) eundum erat.

   _____

2. Exiitne Rōmā Clōdius ad decuriōnēs Arīciae alloquendōs aut ad īnsidiās in Milōnem collocandās?

   _____

3. Mīlitēs in Forō (Pompeiō, ā Pompeiō, Pompeiī) positī sunt ad iūdicēs advocātōsque dēfendendōs.

   _____

4. Milō crēdēbat Clōdium vulnerātum sibi interficiendum esse.

   _____

5. Cicerō dīcit iūdicibus Milōnem līberandum esse; aliī autem adsunt Milōnis convincendī causā.

   _____

   _____

6. Asconius commentārium scrīpsit ad ōrātiōnem (explicandum, explicandam, explicandae); hōc commentāriō legendō, ōrātiōnem multō melius interpretārī possumus.

   _____

   _____

7. Milōnī Rōmā Massiliam statim exeundum erit.

   _____

8. Milō discēdet nē ab amīcīs Clōdiī interficiātur.

   _____

9. Cicerō dīxit servōs Milōnis Clōdium ad dominum vindicandum interfēcisse.

   _____

   advocātus, -ī (*m*), lawyer
   convincō, convincere (3), to convict (of a crime)
   interpretor (1), **interpretārī, interpretātus sum,** to interpret, understand
   Massilia, -ae (*f*), Massilia, the modern city of Marseilles, where Milo was exiled
   vindicō (1), to avenge, get revenge for

Oratory in Republican Politics

(With Chapter 58)

Skill in public speaking, or rhetoric, was a requirement for political success in Rome, for all public offices required speechmaking and the ability to persuade. By Cicero's time, a Roman youth who had completed literary and linguistic studies with **a grammaticus** would finish his education by studying with **a rhētor**, an instructor in public speaking who taught skills in debate and in advocating a particular course of action. The preparation of a speech included gathering of material and its proper arrangement, selection of appropriate language, memorization, and delivery. A good speech had a certain structure to it, including a beginning (**exōrdium**), designed to win the favorable attention of the audience; the body (consisting of **partītiō**, "outline"; **cōnfirmātiō**, "positive arguments"; and **refūtātiō**, "rebuttal"); and the conclusion (**perōrātiō**), designed to summarize the arguments and appeal to the jurors' emotions. In *De oratore*, Cicero wrote:

> Eloquence requires many things: a wide knowledge of very many subjects (verbal fluency without this being worthless and even ridiculous), a style, too, carefully formed not merely by selection, but by arrangement of words, and a thorough familiarity with all the feelings which nature has given to men, because the whole force and art of the orator must be put forth in allaying or exciting the emotions of the audience.

The imperial writer Tacitus reflects nostalgically on the "Golden Age" of Roman oratory during the final years of the Republic:

> For although the orators of today have also succeeded in obtaining all the influence that it would be proper to allow them under settled, peaceable, and prosperous political conditions, yet their predecessors in those days of unrest and unrestraint seemed to accomplish more when, in the general ferment and without the strong hand of a single ruler, a speaker's political wisdom was measured by his power of carrying conviction to the unstable populace. This was the source of the constant succession of measures put forward by the champions of the people's rights, of the harangues of state officials who spent the night on the speaker's platform, of the prosecutions of powerful defendants and hereditary feuds between families, of factions among the aristocracy and never-ending struggles between the Senate and the commons. All this tore the commonwealth in pieces, but it provided a sphere for the oratory of those days and heaped on it what one saw were vast rewards. The more influence a man could wield by his powers of speech, the more readily did he attain to high office, the farther did he, when in office, outstrip his colleagues, the more did he gain favor with the great, authority with the Senate, and name and fame with the common people. With them, moreover, it was a conviction that without eloquence it was impossible for anyone either to attain to a position of distinction and prominence within the community or to maintain it. And no wonder, when they were called upon to appear in public even when they would rather not; when it was not enough to move a brief resolution in the Senate unless one supported one's position with an able speech; when persons who had in some way or other incurred envy or else were charged with some specific offense had to put in an appearance in person; when, moreover, evidence in criminal trials had to be given not indirectly or by affidavit, but personally and by word of mouth.

—Dialogue on Oratory, XXXVII

Study carefully the photographs of statues of Roman orators on page 61 of the student's book.

> **Ō flexanima atque omnium rēgīna rērum Ōrātiō!** *O Eloquence who moves men's minds, queen of all things!* (**Marcus Pacuvius,** *Hermiona*)

Word Study XIV

(With Chapter 59)

Salutations

The salutations used by the Romans in letters reflected those used in conversation. Letters began with **S.V.B.E.** (**Sī valēs, bene est**) or **S.V.B.E.E.V.** (**Sī valēs, bene est; ego valeō**) and ended with **Valē** or **Avē**. **Avē** was often used as a morning salutation and **Valē** in the evening, whereas **Salvē** was used interchangeably. As Latin evolved into the Romance languages, however, greetings such as **Salvē** were replaced with other expressions, as shown in the chart below. For comparison, we have provided the Latin form of these Romance greetings, even though these phrases were not used as greetings in classical Latin.

	Good day!	*Good Evening!*	*Good Night!*	*Good-bye!*
Latin	**Bonus diēs!**	**Bonum sērum!**	**Bona nox!** (noct-)	**Ad deum!**
Italian	Buon giorno!	Buona sera!	Buona notte!	Addio!
French	Bonjour!	Bonsoir!	Bonne nuit!	Adieu!
Spanish	¡Buenos dias!	¡Buenas tardes!	¡Buenas noches!	¡Adios!

Although *jour* and *giorno* might not be obvious derivatives from **diēs**, they arrive through the intermediary Latin word **diūrnus, -a, -um**, which itself came into English as *journal* and *diary*. The Latin adjective **sērus, -a, -um**, adverb **sērō**, and noun **sērum, -ī**, all mean "late in the day," and it is easy to see the relevance of the Spanish *tardes*. The phrase **ad deum**, "to God," and its Romance derivatives may be compared to the English *Good-bye*, which is a contraction of the phrase *God be with you*, the word *good* being substituted for the word *God*.

Participles in the Romance Languages

In later Latin, the gerundive with the ablative singular ending came to be used as the equivalent of the present participle and, in fact, was adopted as such by Italian. Spanish preserved the function of the Latin gerundive and called it the *gerundio*. Compare the French present participle, which derives from the Latin present participle in **-nt-**, in the chart below.

Latin Gerundive (abl. sing.)	*Italian Pres. Part.*	*Spanish Gerundio*	*French Pres. Part.*
amandō	amando	amando	aimant
tenendō	tenendo	teniendo	tenant
vīvendō	vivendo	viviendo	vivant

Exercise

Construct the Latin gerundive equivalents of the following Italian and Spanish forms. The French is given for comparison.

Italian Pres. Part.	*Spanish Gerundio*	*Latin Gerundive (abl. sing.)*	*French Pres. Part.*
desiderando	desiendo	_____	désirant
facendo	haciendo	_____	faisant
preparando	preparando	_____	préparant
scrivendo	escribiendo	_____	écrivant
videndo	viendo	_____	voyant

Genitive and Dative
with Special Verbs

(With Chapter 60 or 61)

In addition to the verbs that take the ablative case (pages 84–85), there are also special verbs that take the genitive and dative cases.

1. *Genitive with Special Verbs*

There are some special verbs that take the *genitive case:*

meminī, meminisse (*irreg.*), to remember (this verb is found only in the perfect, pluperfect, and future perfect tenses; the perfect is translated as a present, the pluperfect as a perfect, and the future perfect as a simple future)

misereor, miserērī (2), **miseritus sum**, to pity, feel sorry for

oblīvīscor, oblīvīscī (3), **oblītus sum**, to forget

potior, potīrī (4), **potītus sum**, to get control of, get possession of

Thus,

Meminit mīlitum. *He remembers the soldiers. He is mindful of the soldiers.*

When the object is a person, as in the example above, the genitive is always used. When the object is not a person, **oblīvīscor** and **meminī** can take either genitive or accusative:

Oblīvīscor **nōmina** *or* Oblīvīscor **nōminum**. *I forget names. I am forgetful of names.*

The verb **potior** can be found with either the genitive or the ablative case:

Caesar **castrīs** potītus est *or* Caesar **castrōrum** potītus est. *Caesar got control of the camp.*

2. *Dative with Special Verbs*

These verbs fall into two main groups:

a. Certain intransitive verbs may be found with the *dative of indirect object.* These verbs cannot take a direct object in Latin:

Caesar **nēminī** cēdit.	*Caesar yields **to no one**.*
Bonīs nocet quī **malīs** parcit.	*He does harm **to the good** who is sparing **to the bad**.*

Sometimes these verbs are translated transitively in English:

Urbī appropinquābant.   *They were approaching **the city**.*

Among the most important of these verbs are:

appropinquāre, to approach*	**nūbere**, to marry
cēdere, to yield	**occurrere**, to meet
cōnfīdere, to rely on, trust	**parcere**, to spare
crēdere, to believe	**parēre**, to obey
diffīdere, not to trust	**persuādēre**, to persuade
favēre, to favor	**placēre**, to please
ignōscere, to pardon	**resistere**, to resist
imperāre, to order	**succēdere**, to relieve
licēre, to be allowed	**succurrere**, to come to the aid
nocēre, to harm	

* This verb may also take **ad** + *acc.*

b. The second group consists of verbs that are compounded with prepositions:

. . . praepositusque (est) **eī** C. Cornēlius Gallus.	. . . *and C. Cornelius Gallus was put in charge of it [Egypt]*. (55B:20–21)
Haec rēs **Caesarī** prōfuit.	*This situation was beneficial to Caesar.*
Servī onera **plaustrīs** imposuērunt.	*The slaves put the loads on the wagons.*

Among the most important of these verbs are:

dēesse, to be lacking
impōnere, to place upon
praecipere, to instruct
praeesse, to be in charge of
praeficere, to place in charge of
prōdesse, to benefit

Notice that the verb **dēesse** requires the person who lacks to be in the dative, and the thing lacked to be the subject:

. . . (exercitus) **cui** semper **omnia** . . . dēfuissent.
. . . *(the army) which always lacked everything* (literally, *to which eveything was always lacking*). (61C:9–10)
Aliquandō **virtūs ducibus** dēest. *Sometimes leaders lack courage* (literally, *Sometimes courage is lacking to leaders*).

The verb **esse** can be used in a similar way with the dative case. This is called the *dative of possession*:

Sunt **Caesarī** paucī equitēs. *Caesar has few cavalry* (literally, *There are few cavalry to Caesar*).
Erant **Antōniō** nāvēs magnae. *Antony had large ships* (literally, *Large ships were to Antony*).

Exercise

Complete each sentence with the proper form of the word in parentheses, and then read aloud and translate. The nominative singular or plural is given.

1. Meminit _____, sed oblīvīscitur _____. (ego) (tū)

   _____

2. Centuriōnēs semper pārent _____. (imperātor)

   _____

3. Caesar praefēcit Marcum Antōnium _____ _____. (multī mīlitēs)

   _____

4. Miserēminī _____ quī in proeliō mortuī sunt. (hominēs)

   _____

5. Pompeius imperāvit _____ ut _____ pārērent. (omnēs suī) (tribūnī)

   _____

6. Potestne Caesar meminisse _____ cuiusque omnium centuriōnum? (nōmina)

   _____

7. Cum Pompeiānī acerrimē pugnāvissent, Caesariānī _____ parcere voluērunt. (eī)

   _____

8. _____ nōn licet oblīvīscī _____ (nōs) (Caesar)

   _____

9. Pompeiānī _____ fortiter resistēbant; _____ nōn iam persuāsum est ut arma dēpōnerent. (hostēs) (eī)

   _____

10. Caesar _____ Pompeiī appropinquāvit et dīxit "Hoc _____ placet." (castra) (ego)

    _____

Practice with Fear Clauses and Impersonals

(With Chapter 61)

Read aloud and translate into good English:

1. Caesar verēbātur nē equitātus Pompeiī aciem suam turbāret.

   _____

2. Ab equitibus Pompeiī concursum est; ā peditibus Caesaris nōn repugnābātur.

   _____

3. Pompeius timet ut in proeliō Caesarem vincat.

   _____

4. Pompeius victus in Graeciā manēre timuit; magnopere enim metuit ut Caesariānōs effugere posset.

   _____

5. Circum castra Pompeiī graviter contentum est.

   _____

6. Equitibus Pompeiī fugātīs, ā Caesare magnopere gavīsum est.

   _____

7. Maximā celeritāte ad lītus ā Pompeiānīs fugitum est.

   _____

8. Multī Rōmānī verēbantur nē Caesar sē dictātōrem faceret atque ut Senātus eum impedīre posset.

   _____

9. Caesar metuit nē rēx Aegyptī auxilium Pompeiō ferret.

   _____

10. Rōmae erat maximus metus nē Caesariānī venīrent ad urbem dīripiendam.

    _____

> **contendō, contendere** (3), **contendī, contentum,** to fight, struggle
> **Caesariānī, -ōrum** (*m pl*), soldiers of Caesar
> **Pompeiānī, -ōrum** (*m pl*), supporters of Pompey
> **dīripiō, dīripere** (3), to plunder, ravage

The Deaths of Caesar and Cicero

(With Chapter 61)

The Ides of March

On 15 March 44 B.C., Julius Caesar was murdered by a faction of the senatorial nobility because, as dictator, he threatened senatorial control of the government of the Republic. Of the events that took place on the Ides of March, no eyewitness account survives. Nicolaus of Damascus came to Rome sometime during Augustus' reign and had the opportunity to interview those who may have witnessed the murder. He wrote as follows:

> The Senate rose in respect for his position when they saw him entering. Those who were to have a part in the plot stood near him. Right next to him went Tullius Cimber, whose brother had been exiled by Caesar. Under pretext of a humble request on behalf of his brother, Cimber approached and grasped the mantle of his toga, seeming to want to make a more positive move with his hands upon Caesar. Caesar wanted to get up and use his hands, but was prevented by Cimber and became exceedingly annoyed. That was the moment for the men to set to work. All quickly unsheathed their daggers and rushed at him. Caesar rose to defend himself. They were just like men doing battle against him. Under the mass of wounds, he fell at the foot of Pompey's statue. Everyone wanted to seem to have had some part in the murder, and there was not one of them who failed to strike his body as it lay there, until, wounded thirty-five times, he breathed his last.

> —Nicolaus of Damascus, *Historici Graeci minores* par. 24

The following hasty note of congratulations to Basilus is thought to have been written by Cicero on the day of the assassination, in reply to a report received from Basilus. L. Minucius Basilus was an officer in Gaul under Caesar and was one of his assassins. Translate Cicero's message.

CICERO BASILO SAL.

Tibi grātulor, mihi gaudeō; tē amō, tua tueor, ā tē amārī et quid agās quidque agātur certior fierī volō.

> —Cicero, *Epistulae ad familiares* VI.15

> **tueor, tuērī** (2), **tuitus sum**, to look out for, protect
> **certior fierī**, to be informed.

The Death of Cicero

On 7 December 43 B.C., Cicero bravely faced death at the hands of assassins sent by Marc Antony, who was angry at Cicero for having delivered a series of speeches, called the *Philippics*, attacking him. Livy describes his death as follows:

> Cicero, realizing that he could not be rescued from the hands of Antony, first made for his estate at Tusculum and, from there, by traveling crossways across the peninsula, he set out for Formiae to board a ship leaving Gaeta. There, weariness of both flight and life itself seized him, for, having set out to sea several times, contrary winds had brought him back and then the tossing of the ship had become unendurable. On returning to his villa, he exclaimed, "I will now die in the land I have so often served." It is a fact that he ordered his slaves, willing to fight bravely and loyally to the finish, to put down his litter and to endure without resistance what an unjust fate had laid upon them all. As he stretched himself out from his litter and offered his neck without hesitation, his head was cut off. Charging that his hands had written things against Antony, the assassins cut off those as well. And so the head was carried back to Antony and by his order was placed between Cicero's two hands on the Rostra where, as former consul, he had spoken with remarkable eloquence against Antony that very year.

> –Livy, *Periochae*, CXX

A Casualty of War

(With Chapter 61)

In A.D. 9, three Roman legions under the command of Quinctilius Varus were annihilated by the Germans. The following epitaph commemorates a centurion who fell in this battle against the Germans. The epitaph was inscribed on a cenotaph, that is, a tomb with no remains, probably erected shortly after the disaster. After translating the inscription, write a brief obituary of the deceased.

M CAELIO T F LEM BON
O LEG XIIX ANN LIII^S
CECIDIT BELLO VARIANO OSSA
INFERRE LICEBIT P CAELIVS T F
LEM FRATER FECIT

**M(arcō) Caeliō T(itī) f(īliō), Lem(ōniā) (tribū), (domō) Bon(ōniā),
c(enturiōnī) Leg(iōnis) XIIX, ann(ōrum) LIII s(ēmissis);
cecidit bellō Variānō. Ossa
īnferre licēbit. P(ūblius) Caelius T(itī) f(īlius),
Lem(ōniā) (tribū), frāter fēcit.**

Lemōnia, one of 16 tribes into which
    Roman citizens were divided
tribus, -ūs (*f*), tribe
Bonōnia, -ae (*f*), Bononia, modern Bologna
O = centum, for **centuriō**
XIIX = XVIII

sēmis, sēmissis (*m*), one-half
Variānus, -a, -um, of Quinctilius Varus
os, ossis (*n*), bone, remains
īnferō, īnferre (*irreg*.), **intulī, illātum,**
    to put, place in or on

Comparison of Sculptures

(With Chapter 62)

You have already looked briefly at the statue of Augustus (page 94). This statue, one of the most famous of Roman statues, was modeled on another famous statue, the Doryphorus or Spear-bearer by the Greek sculptor Polyclitus. In this activity, you will compare the Greek statue with the Roman one which was modeled on it; by doing so, you can gain a deeper appreciation of how effectively Augustus used art to create the desired image of himself in the minds of his subjects, and of some of the important differences between the art of the Greeks and that of the Romans.

After studying the photos of both statues on the following page, compare and constrast the statues on each of the points listed.

Doryphorus (Spear-bearer)	Augustus from Prima Porta
Polyclitus (Roman copy of Greek original carved ca. 450-440 B.C.)	unknown sculptor, ca. 20 B.C.

Both statues are marble, over six feet tall.

clothing	
pose	
orientation	
focus/relation- ship to viewer	

specificity
 	
  of person
 	
  of history	

realism	
purpose	

107

Doryphorus

Augustus from Prima Porta

Credit Where Credit is Due

(With Chapter 62 or 63)

Many wealthy Romans felt that they had a duty to do things that benefited their fellow citizens, such as sponsor games, provide money for the construction of public buildings, or give a free meal for all citizens. In return, they fully expected to have their generosity recognized by the public; this often took the form of honorary or dedicatory inscriptions. In Reading 62D you read Augustus' boast that he rebuilt the Theater of Pompey **sine īnscrīptiōne nōminis meī**. Here are two typical inscriptions which *do* give credit to the donors:

A Town Councilman from Pompeii

The following inscription commemorates the civic generosity of Numerius Popidius Celsinus, who rebuilt the Temple of Isis. Translate it.

> N(umerius) Popidius N(umeriī) f(īlius) Celsīnus
> aedem Īsidis terrae mōtū conlāpsam
> ā fundāmentō p(ecūniā) s(uā) restituit. Hunc decuriōnēs ob līberālitātem
> cum esset annōrum sex ōrdinī suō grātīs adlēgērunt.
>
> —*Corpus Inscriptionum Latinarum*, X.846

aedis, aedis (*f*), temple, building, (plural) house
Īsis, Īsidis (*f*), Isis, an Egyptian goddess whose worship had spread all over the Mediterranean
fundāmentum, -ī (*n*), foundation
decuriōnēs, the town councilors in a Roman town
ob (+ *acc.*), because of
līberālitās, līberālitātis (*f*), generosity
cum, although. The real donor was Celsinus' father, Numerius Popidius Ampliatus, who was ineligible for election to the town council because he had been born a slave.
ōrdō, ōrdinis (*m*), order, membership
grātīs, for free. In many cases the newly elected **decuriō** paid a fee in honor of his election.

The Career of Pliny the Younger

You will read some of Pliny's letters in Chapters 63, 64, 66, and 67. Here is part of an inscription that was placed in the baths at Comum, Pliny's home town, in recognition of his civic generosity:

Gaius Plinius Caecilius Secundus, son of Lucius of the tribe Oufentina, consul, augur, praetorian commissioner with full consular power for the province of Pontus and Bithynia, sent to that province in accordance with the Senate's decree by the Emperor Nerva Trajan Augustus, curator of the bed and banks of the Tiber and the sewers of Rome, official of the Treasury of Saturn, official of the military Treasury, praetor, tribune of the people, quaestor of the Emperor, commissioner for the Roman knights, military tribune of the Third Gallic Legion, magistrate of the Board of Ten, left by his will public baths at a cost of . . . and an additional 300,000 sesterces for furnishing them, with 1,866,666 sesterces to support a hundred of his freedmen, and subsequently to provide an annual dinner for the people of the city . . . . Likewise in his lifetime he gave 500,000 sesterces for the maintenance of boys and girls of the city and also 100,000 for the upkeep of the library.

—*Corpus Inscriptionum Latinarum*, V.5262

Geography Ancient and Modern

(With Chapter 63)

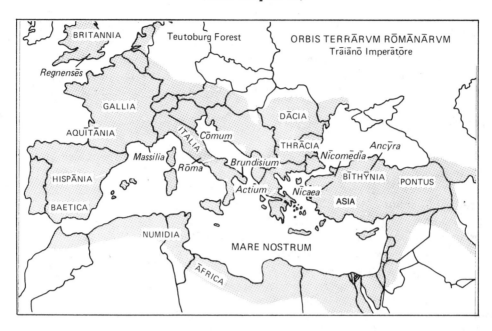

During the principate of Trajan, the Roman Empire reached its greatest size. The map above shows all the territory that was ruled by Rome at Trajan's death.

Exercise 1
Compare this map with the map on page 31 of the student's book, which shows the boundaries of the Empire at Augustus' death. List those territories that had been added by Trajan's time.

Exercise 2
Make a list of all the modern countries wholly or partly contained within the boundaries of the Roman Empire during the time of Trajan, as illustrated by the map above. Consult a modern atlas for assistance, as necessary.

Exercise 3
Many cities trace their origins to the Roman imperial period. In the first blank on each line, write the lower-case letter to show the modern city that corresponds to the Roman one. In the second blank, write the upper-case letter to show the country in which it is found (use an atlas as necessary).

	ROMAN CITY		MODERN CITY		MODERN COUNTRY*
____, ____	Ancyra	a.	London	A.	Austria
____, ____	Burdigala	b.	Cadiz	B.	England
____, ____	Carthago Nova	c.	Milan	C.	France
____, ____	Colonia Agrippinensis	d.	Vienna	D.	Germany
____, ____	Gades	e.	Cologne	E.	Israel
____, ____	Hierosolyma	f.	Ankara	F.	Italy
____, ____	Londinium	g.	Cartagena	G.	Rumania
____, ____	Mediolanum	h.	Naples	H.	Russia
____, ____	Neapolis	i.	Bordeaux	I.	Spain
____, ____	Vindobona	j.	Jerusalem	J.	Turkey

* Some countries are used more than once.

Two Inscriptions from Britain

(With Chapter 63)

As time went by, the various provinces of the Empire gradually became "Romanized"—that is, what were originally pieces of conquered territory (cf. **vincere**, the root of **prōvincia**) took on the language and customs of their conquerors. The Romans systematically encouraged this process by rewarding provincial leaders who adopted the Roman way of life. The following dedicatory inscription from a Roman temple at Chichester in Britain illustrates the influence of Rome on Cogidubnus, an important British client king of the first century A.D., who had been made a Roman official by the Emperor Claudius. Translate the inscription, and then write answers to the questions that follow.

> Neptūnō et Minervae
>   templum
> prō salūte domūs dīvīnae
> ex auctōritāte Ti. Claud(ī)
> Cōgidubnī R(ēgis) Lēgāt(ī) Aug(ustī) in Brit(anniā)
> collēgium fabrōrum et quī in eō
> sunt dē suō dedērunt dōnante āream
> Clēmente Pudentīnī fīliō

domūs dīvīnae, the family of the Emperor Claudius
Cōgidubnus, king of the Regnenses tribe
collēgium, -ī (*n*), guild, union

faber, fabrī (*m*), metalworker
dē suō, at their own expense
ārea, -ae (*f*), open space, site

Questions

1. To what deities was this temple dedicated? What does this reveal about the progress of Romanization in Britain?
2. What Latin words reveal the feelings of the donors toward the emperor?
3. Under whose authority was this dedication made? What do his name and titles reveal about his relationship with Rome?
4. Who provided the funds for the temple? What does this imply about the extent of technology in this province?
5. Where did the land for the temple precinct come from?

Roman gods were sometimes adopted wholesale in the provinces and fused with local deities. This can be seen clearly in Britain, where the Roman army was the main vehicle of Romanization. Here is an inscription from a small altar dedicated by a soldier in payment of a vow to **Mars Brāciāca**, "Mars in Pants." The word **brācae** refers to the trousers worn by Gallic barbarians, but never by Greeks or Romans. Although the altar was found in Britain, the soldier was serving in a unit of provincial auxiliaries from Aquitania, in southwestern Gaul (see the map on page 31).

Deō Martī Brāciācae
Q. Sittius Caeciliān(us) Praef(ectus) Coh(ortī) I. Aquītānō
V(ōtum) S(olvit)

> **praefectus, -ī** (*m*), prefect, official in charge
> **I.:** = **prīmō**

Epitaph of a Young Christian Boy

(With Chapter 64)

This early epitaph of a Christian child came from the Catacomb of Commodilla, just off the Appian Way, and is now in the Vatican Museum. What can you learn about the deceased?

Innocus puer nōmine Siddī hīc bīxit mēsēs quator, diēs bīgintī quator, petītus in pāce III Īd(ūs) Aprīlīs Aniciō Aucheniō Basō cōnsule.

> **innocus = innocuus, -a, -um**, harmless, innocent
> **bīxit = vīxit**
> **mēsēs = mēnsēs**
> **quator = quattuor**
> **petītus**: "taken," "summoned"
> **Anicius Auchenius Bassus**, consul for A.D. 408
>
> **ω** = *omega*, last letter of the Greek alphabet
>
> **A** = *alpha*, first letter of the Greek alphabet
>
> ☧ = the Greek letters *chi* (X) and *rho* (P), the first two letters of the name *Christos* in Greek

1. How old was Siddus when he died?
2. According to the modern calendar, on what date did he pass away?
3. What significance might the phrase **petītus in pāce** have for a Christian?
4. What is the special significance of each of the symbols?
5. In modern Spanish, the letter *v* is pronounced as *b*, that is, *victoria* is pronounced "bictoria." Also, the letter *n* has dropped out of many words; the Latin **mēnsa** (table) comes into Spanish as *mesa*. What evidence can you find in this inscription that both of these phonetic changes were already taking place by the fourth century A.D.?
6. What features of the inscription suggest that the stonecutter was not well educated? What does this suggest about the economic status of Siddus' family?

Word Study XV

(With Chapter 64)

The Days of the Week

At first glance, the names of the days of the week in English look very different from the corresponding ones in the Romance languages (see table below). In reality, though, our words are the same in origin as the Romance ones. The Romans named the days of the week after the seven "planets" (without Uranus, Neptune, and Pluto, which they did not know, and including the sun and moon). The planets, in turn, had long been associated with certain divinities of the Greco-Roman pantheon. Thus we find a Pompeian graffito (first century A.D.) listing the market-day (**nūndinae**) at Pompeii and neighboring towns.

Diēs	Nūndinae
Sāturnī	Pompeiīs
Sōlis	Nūceriae
Lūnae	Atīlae
Martis	Nōlae
Mercurī	Cūmīs
Iovis	Puteolīs
Veneris	Rōmae, Capuae

And a little girl's epitaph sadly records the ironic coincidence between her name and the day of her birth and death:

D. M. Sāturnīnae, diē Sāturnī nātae, diē Sāturnī diē fūnctae; vīx(it) annīs III, m(ēnsibus) V, d(iēbus) XX.

— *Corpus Inscriptionum Latinarum* X.2933

diē fūnctae: = mortuae

The Romance languages took over the Roman day-names, except for the Judaeo-Christian innovations **dominica diēs** and **sabbatī** (or **sambatī**) **diēs**. English, however, being a Germanic language, replaced the Roman divinities with their counterparts in Germanic mythology. The thunder god Thor, for example, was regarded as the equivalent of the Roman Jupiter (Jove).

The Days of the Week

LATIN	ITALIAN	SPANISH	FRENCH	ENGLISH
Solis diēs				Sun-day
dominica diēs	dominica	domingo	dimanche	
Lūnae diēs	lunedi	lunes	lundi	Moon-day
Martis diēs	martedi	martes	mardi	Tiw's-day
Mercurī diēs	mercoledi	miércoles	mercredi	Woden's-day
Iovis diēs	giovedi	jueves	jeudi	Thor's-day
Veneris diēs	venerdi	viernes	vendredi	Freya's-day
Sāturnī diēs				Saturn's-day
sa(m)(b)atī diēs	sabato	sábado	samedi	

Answer the following questions in English:

1. What is the only day named for a goddess?

   _____

2. What was her name in Latin and Romance? In German and English?

   _____

3. Why is Wednesday spelled with an unpronounced *d*?

   _____

4. Which Romance day-name is Christian in origin? Translate the Latin phrase.

   _____

5. Which Romance day-name is Jewish in origin? Translate the Latin phrase.

   _____

6. On what day of the week was market held in Pompeii? In Rome? In Nola?

   _____

7. Which English day is named after a Roman god?

   _____

8. What do you deduce is the word for "moon" in Italian, Spanish, and French?

   _____

9. Which English day-name is of Christian or Jewish origin?

   _____

10. What do you deduce was the nature of the Germanic divinities Tiw and Freya?

   _____

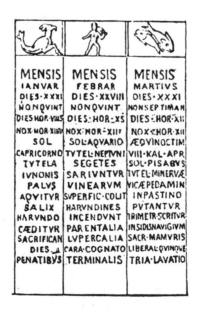

Roman Names

(With Chapter 65)

A. Names of Slaves and Freedmen

You have already learned about the **tria nōmina** of the Roman citizen (Chapter 51, page 94). Other elements of Roman society such as slaves, women, and animals (and they were the majority) had only one name. While women were known by the name of their **gēns** (*Claudia, Iūlia*), animals and slaves were named in a variety of ways. Some slaves were called after a personality trait, real or hoped for; hence the names **Hilarus** and **Hilariō**, Cheerfulness, a very desirable characteristic in a servant. Names connoting good luck were especially popular: **Fortūnātus (-a), Fēlīx, Fēlīcula**, and Greek equivalents such as **Tychē** (*Luck*), **Eutychēs**, or **Tychicus** (*Lucky*). Once freed, a slave proudly adopted the **tria nōmina**, which became a kind of capsule history of his life. For his **cognōmen** he used his slave name; for his **prōnōmen** and **nōmen** he adopted those of the master who had freed him. If he had earlier belonged to another master, he might use that man's name, in adjectival form, as an **agnōmen**. A freedwoman, too, retained her slave name but might also adopt the feminine form of her former master's **nōmen** (e.g. **Iūlia**).

1. What would be the name after manumission of a slave named **Hilarus** who belonged to Pompey (**Cn. Pompeius Magnus**)?

   _____

2. What would be the name after manumission of a slave-woman named **Tychē** freed by Caesar?

   _____

3. What would be the name after manumission of a slave named **Fortūnātus** freed by Caesar but previously owned by Cicero (**M. Tullius Cicerō**)?

   _____

4. Explain the significance of each of the four names Trimalchio wants included in his epitaph (**C. Pompeius Trimalchiō Maecēnātiānus**).

   _____

   _____

   _____

B. Names Reveal the Family Tree

*The following epitaph of two children who lived in **Lugdūnum** (Lyons in southern France) tells a touching story of parental hopes disappointed. It is also an interesting example of the way Roman naming practices can be used to reconstruct family history. After you have read and translated the epitaph, do some detective work and construct a family tree of the people mentioned. The questions that follow the text will help you.*

D.M. Memoriae aeternae Valeriae Leucadiae īnfantis dulcissimae, quae vīxit annīs VI d(iēbus) XXX, et Vireī Vitālis, iuvenis incomparābilis ingenī, artis fabricae ferrāriae, frātris eiusdem Leucadiae, quōrum mortem sōlī XXX diēs interfuērunt, quī vīxit ann(īs) XVIIII m(ēnsibus) X d(iēbus) VIIII, cuius sapientia omnibus amīcīs et parentib(us) admīrābilis fuit. Val(erius) Maximus vītricus quī eum sibi fīlium adoptāverat et arte ēducāverat, in quō spem aetātis suae conlocāverat, et Iūlia Secundīna māter īnfēlīcissima, quī sibi ab eīs id fierī spērāverant, et Vireiī Marīniānus et Secundiānus et Val(erius) Secundīnus frātrēs p(ōnendum) c(ūrāvērunt).

dulcis, -is, -e, sweet
artis . . . ferrāriae, "(skilled in) the art of ironwork."
intersum, interesse (*irreg.*), **interfuī**, to be between, separate
sapientia, -ae (*f*), wisdom, skill
vītricus, -ī (*m*), stepfather
spēs, speī (*f*), hope
aetās, aetātis (*f*), age, old age
conlocō (1), to place, put
sibi . . . fierī: "that it (i.e., burial) would be done for them (the parents) by them (the children)"
Vireiī: two men with the **nōmen** Vireius, i.e., **V. Marīniānus** and **V. Secundiānus**
pōnendum cūrāvērunt: "took the responsibility of setting up (this monument)"

1. How many children did Julia Secundina have?

   _____

2. Which were the children by her first husband? What was his (partial) name?

   _____

   _____

3. Which were the children by her second husband? What was his name?

   _____

   _____

4. Which children's names reflect that of their mother?

   _____

5. Which children's names reflect that of their father?

   _____

Now insert the names into the genealogical chart below.

(1)   (2)

Julia = _____   = _____

116

Word Study XVI

(With Chapter 65)

Romance Derivatives: Survival of the Simplest

Many Romance words derive from colloquial, rather than literary ("classical") Latin. Some common literary words were short, irregular, and/or easily confused with other words; ordinary speakers of Latin preferred synonyms that were easier to recognize and to decline or conjugate. Hence:

1. **Ōs, ōris** (*n*), "mouth," was a very short word and liable to be confused with **os, ossis** (*n*), "bone"; it lost out, in popular speech, to **bucca, -ae** (*f*), "cheek," from which derive It. *bocca,* Sp. *boca,* and Fr. *bouche.*

2. **Rēs, reī** (*f*), "thing," another short word and member of the relatively rare 5th declension, was replaced by **causa,** which eventually produced It. and Sp. *cosa* and Fr. *chose.*

3. Where a classical verb had an alternative form in the 1st conjugation, the latter tended to survive, as being easier to conjugate; hence the Romance verbs for "to sing" derive not from **canere** but from the frequentative form **cantāre**: It. *cantare,* Sp. *cantar,* Fr. *chanter.*

4. The classical verb **edō, edere** or **esse** "to eat" was short, irregular, and likely to be confused with the verb "to be." In Spanish a compound of this verb has survived (*comer* from **comedere,** and the noun *comida* "food"), while the Italian and French verbs for "to eat" (*mangiare* and *manger*) are derived from a slang use of the Latin verb "to chew," **manducāre** (this verb is a variant of the basic verb **mandere,** which again illustrates the preference for 1st conjugation forms).

5. Some short words were easier to remember and inflect in their diminutive form: classical **auris, -is** (*f*), "ear," (not to be confused with **aura,** "breeze," or **aurum,** "gold") gave way to its diminutive form **auricula,** from which derive Sp. *oreja,* It. *orecchio,* and Fr. *oreille.*

6. Some of the commonest classical words seem to have been rejected by ordinary people as being too literary or "fancy." To them, **equus** sounded something like "steed," and you don't hitch a "steed" to a plow or a wagon; they called the beast a **caballus** ("nag" in the literary language); hence It. *cavallo,* Sp. *caballo,* and Fr. *cheval.* Likewise, classical authors who aimed at an elegant style used **magnus,** while everyday speakers preferred **grandis** (leading to Fr. *grand* and It. and Sp. *grande*). An amusing illustration of the ordinary person's preference for the slang word over the literary word is provided by the It. *testa* and Fr. *tête,* "head." These words come from **testa, -ae** (*f*), whose literal meaning was "a ceramic pot" but which was used jokingly of the human head until it eventually replaced the classical **caput** altogether.

7. Neuter nouns were a great source of confusion. Since most of their forms were identical to those of masculine nouns, speakers were often not sure which nouns belonged to which type (recall Trimalchio's **malus fātus** and **candēlabrus** for **malum fātum** and **candēlabrum**). As a result, in Romance neuters were eliminated, most of them going to the masculine gender. Deponent verbs, another source of doubt (cf. Trimalchio's **exhortāvit** for **exhortātus est**), were likewise eliminated in Romance.

These modern Romance words bear eloquent witness to the difficulties and frustrations ordinary Romans experienced in handling their language. Like us, they found look-alike words confusing, they liked simplicity and regularity, and they bypassed "fancy" or "poetic" words.

Practice with Conditionals

(With Chapter 66)

Exercise 1

Categorize each of the following conditions as simple, future more vivid, future less vivid, present contrary to fact, or past contrary to fact, and translate each sentence:

1. Miser sum, nisi tē videō._____

    _____

2. Miser eram, nisi tē vidēbam._____

    _____

3. Miser sim, nisi tē videam._____

    _____

4. Miser fuissem, nisi tē vīdissem._____

    _____

5. Miser fuī, nisi tē vīdī._____

    _____

6. Miser erō, nisi tē vīderō._____

    _____

7. Miser erō, nisi tē vidēbō._____

    _____

8. Miser essem, nisi tē vidērem._____

    _____

Sometimes conditional sentences are "mixed," that is, they contain different tenses in protasis and apodosis, as in the following example:

9. Miser essem, nisi tē vīdissem._____

    _____

Exercise 2

Complete the following sentences with the correct forms of **dīcere** *in the if-clauses and* **crēdere** *in the main clauses, as the rules and the sense dictate. Then translate each sentence.*

1. Etiamsī tū vēra _____, nēmō tibi _____. (present contrary to fact)

_____

2. Etiamsī tū vēra _____, nēmō tibi _____. (future less vivid)

_____

3. Etiamsī tū vēra _____, nēmō tibi _____. (past contrary to fact)

_____

4. Etiamsī tū vēra _____, nēmō tibi _____. (simple present)

_____

5. Etiamsī tū vēra _____, nēmō tibi _____. (future more vivid)

_____

6. Etiamsī tū vēra _____, nēmō tibi _____. (mixed contrary to fact)

_____

Exercise 3

Translate each of the following quotations from Latin authors:

1. Sī vīs amārī, amā! (Seneca)

_____

2. Dī nōn cūrant quid agat hūmānum genus. Nam sī cūrent, bene bonīs sit, male malīs. Quod nunc abest. (Ennius)

_____

_____

3. Sī vīveret, verba eius audīrētis. (Cicero)

_____

4. Dīcēs "Ēheu!" sī tē in speculō vīderis. (Horace)

_____

      speculum, -ī (*n*), mirror

Summary of Case Usages

(With Chapter 66 or 67)

Genitive

1. Possessive: **fundōs omnēs, quī patrōnī meī fuerant** (65C:23)
2. Objective: **Augēbat factī invidiam uxor Clōdiī.** (57C:30–31)
3. Partitive: **nihil factī** (65C:14)
4. With **causā** or **grātiā**: **Ardeat amōris et dēsīderī meī causā.** (Ex. 65b:6)
5. Descriptive: **Marcus Ulpius Trāiānus, . . . inūsitātae cīvīlitātis et fortitūdinis** (63B:1–2)
6. With impersonal verbs: **Mē taedet solitūdinis** (49:3)
7. With special verbs: **oblīvīscātur patris et mātris** (Ex. 65b:3–4)
8. With special adjectives: **Immemor terrōris nocturnī, fābulam nārrābat.** (21:4)

Dative

1. Indirect object: **quae . . . vōbīs ostendam** (65D:41–42)
2. Of possession, with the verb **esse**: **servus quīdam cui nōmen est Pseudolus** (29:5–6)
3. Of agent, with gerund or gerundive: **ubi diūtius nōbīs habitandum est** (65A:18)
4. Of reference: **quī illī . . . gravior et sonantior erat** (67C:43–44)
5. Of purpose: **Spectātōribus admīrātiōnī fuērunt leōnēs.** (47:1–2) (When a dative of reference and a dative of purpose occur together, as in this example, they are called the *double dative.*)
6. Of separation: **signa . . . quae Crassō victō adēmerant.** (56B:8–9)
7. With compound verbs: **Aegyptus . . . imperiō Rōmānō adiecta est praepositusque eī C. Cornēlius Gallus.** (55B:19–21)
8. With special verbs: **crēdite mihi** (65D:42)
9. With special adjectives: **habitus corporis quiēscentī quam dēfūnctō similior** (67D:72–73)

Ablative

1. Place from which (with **ab, dē, ex**): **ex Asiā vēnī** (65C:2)
   Without preposition (names of towns, small islands): **Rōmā subitō ipse profectus prīdiē est** (58A:4–5)
2. Of separation: **ut sē tantō discrīmine ēriperet** (67A:14–15)
3. Of respect: **Graeculiō Serāpa nōmine** (65D:29)
4. Of comparison: **nox omnibus noctibus nigrior dēnsiorque** (67D:59–60)
5. Place where (with **in, sub**): **In castrīs Pompeiī . . .** (61C:1)
   Without preposition: **plūrimīs locīs lātissimae flāmmae altaque incendia relūcēbant** (67C:37–38)
6. Time when: **ūnō diē** (65C:12)
7. Means: **catellam cingulō alligātam** (65B:28)
8. Price: **Bona eius . . . sēmiunciā vēniērunt.** (58E:7–8)
9. Agent: **Victus est ab Augustō** (55B:15)
10. Cause: **agrestium trepidātiōne ignēs relictōs . . . dictitābat** (76C:37–38)
11. Accompaniment: **putāssēs illum semper mēcum habitāsse** (65D:33)
12. Manner: **cum . . . sē acrī animō dēfenderet** (58C:25–26)
13. Description: **quī animō fidēlī in dominum . . . fuērunt** (58D:31–32)
14. With certain deponents: **. . . commemorāvit testibus sē mīlitibus ūtī posse, . . .** (60A:3)
15. Degree of difference: **Multō libentius tē vidēbō.** (34:10)
16. Ablative absolute: **ingemēscente familiā** (65A:9)

Exercise

Read aloud and translate the following sentences. Then identify the usage of each noun in italics.

1. *Uxōrī Clōdiī* nūllus metus *mortis* erat.

   _____

   Uxōrī: _____ Clōdiī: _____ mortis: _____

2. Illum paenitēbit *scelerum*. scelerum: _____

   _____

3. Nē oblīvīscātur *amīcārum*. amīcārum: _____

   _____

4. Ars grātiā *artis*. (Motto of MGM Films) artis: _____

   _____

5. Hic liber nōn est *discipulīs* idōneus. discipulīs: _____

   _____

6. Milō *Pompeiō* nōn crēdēbat. Pompeiō: _____

   _____

7. Rēs pūblica *Cicerōnī cūrae maximae* erat.

   _____

   Cicerōnī: _____ cūrae maximae: _____

8. Aurum *tibi* tangendum nōn est. tibi: _____

   _____

9. Clōdius et Milō *sceleribus* parēs erant. sceleribus: _____

   _____

10. Poēta dōnum *maximō gaudiō* accēpit.

    _____

    maximō gaudiō: _____

    _____

11. Mārtiālis poēta *multō* melius *Cicerōne* fuit.

    _____

    multō: _____ Cicerōne: _____

12. Cicerō *litterīs Graecīs* ūtēbātur. litterīs Graecīs: _____

    _____

13. Poēta librum *decem sēstertiīs* ēmit. decem sēstertiīs: _____

    _____

14. C. Iūlius Caesar, vir *ēgregiā scientiā reī mīlitāris*, multa proelia commīsit.

    _____

    ēgregiā scientiā: _____ reī mīlitāris: _____

15. Mīlitēs *timōre* ex agrō Pharsālicō effūgērunt.

    _____

    timōre: _____

Word Study XVII

(With Chapter 67)

Latin Suffixes in the Romance Languages

You have learned some of the ways in which words are formed from other words in Latin by the addition of prefixes and suffixes. Knowing the principles of word-formation, as you have discovered, makes it possible to increase your Latin vocabulary with a minimum of memorizing. These same principles will also enable you to recognize hundreds of words in the Romance languages. Some of the Latin suffixes you have already learned, and their Romance equivalents, are shown below.

LATIN	ITALIAN	SPANISH	FRENCH
-tās, -tātis *(f)* ūnitās	-tà *(f)* unità	-dad *(f)* unidad	-té *(f)* unité
-tiō, -tiōnis *(f)* nātiō	-zione *(f)* nazione	-ción *(f)* nación	-tion *(f)* nation
-tor, -tōris *(m)* ōrātor	-tore *(m)* oratore	-dor *(m)* orador	-teur *(m)* orateur
-entia, -ae *(f)* scientia	-enza *(f)* scienza	-encia *(f)* ciencia	-ence *(f)* science
-ōsus, -a, -um verbōsus	-oso, -a verboso	-oso, -a verboso	-eux, -euse verbeux

Note that the Romance forms often bear a closer resemblance to the Latin ablative case form than to the nominative form.

The adverb in the Romance languages is an interesting special case: it derives from Latin phrases of the type (adjective) **mente**, e.g., **firmā mente**, "with a firm mind," "firmly." This type of ablative of manner was used so extensively that **mente** eventually lost most of its original meaning and became a suffix changing the preceding adjective into an adverb.

LATIN	ITALIAN	SPANISH	FRENCH
_____ mente firmā mente	_____-mente fermamente	_____-mente firmemente	_____-ment fermement

Exercise 1

Give the Latin root, and the meaning, of each of the following groups of words in Romance:

FRENCH	SPANISH	ITALIAN	LATIN	MEANING
cité	ciudad	cività	_____	_____
glorieux	glorioso	glorioso	_____	_____
liberté	libertad	libertà	_____	_____
empereur	emperador	imperatore	_____	_____
sévèrement	severamente	severamente	_____	_____
ambiteux	ambicioso	ambizioso	_____	_____
sénateur	senador	senatore	_____	_____
pestilence	pestilencia	pestilenza	_____	_____
librement	libremente	liberamente	_____	_____
position	posición	posizione	_____	_____
location	locación	locazione	_____	_____
ignorance	ignorancia	ignoranza	_____	_____

Exercise 2

*Here are some **sententiae** written in French, Italian, and Spanish, together with their English translations. Using the related Romance words, write the same **sententiae** in Latin (some help with Latin words is given at the end of the exercise):*

1. O Liberté, O Liberté, que de crimes on commet en ton nom! (French)
   O Liberty, O Liberty, how many crimes are committed in your name!

   _____

2. Non ogni fiore fa buon odore. (Italian)
   Not every flower makes a sweet smell.

   _____

3. Rey nuevo, ley nueva. (Spanish)
   New king, new law.

   _____

   crīmen, crīminis (*n*)
   lībertās, lībertātis (*f*)
   flōs, flōris (*m*)
   odor, odōris (*m*)